THE EDGE

THE EDGE

The War against
Cheating and Corruption in
the Cutthroat World of Elite Sports

ROGER PIELKE, JR.

ROARING FORTIES
PRESS

Berkeley, California

Roaring Forties Press
1053 Santa Fe Avenue
Berkeley, CA 94706
www.roaringfortiespress.com

Cover design by Nigel Quinney and Jeff Urbancic; interior design by Nigel Quinney.

Cover photos: (top) Mr.Big-Photography/Getty Images; (bottom) Jahre Photography/Shutterstock.

Library of Congress Cataloging in Publication Data is available.

ISBN 978-1-938901-57-7 (print)
ISBN 978-1-938901-61-4 (pdf)
ISBN 978-1-938901-62-1 (epub)
ISBN 978-1-938901-63-8 (Kindle)

To Amelia Martelo Coleman, 1919–2015

CONTENTS

PART III: WINNING THE WAR FOR SPORT

Preface

Simon Kuper

A few years ago in Paris, I met an American political scientist who had decided to devote his considerable brainpower to sports. Roger Pielke Jr. had spent most of his career working on the politics of climate change. But over a delicious French lunch, he explained that he had almost given up hope of anything being done about that problem.

"That's exactly how I feel about sport," I said. The many problems of sporting governance seemed as eternal as death and taxes. Sports authorities governed themselves and didn't care what the rest of us said. That allowed sports officials to be stupid, pompous, corrupt, or all three. The consequences are the scandals that Pielke charts in this excellent book, from the NFL's "Deflategate" through the doping that pervades most sports to the bizarre spectacle that is FIFA.

But with hindsight, it seems he was right to be hopeful. As he explains in this book, sport's age of impunity may now be ending. The dawn raids by Swiss police on FIFA officials in the Baur au Lac hotel in Zurich on May 27, 2015, symbolized a new era: the "autonomy of sport"; the right of sports organizations to do whatever they want has gone. Now is the moment to replace what Pielke calls the outdated values of sports governance: "amateurism, purity, uncertainty, and autonomy."

Some sports fans may ask why they should care. After all, most of us are a lot more interested in the sports themselves than in the old men who run them. But as Pielke shows, there's a close link between misrule off the field and cheating on it.

My own favorite example is the Ecuadorean soccer referee Byron Moreno. Upon landing "visibly nervous" at JFK airport in New York in 2010, Moreno was arrested after a customs official found "hard objects on the defendant's stomach, back, and both of his legs." Moreno turned out to be carrying ten plastic bags of heroin. He was sentenced to thirty months in a Brooklyn jail, but was released early for good behavior.

In the South Korea–Italy quarterfinal at the World Cup of 2002, Moreno had disallowed a legitimate Italian "golden goal," given Korea a penalty, and sent off Italy's Francesco Totti. Moreno personally may have prevented a strong Italian team from winning that World Cup. Three months after the tournament, the Ecuadorean soccer federation gave him a twenty-game ban for an exceptional display of bizarre refereeing that featured (among other things) two controversial penalties, two red cards, and thirteen minutes of extra time. Soon after he returned to soccer in 2003, he was suspended again after sending off three Deportivo Quito players in a game. He then resigned from refereeing.

We now know Moreno was a crook. The question is: Who in FIFA appointed him to referee a crucial World Cup match, and why? And he's not the only corrupt referee: another of his colleagues at that World Cup, the Chinese Lu Jun, was later jailed in his own country for match fixing.

Fixing is one of the big battlefields Pielke identifies in modern sport, along with amateurism (chiefly in American college sports), doping, technology, and sex testing. The next big issue coming down the pike may be genetically enhanced athletes. Sports authorities as currently constituted are not equipped to make good decisions on any of these issues.

From his years in climate politics, Pielke has a subtle sense of the role of experts in these debates. Science, he notes, can't "solve" any of these problems. It cannot, for instance, eradicate doping or settle whether the risk of concussion is great enough to justify banning teenagers from playing football. But science can inform the debates and help show sports officials what their options are.

Pielke urges sports to adopt new values: professionalism, pragmatism, transparency, and accountability. Making the shift will require the help of people like him. This is a book that should reach informed experts on sports governance as well as ordinary curious fans. Pielke writes with an academic's erudition and a journalist's style and eye for detail. Sport is lucky to have him.

Prologue

This book is about a war—a war for the soul of sport. Sport depends for its very existence on rules; take the rules away, and what you have left might be a fistfight or a workout, but it won't be sport. Today, however, the edge between what is acceptable in sport and what is not has become blurred, and this blurred edge threatens the soul of sport itself.

The search for a sporting edge brings many to the brink, both the men and women who play sports and the administrators, businesspeople, and politicians who regulate it. And once they are at the brink, the temptation to jump to the other side, to cross the line, can be hard to resist. Sport has never been immune from corruption, cheating, or greed, but these days it seems to be riddled with these vices. Just take a look at the headlines.

The media are abuzz with disturbing reports about the world's elite athletes and the governing sports bodies, which have been investigated repeatedly about the rampant use of prohibited performance-enhancing drugs. The NFL has been embroiled in the so-called Deflategate scandal over cheating by Tom Brady and the New England Patriots. Tennis authorities have suspended players for fixing matches and using performance-enhancing drugs. Victor Conte, who founded a performance-drug company called BALCO (for Bay Area Laboratory Co-operative), went to jail for supplying Olympic sprinter Marion Jones, baseball superstar Barry Bonds, and others with illegal drugs.* Conte alleges that the "majority of world track and field records were set" by athletes taking such prohibited substances.[1] The list goes on and on. I haven't yet mentioned soccer's governing body FIFA (Fédération Internationale de Football Association) and its longtime president Sepp Blatter, who stepped down

---

*   Specifically, for steroids. Conte also pled guilty to a money-laundering charge. He served four months in jail.

amid a series of scandals and arrests connected to a culture of corruption at the very heart of international soccer.*

The various allegations that sport is dealing with are explosive. For instance, a 2015 German TV series claims that pervasive doping took place in the Olympics over the past decade and that, remarkably, the organizations that are supposed to police such cheating turned a blind eye. The series alleges that one-third of all medals won at the Olympics (and the track and field World Championships) from 2001 to 2012 were awarded to athletes who subsequently had suspicious blood results. Russia and Kenya were identified as having an especially large number of athletes with suspicious test results, but the shadow of suspicion falls on athletes around the globe.[†]

In the meantime, two athletes who experienced incredible performances during the summer of 2015 were Alex Rodriquez, a baseball player for the New York Yankees, and Justin Gatlin, an American sprinter. The good news is that both athletes were performing better than they ever had, and at ages well past the point when such performances might be expected. The bad news is that both had previously served suspensions for doping offenses. Their stellar accomplishments had people wondering about what, exactly, they were seeing. Were these rousing stories of athletic triumph or sordid tales of undeserved benefits collected by those who had gone over the edge?

Other debates are under way as well. Just one week before the broadcast of the German doping series, the Court of Arbitration for Sport (CAS) in Switzerland issued a landmark ruling on "sex testing" by the International Association of Athletics Federations

---

* Throughout this book, I use the term "soccer" to refer to what most people around the world consider to be "football." To understand the origins of both terms and the evolution of their use, see Steve Hendricks, "A 'Soccer' Lesson," *Sporting Intelligence,* December 6, 2015, http://www.sportingintelligence.com/2015/12 /06/letter-from-america-happy-130th-birthday-to-english-soccer-071201/. The origin may not be what you think

† A World Anti-Doping Agency (WADA) investigation of these claims concluded that more than 150 such medals had been awarded to athletes with suspicious blood values. See WADA, *Independent Commission Report Part 2,* 2016, https:// www.wada-ama.org/en/resources/world-anti-doping-program/independent-commission-report-2.

(IAAF), which oversees track and field. For more than half a century, athletics organizations have tried—and consistently failed—to figure out how to determine eligibility for participation in women's events in athletics. It turns out that biological sex is not a simple binary set of categories, but is far more complex and better depicted in shades of gray than in black and white. Since 2011, the IAAF had used a policy based on female testosterone levels. The arbitration court struck that policy down in 2015, leaving the sport in limbo.

In short, the sports world of today is characterized by battles on multiple fronts, each characterized by a need for rules and regulations to govern what happens when the quest for a performance edge meets the boundary of what is allowed or acceptable.

This book is designed to help people make sense of these battlegrounds. There are a number of excellent books about athletic performance and doping.* And there are plenty of narratives written about colorful but flawed characters in sport, such as Lance Armstrong and Marion Jones. But there is no book that looks at the edge, the place where the quest for athletic advantage runs into the rules governing what is allowed, what is fair, what isn't, and what is really behind the "spirit of sport."

The fact that there just isn't a book like this is pretty exciting for an author. Over the past decade, I have moved the focus of my research on science, policy, and decision making away from space exploration and climate change and toward issues related to sport. Policy researchers are like sharks in the sense that if we are not moving forward, we can't thrive. We are also like sharks in the sense that we are attracted to blood in the water, something (metaphorically speaking) that sport has plenty of these days.

But it's not just the blood that appeals—it's also the sweat and the tears that sport produces. When I was a child in the early 1980s, my father, then a professor at the University of Virginia in Charlottesville, would often take me to campus with him when I was on holiday from school. I would wander the campus while he taught or did research. I would marvel at the rotunda, and regularly made a point of checking out the astronomy department (then my favor-

---

* You can find recommendations for further reading at the end of this book.

ite). But most of all, I'd hope for a chance to catch a glimpse of Ralph Sampson or Jeff Lamp, stars of the Wahoo basketball team.

The apple doesn't fall far from the tree, and more than thirty years later I am a college professor. I am also one of those college professors who landed a job at his alma mater. I attended the University of Colorado in the late 1980s and early 1990s, earning three degrees along the way. The era of big hair and New Wave was also the time when the Colorado football program rose from obscurity to winning a national championship. It was an exciting time to be a student at CU.[2]

When I am older and most memories have long faded, I have no doubt that one that will remain will be a sunny September afternoon in 1989 when the Colorado Buffaloes had their way in a 38–7 victory over the University of Illinois. I remember defensive linemen Alfred Williams and Kanavis McGhee tormenting Illini quarterback Jeff George, and those of us in the student section tormenting him too. Seeing Williams and McGhee on the Boulder campus was a thrill then just like it had been for me in the early 1980s to catch a glimpse of 7' 4" Ralph Sampson eating at the University Cafeteria near UVA.

An uncomplicated world is one of the benefits of being a teenager, I suppose. With age comes learning and experience, and the teenager's simple view of the world inevitably grows more complicated. One week after that beautiful fall day and thrashing of the Illinois football team, the quarterback who had led the Buffaloes the previous two seasons, Sal Aunese, died from inoperable stomach cancer.

Occasionally during the previous few years, before he got sick, I had played basketball with Aunese and other football players at our neighborhood court on Canyon Boulevard, just off campus. From my perspective as a fellow student, one moment Aunese was young, strong, famous, and seemingly invincible. The next he was gone. Just like that. For me as a twenty-year-old, it was a brutal reminder that the fantasy world of sport and the real world of life are not so far apart. It wouldn't be the last time that I learned this lesson.

I earned an undergraduate degree in mathematics and ultimately decided to pursue an academic career in science policy—that
messy place where science and decision making meet. As a graduate student, I earned some money by working as a "mentor-tutor"
at the university's athletics department. The job involved working
with specific students on specific subjects. Because I was pretty
good at both math and writing, which every student had to take,
and because I liked teaching, eventually I earned the privilege of
working with some of the scholarship athletes who most needed
tutoring help. In particular, I was assigned to the men's and wom-
en's basketball teams, and even sat on the bench with the CU men's
basketball staff at the 1993 Big 8 tournament in Kansas City.* This
experience marked my transition from starry-eyed sports fan to a
budding academic with a deep interest in how we govern sport and
its role in broader society.

Over the years that I have immersed myself in scholarship related to sports, I have come to appreciate that there are lots of smart,
thoughtful, and creative scholars working on a remarkable array of
issues related to the governance of sport. Sport probably receives
more commentary and analysis outside of academia than any other
human endeavor, except perhaps politics.

But at the same time, sport suffers a certain kind of prejudice
in academia. In the United States, at least, more than a few university academics are offended by, if not openly hostile to, big-time college sports on their own campuses. This is perhaps understandable,
given the amount of time and money that college administrators
invest in athletics. (To take just one example: In 2016, Nick Saban,
the superstar football coach at Alabama, received a salary equivalent to that of about seventy professors.)† As well, many academics
look down their noses at sport. As this book explains, this prejudice
has deep roots in class and culture that date back to the nineteenth
century and that persist today. Although there are plenty of univer-

---

*   It was a short tournament for the Buffs, who were blown out 82–65 by Kansas in
      the first round.
†   In 2016, Saban made about $7 million, enough for seven professors at $100,000
      per year.

sity research centers focused on (to pick one I'm familiar with) the environment, there are only a few focused on the study of sport.

Yet sport is everywhere. Arguably, the enjoyment of sport offers as close as a universal value we can find among the more than 7 billion of us who inhabit planet Earth. Consider that nations as diverse as Iran, China, North Korea, and the United States are among the 183 countries that have signed on to the International Convention against Doping, which covers the use of banned performance-enhancing drugs in sport.[3] The soccer World Cup represents 209 footballing nations, and the Olympics represents 206 sporting nations; the United Nations has only 193 member states. Look around and you'll see sport almost everywhere. And where you find sport, you find all the messiness and complexity of any human endeavor.

Which brings us back to the edge.

Drawing on controversies straight out of the headlines as well as a broad base of academic literature, this book synthesizes a vast amount of information to explore the edge, to try to make some sense of it all, and to offer the reader a provocative but clear new understanding of twenty-first-century sport.[*]

Make no mistake: although this book dives into the incredibly complex and interesting topic of sports governance, we don't get close to the bottom of it. The book's goal, however, is not to provide answers. The objective is to open a door to a fascinating topic so you can think about sport in new ways. Sport needs more thinking, more debate, and more out-in-the-open discussion. Many of the answers to the difficult questions facing sport won't come from experts or authorities. Those answers—especially to the most important questions—will be shaped by all of us who care deeply about sport and

---

[*] This book does not consider issues associated with the rapidly growing world of "e-sports," which refers to the playing and watching of video game competitions. This is a growing area, expected to reach $1.9 billion in revenue by 2018. It faces many of the governance challenges faced by more traditional sports, such as match fixing, doping, and accountability. For an overview, see Andrew Visnovsky, "Growth of Esports: Regulatory Concerns," *The Sports Integrity Initiative* (December 16, 2015), http://www.sportsintegrityinitiative.com/growth-of-esports-regulatory-concerns/.

its role in our society and our world. It is we who will ultimately decide what values we want sport to embrace and reflect.

This book covers some troubling territory. It is enough to make even the seasoned policy analyst more than a bit cynical. But please be aware at the outset that the book ends optimistically. If there is one thing that sport desperately needs in the second decade of the twenty-first century, it is a bit of optimism. But getting to that perspective requires an open-eyed look at the battles that confront sport. What we will see there won't be pretty. But the first step in addressing any difficult challenge is to understand what we are up against. So let's take a look.

PART I

THE WAR FOR THE SOUL OF SPORT

Chapter 1

A Little Edge Can Make a Big Difference

Pop quiz. What do Nellie Kim, Yohan Blake, and László Cseh have in common?

If you said that they each won a silver medal at the Olympics, then you get an A+. But I'd bet you are more likely to recognize the names of Nadia Comăneci, Usain Bolt, and Michael Phelps. These are the three athletes who beat Kim, Blake, and Cseh, winning gold medals, not silver.

We live in a winner-take-all world where, as popularized by legendary football coach Vince Lombardi, "winning isn't everything; it's the only thing!"[1] As the late National Association for Stock Auto Car Racing (NASCAR) driver Dale Earnhardt, Sr., used to say, "Second place is the first place loser."[2] The difference between winning and coming in second can be exceedingly small. In three different swimming events in the 2008 Olympics, László Cseh won three silver medals when his finishing times were a mere 0.6 percent, 1.7 percent, and 1.0 percent behind those of Michael Phelps, but faster than everyone else on the planet.* Yet outside his native Hungary, Cseh is little known.

More than sporting pride is at stake between winning and coming very close to winning. Consider Heath Slocum, a golfer who

---

* Cseh was 0.67 seconds behind Phelps in the 200-meter butterfly and 2.29 and 2.32 seconds behind Phelps in the 200-meter and 400-meter individual medleys, respectively; http://www.olympic.org/olympic-results/beijing-2008/swimming.

turned professional in 1996, the same year that Tiger Woods did.[3] From 1996 to the end of 2013, Slocum's scoring average for each round on the Professional Golfer's Association (PGA) Tour was 70.9, which he was able to translate into four victories and a cool $17 million in winnings (inflation adjusted), making him one of the top 100 money winners ever on the PGA Tour. Over the same eighteen-year period, Tiger Woods averaged about 1.6 strokes per round better than Slocum, turning that small score differential into a difference of $110 million in tournament prize money and becoming one of the most recognizable faces on the planet.

Here is another way to think about those numbers: Over eighteen years, Woods turned his 2.2 percent better scoring average into a 650 percent advantage in prize winnings over Slocum. (Slocum shouldn't feel too bad; Woods did the same to everyone on the Tour over the same period.)* In sport, the smallest performance difference can be a very big deal indeed. No wonder athletes are always looking for that little bit of an extra edge.

Seemingly small differences in sporting outcomes can translate into outsized differentials in rewards. And that's true not just for athletes. Coaches have long reaped the rewards of big-time sporting successes. In 1905, the twenty-six-year-old coach of Harvard's football team earned a salary of $7,000, which was $2,000 more than Harvard's highest-paid professor, and only $1,000 less than Harvard's president.[4] Eighty-six years later, in 1991, an academic observed that "today, a salary above $100,000 is not uncommon for the successful collegiate coach."[5] In 1987, Jerry Tarkanian, head coach of the highly successful University of Nevada, Las Vegas, basketball team, received a salary of $174,000 plus the use of a Cadillac. Swanky. But even those more recent numbers seem quaint today, when coaches are paid far, far more than professors and college presidents, and even more than many CEOs.

---

* Slocum likely has Woods to thank for more than $8 million of his career earnings, due to what I call the "Tiger effect" of Woods's popularity on Tour purses. See Roger Pielke, Jr., "Measuring the 'Tiger Effect': Doubling of Tour Prizes, Billions into Players' Pockets," *Sporting Intelligence*, August 6, 2014, http://www.sportingintelligence.com/2014/08/06/measuring-the-tiger-effect-doubling-of-tour-prize-money-billions-extra-into-players-pockets-060801/.

In 2013, Deadspin.com produced a map (see figure 1.1) showing the highest-paid public employees in each of the fifty United States. In forty states, that person was a head coach of a college football (twenty-seven) or basketball (thirteen) team.[6] The head football coaches of the Army, Navy, and Air Force academies are paid far more than any general or admiral, or anyone else, in the US military, including its commander in chief, the US president.[7]

Figure 1.1. Highest-Paid Public Employees by State, 2013

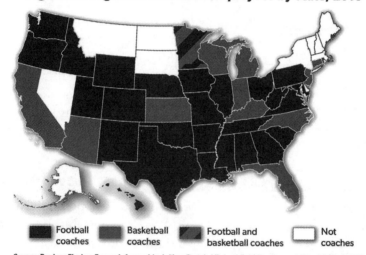

Football coaches   Basketball coaches   Football and basketball coaches   Not coaches

Source: Reuben Fischer-Baum. Infographic: Is Your State's Highest-Paid Employee A Coach? (Probably). http://deadspin.com/infographic-is-your-states-highest-paid-employee-a-co-489635228, May 9, 2013.

Within most professional sports, differences in compensation are dramatic. Figure 1.2 shows the distribution of all player salaries for five major US professional sports leagues in 2014. The top earners in each of these leagues far exceed those in the middle, who (with the exception of Major League Soccer) are all extremely well rewarded compared to most people. Moving just a little bit from left to right on this scale means a dramatic increase in earnings potential. Even within the boundaries of elite sport, a little edge goes a long way. And in sport, by its very nature, there is always a little more edge to achieve.

On-the-field success often translates into off-the-field earnings power. Table 1.1 presents estimates of what the world's top-

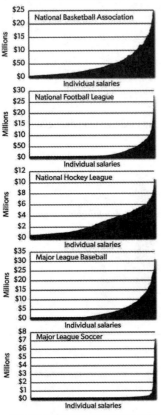

Figure 1.2. Players' Salaries in the Top Five US Leagues, 2014

National Basketball Association

Individual salaries

National Football League

Individual salaries

National Hockey League

Individual salaries

Major League Baseball

Individual salaries

Major League Soccer

Individual salaries

Source: National Basketball Association, National Football League, National Hockey League, Major League Baseball, and Major League Soccer.

earning athletes made from endorsements in 2015, as well as the estimated commercial value of a single tweet.[8] Roger Federer is at the top, with an estimated $58 million in endorsements, followed by plenty of familiar names, all of whom are characterized by extraordinary athletic success. Cristiano Ronaldo, the superstar striker for Real Madrid, can earn more than $250,000 just by sending out a product endorsement via Twitter to his 38 million followers.* Not a bad return on typing 140 characters or less.

Old Rules, New Values

Here is another pop quiz. What do Ben Johnson, Marion Jones, and Alex Rodriguez have in common?

That one is easy. Each was penalized for taking prohibited performance-enhancing drugs—otherwise known as "doping." Their efforts to become champions went over the edge. They violated the "spirit of sport" as codified in the rules that they agreed to follow within their respective sports. As you will discover in chapter 2, the spirit of sport is an important but fuzzy concept, the impre-

---

*   Ronaldo's followers make up about 12 percent of *all* Twitter's active followers every month (about 320 million in early 2016; see https://about.twitter.com/company). As of this writing, only twelve Twitter personas had more followers than Ronaldo: seven of those were singers, one was a talk show host, one was Barack Obama, and three were companies.

Table 1.1. Endorsements by Top-Earning Athletes

Athlete	Sport	2015 estimated endorsement earnings in millions	2015 Opendorse estimated cost per tweet
1. Roger Federer	Tennis	$58	$16,762
2. Tiger Woods	Golf	$50	$27,728
3. Phil Mickelson	Golf	$44	n/a
4. Lebron James	Basketball	$44	$140,119
5. Kevin Durant	Basketball	$35	$66,764
6. Rory McIlroy	Golf	$32	$14,367
7. Novak Djokovic	Tennis	$31	$26,530
8. Rafael Nadal	Tennis	$28	$58,240
9. Cristiano Ronaldo	Soccer	$27	$260,490
10. Mahendra Singh	Cricket	$27	$24,871
11. Kobe Bryant	Basketball	$26	$42,398
12. Maria Sharapova	Tennis	$23	$9,021
13. Lionel Messi	Soccer	$22	n/a
14. Usain Bolt	Track	$21	$21,123
15. Neymar	Soccer	$17	$135,900
16. Andy Murray	Tennis	$16	$18,788
17. Floyd Mayweather, Jr.	Boxing	$15	$34,924
18. Derrick Rose	Basketball	$15	$11,350
19. Kei Nishikori	Tennis	$15	$1,721
20. Serena Williams	Tennis	$13	$30,558
21. Manny Pacquiao	Boxing	$12	$14,617
22. Dwyane Wade	Basketball	$12	$28,276
23. Peyton Manning	Football	$12	n/a
24. Justin Rose	Golf	$12	$2,430 ·
25. Drew Brees	Football	$11	$12,562

cision of which sometimes leads to inconsistencies and even irra-tionality in the rules of sport. What is OK in the National Football League is not necessarily OK in the Olympics. The severity of sanc-tions differs across sports. For instance, get caught taking human growth hormone in the Olympics and you can be suspended for four years, but in the NFL, the penalty is four weeks.*

Sport is characterized by frequent appeals to admirable aspirations, such as purity of motive and self-regulation. However, such aspirations have proven problematic when they morph from fuzzy, overarching values into concrete rules and regulations. The sports values that we have inherited have a long history. The founder of the modern Olympic Games, Pierre de Coubertin, explained in 1927 that "our object in reviving an institution twenty-five centuries old was that you should become new adepts of the religion of sports, as our great ancestors conceived it." Athletes became members of that religion by "the swearing of an oath of fidelity to the rules and unselfishness, and above all in compelling themselves to strict adherence thereto."[9]

Pierre de Coubertin, founder of the modern Olympic Games.

Without rules, our society would be impossible. Think about driving. In the United States, we drive on the right side of the road and agree to follow numerous rules that govern how we drive. Red means stop, green means go. If people chose to make up whatever rules they wanted, not only would our safety be imperiled, but our ability to move about would be compromised. Rules—and following them—help make the world go round. They also make sport possible.

Not everyone follows the rules, however, so there are traffic cops and traffic courts, speed

---

* In the NFL, the penalty is technically four games, which could occur in consecutive weeks.

cameras, and parking tickets. A vast array of institutions is in place to govern the rules of driving. Sport is no different. The sports world has many institutions, ranging from referees and umpires to players organizations, leagues, associations, federations, and even scholarly groups and fan clubs. Sport is surrounded by an ecosystem of business and commercial interests that, as we will see, is not particularly large in comparative economic terms but that has outsized influence in culture and the media. Also involved in overseeing sport are governments and at least one international treaty. Sometimes these institutions break down or fail to do their job. Indeed, as we are often reminded, sports officials are occasionally complicit in helping athletes avoid the rules, and at other times they break the rules when athletes want them followed.

This chapter introduces the struggle that lies at the heart of this book: the battle between a performance edge and an ethical edge. The battle takes place in the language and practice of rules. And the rules, in turn, reflect a battle to preserve certain values. The trouble is, today the values that underpin sport are outdated, which places rules on a shaky foundation.

The aspirational values that underlie modern sport can be distilled down to four: amateurism, purity, uncertainty, and autonomy. Unfortunately, all four are either out of step with modern society or have always been mythological. As I argue in chapter 2 (and throughout the book), sport needs to be governed based on a new quartet of values: professionalism, pragmatism, accountability, and transparency.

Rapid developments in the twenty-first century and outdated sports governance have revealed the tension between sports' outdated values and the demands of the new era. This tension has left sport in a state of crisis. Increasingly, athletes, teams, and administrators seek a competitive edge in the cutthroat world of elite sport—and sometimes they go *over* the edge in their pursuit of one. Sustaining what we love most about sport requires that how we think about sport keep pace with the changes in sport in the twenty-first century.

Squidgy Balls, Fuzzy Edges, and Hazy Rules

The travails of Tom Brady and his (allegedly) deflated footballs illus-trate what happens when old principles and new attitudes collide: the rules get broken or blurred, the institutions supposed to enforce the rules do a bad job and get a bad rap, and no one can agree what it means to "cheat."

Tom Brady is among the most successful athletes in American history. As of this writing, he has led the NFL's New England Patri-ots to four Super Bowl victories, earning the award for most valu-able player in three of them. By the end of the 2015–16 NFL season, only four other NFL quarterbacks had ever passed for more yards and no one had ever passed for more in the playoffs.[10] His magnetic smile and movie star good looks befit the leader of his generation's winningest team in America's favorite sport.

Yet, when Brady came out of college at the University of Michi-gan, he seemed highly unlikely to make it in the NFL, much less as-semble one of the most remarkable careers in league history. Skinny for a professional football player and lacking much in the way of obvious muscle tone, young Tom Brady did not look the part of a future sports hero.

The numbers bear out that perception. Each year, before NFL teams draft eligible players from the college ranks, they evaluate the players' athleticism at what is called the NFL Combine. Consider these remarkable statistics: Of the 327 quarterbacks who partici-pated in the NFL Combine from 1999 to 2014, Brady recorded the 325th fastest time in the forty-yard dash, at 5.28 seconds.[11] Only two prospective quarterbacks ran slower. He also had the 6th worst vertical leap, at 24.5 inches.

With this performance, it is not surprising that Brady was the 199th player, and the 7th quarterback, chosen in the 2000 NFL draft. But in the years that followed, Brady surprised everyone, especially those teams that passed on taking him in the draft that year. The six quarterbacks selected ahead of Brady collectively started 191 games in their NFL careers, a total that Brady surpassed in 2014. The skinny, slow kid from Michigan outperformed them all. In fact, he has outperformed almost every quarterback who has ever played the game.

There could not be a better example than Brady to illustrate that achieving a competitive edge in sport is about much more than physical appearance or even the analytical quantification of athleticism in raw numbers. Attaining that edge, whether you are Tom Brady or the New England Patriots, requires a sometimes-mysterious combination of skill and luck. Cracking that code, or just being the right person in the right place at the right time, can lead to on-the-field glory and off-the-field rewards.

Tom Brady cracked that code. Today, Brady has a reported net worth of more than $130 million. He is married to a Brazilian supermodel. A postfootball career in politics—which Brady has hinted at every so often—seems possible. Brady's opulent lifestyle and fame provide an easy answer to the question of why athletes seek to achieve a competitive edge. Sure, winning and basking in its glory are great. But the winnings are found not only on the field.

In the 2015 Super Bowl, the Patriots pulled off an improbable, last-minute victory over the Seattle Seahawks (whose coach decided—in what many people thought a moment of madness or hubris—to throw the ball rather than run it, even though the ball sat a mere thirty-six inches from the Patriot's goal line). Another chapter

Tom Brady playing for the New England Patriots in 2009.

was added to Brady's storybook career. But then the entire fairy tale appeared to be threatened by a most bizarre turn of events.

It turned out that less than two weeks before the Super Bowl, an equipment manager for the Indianapolis Colts—whom the Patriots had beaten in the American Football Conference (AFC) championship game to get to the Super Bowl—had contacted the NFL with concerns that the balls used by the Patriots had been intentionally underinflated. In the NFL, each team provides the game balls that it uses when on offense, and the equipment manager suspected that the Patriots were using nonconforming balls to gain a competitive advantage. The Patriots were accused of preparing the footballs that they were using in a way that would make the balls easier to throw, catch, and grip. Specifically, the Patriots were charged with letting some air out of each ball, thereby making them a bit softer and easier to handle on a cold, rainy New England winter day.

The combustible mix of America's most popular sport, one of its most high-profile teams, and its wildly successful and photogenic quarterback at the center of the controversy ignited into what came to be called "Deflategate." The controversy led the NFL to investigate, which resulted in a 243-page report that suggested some sort of cheating by Brady and the Patriots. The NFL responded to the findings of its report by suspending Brady for four games.

Deflategate blows up. New York *Daily News*, May 7, 2015.

But that was far from the end of the story. It was actually just the beginning. Brady challenged the suspension, which the NFL subsequently upheld. Then the National Football League Players Association (NFLPA) took the NFL to court. The dispute thus moved from an internal NFL disciplinary proceeding to a legal action under US law. All this over allegedly deflated footballs used in a game.

In court, the NFLPA accused the NFL of failing to play by the rules of its own disciplinary proceedings through a lack of independence in its investigation, misrepresentation of evidence, and errors in its analysis that called into question the NFL's findings. The science of ball pressurization underlying the NFL's report on the alleged deflated footballs was challenged, and competing hired experts aired their different views. A cottage industry of analysts found a home on the Internet, and included everyone from skilled technical experts to far-out conspiracy theorists. The issue became characterized as NFL commissioner Roger Goodell's rush to judgment versus Brady's alleged cheating. Just before the next season began in September 2015, the court vacated the NFL suspension, freeing Brady to play, but the cloud over Brady lingered. The issued dragged on, and in the spring of 2016 a court reinstated Brady's suspension, withholding judgments on the merits of the dispute but supporting Goodell's disciplinary authority.

Tom Brady and the Patriots may indeed have been guilty of violating the rules in search of an advantage—consider that one of their equipment men was nicknamed "the Deflator."* However, what is unambiguous is that the NFL, in its procedural missteps in conducting its investigation and meting out punishment, failed in its basic duty to fairly enforce the rules of the game that it oversees. Writing for Yahoo Sports, Dan Wetzel summed up the controversy, explaining that the NFL's missteps helped the controversy evolve to become about much more than simply underinflated footballs: "How does anyone in the NFL—owner, coach, player, or fan—possibly trust the league office to investigate and rule on anything ever again?"[12]

All is fair in love and war, but not in sport. Sport is based on rules. Without rules, there can be no sport. Without trust in the enforcement of rules, the rules risk becoming meaningless, or worse, the rules actually contribute to a diminishment of the integrity of sport.

---

* The Patriots insist that there is a perfectly innocent explanation for this remarkable coincidence; see Sean Wagner-McGough, "Patriots: Ball Boy Called Self 'Deflator' Because Wanted to Lose Weight," CBSSports.com (May 14, 2015), http://www.cbssports.com/nfl/eye-on-football/25185129/patriots-attendant-called-himself-deflator-because-he-was-trying-to-lose-weight.

Whatever may have happened with those footballs, the violation itself doesn't threaten the integrity of sport. But if the NFL fails to uphold the rules of the game or the rules that it has in place for investigations and punishments, then the integrity of the game itself may be threatened.

When the organization in charge of establishing and enforcing the rules fails to do its job, the spirit of sport is threatened. We may never know the truth behind Deflategate. But the NFL rules that governed equipment for football games set the stage for the Deflategate, and the NFL did professional football no favors in how it responded to the claims of the Patriots' subterfuge. As the entities responsible for coming up with the rules governing the preparation of footballs, the NFL and NFLPA share the ultimate responsibility for the lingering controversy. The NFL rules allowed each team to prepare its own footballs, for use when on offense, with very little in the way of oversight or accountability. That created an opportunity for mischief while denying the NFL the ability to enforce these rules when a situation like Deflategate arose.

It need not have been so. Had the NFL had in place better procedures for overseeing how footballs are prepared by each team—basic accountability—Deflategate might never have occurred. And if allegations were raised about rule breaking, greater transparency about the handling of the footballs would have rendered moot future scientific debates in courtrooms about the application of the Ideal Gas Law to the behavior of wet footballs.

Reactions to the Deflategate controversy help characterize two commonplace positions when it comes to enforcing rules in sport.

One is that rules are meant to be broken, and if you get caught, too bad for you. NFL Hall of Fame quarterback Joe Montana expressed this view when he said that even if the Patriots altered balls for advantage, Deflategate was not a big deal:

> It is one of those things that is a rule, right? It might be a dumb rule, but it doesn't matter. [Brady] didn't deflate them himself, but you can pick up the ball and can tell if it is underinflated, overinflated, or what you like. Everybody is afraid to say it, but if the guy did it, so what. Just pay up and move on. It's no big deal. . . . Our offensive

linemen used to spray silicone on their shirts until they got caught. Once you get caught, you get caught. Period. It doesn't take anything away from Tom's game.[13]

Players, Montana tells us, go right up to and sometimes over the edge, and if they do, they sometimes get caught. Big whoop. If you are caught you are penalized. That is what rules are for, right? Accept the penalty and move on.

The other position on Deflategate has been voiced by, among others, Charles Haley, another NFL Hall of Famer and the only player to earn five Super Bowl rings (two with San Francisco and three with Dallas). Haley, who played linebacker and defensive end, positions that often require chasing after quarterbacks (perhaps protected by linemen with silicon on their shirts!), called Brady a cheater: "I've lost all respect [for Brady]. When your integrity is challenged in the game of football, to me, all his Super Bowls are tainted."[14] Similar comments were made by Jerry Rice, the Hall of Fame receiver who caught a lot of Joe Montana's passes, in siding with Haley: "I'm going to be point blank, I feel like it's cheating."[15]

Edge Battles

We all think we know what it means to cheat, right? It means to take something unfairly or act dishonestly or unfairly to get an advantage—to cheat is to gain an edge improperly. Right?

Defining what it means in practice to cheat in sports can be fiendishly difficult. Consider these cases:

- Before a race, a sprinter takes three caffeine pills, prepared specifically by sport scientists to give her a notable performance boost.

- A soccer player bets on the timing of a game's first throw-in and kicks the ball out of bounds at exactly that time (and then he scores one of his team's two goals and his team goes on to win).

- A popular college athlete accepts money for his signature.

- A woman with elevated but natural testosterone level competes against women whose testosterone level is more common.

- A soccer player (who is not the goalie) intentionally uses his hands to stop the ball from entering his goal in a tied game near the end of the match (and he gets a red card from the referee, meaning he is kicked out of the match). The opposing team misses the subsequent penalty kick and then ultimately loses the game in a penalty shootout.

- A tennis player is losing a match—and her composure. She takes an allowed ten-minute medical timeout even though she is uninjured. She regains her composure, returns to the court, and promptly wins the match.

- A bicyclist takes a prohibited performance-enhancing substance, knowing that virtually everyone else in the peloton is taking the same stuff. He receives a lifetime ban from the sport, while other riders who took the same drug are given much shorter bans.

- A man born without lower legs uses prosthetic blades to compete in the Olympics against athletes who have no such technological aids.

- A young boy is given human growth hormone by a famous soccer club to aid his physical development. He goes on to stardom.

- A badminton doubles team purposely loses a match early in the tournament in order to get a better seeding in the later knock-out phase of the competition.

- A basketball player "flops"; a soccer player "dives"; a baseball catcher "frames" a pitch.

Each of these examples is taken from a real-world situation. And each is discussed in the following chapters. Whether or not each case reflects cheating, going over the edge, or not, is hotly contested. For example, a top official of the World Anti-Doping Agency (WADA), the international body that oversees doping regulations in Olympic sport, has suggested that caffeine ingested as a triple espresso is allowable, but the exact equal amount of the drug in pill form should not be allowed. The tennis player who abused injury rules was accused of gamesmanship and cheating by some, while others applauded her cleverness. A soccer team that plays for tournament positioning in group play is usually characterized as being sensibly "strategic"; but the badminton players engaging in exactly the same behavior were sent home from the Olympics.

Where is the ethical edge that separates effective tactics from cheating? Sometimes it's literally impossible to tell, because there is no written or unwritten rule stating where that edge lies. That is why institutions of sports governance are so important—it is their job to define where that edge lies and to hold athletes, officials, and administrators to account.

The sporting world today is overwhelmed by what might be called "edge battles." Edge battles are to be expected in sport, because sport is all about securing an edge—over history, over an opponent, over what has been done before. Pushing limits and exceeding them is a defining characteristic of sport and even a fulfillment of what it means to be human. Such battles might not be so problematic except for the fact that ample evidence suggests that more than a few institutions of sports governance are either not doing their jobs or doing their jobs extremely poorly. Consequently, it is no overstatement to say that today's edge battles are part of a larger war for the soul of modern sport.

Part II of this book zeroes in on five edge battles—probably the top five in terms of their current impact on sport and on what we think sport is or should be. The chapters in part II look in turn at battles over amateurism, match fixing, doping, technology, and sex testing. The chapters also offer some constructive and pragmatic ideas about how these battles might be won in a way that makes sports no less exciting and competitive (no less edgy) but more ethical and pragmatic (more in keeping with the spirit of sport).

Amateurs: Who Is Being Cheated?

College sports in the United States are governed by an organization called the National Collegiate Athletic Association, or the NCAA. The NCAA asserts that "amateurism" is the "bedrock principle" of college athletics.[16] Under the NCAA, amateurism means that "young men and women competing on the field or court are students first, athletes second."

But what amateurism means in practice is increasingly complicated. In the 1950s, the NCAA introduced the athletic scholarship,
which in recent years has been augmented by many other perks
and benefits that are provided to athletes in exchange for playing.
Athletes are not paid salaries, but they are certainly compensated.
In 2013, the American Institutes for Research, a Washington, DC–
based nonprofit organization, estimated that major universities
spent an average of about $14,000 per enrolled student per year
in support of their education. For scholarship athletes, however,
they spent an additional *$95,000* per student per year.[17] University
spending on college athletes is increasing faster than spending on
students generally, mainly because athletics departments are able
to secure external funding support well beyond that provided by
tuition alone.

As more and more money has poured into college athletics, due
largely to men's basketball and football, athletes and their representatives have demanded a greater share. Some have even called for
salaries to be paid to scholarship athletes. The NCAA has responded
by increasing athletes' food allowances and implementing a stipend
system (called "cost of attendance"), which *USA Today* estimated to
resulted in $160 million in additional benefits in 2015–16.[18]

As we shall see, the efforts by the NCAA to maintain a façade of
amateurism while college sports becomes increasingly professional-
ized has created tensions that threaten the very existence of college
athletics. It may be time for the NCAA, like the Olympics before it,
to move beyond the ideal of amateurism and embrace professionalism in a way that makes practical sense but preserves the unique
identity of college sports. If the NCAA does not change, then change
will be forced upon it. I make some pragmatic, common-sense suggestions that might help preserve what is so beloved about college
sports while recognizing the professional characteristics of elite
programs.

Match Fixing: Cheating to Lose

Match fixing, the manipulation of game results often associated with organized crime and gambling, poses threats to the integrity of what we see in sport, threatening in some cases to turn it from unscripted competition to staged performance. The start of 2016 saw the tennis world thrown into upheaval with remarkable claims of widespread match fixing at the highest levels.[19] The specter of match fixing has on occasion blighted the National Basketball Association (NBA) and the NCAA. Soccer and cricket have for years been embroiled in controversies over contrived results. As Simon Kuper relates in the preface, even the World Cup has not been immune to such claims.

In 2015, prior to the Cricket World Cup jointly hosted by Australia and New Zealand, the New Zealand cricket team participated in a training session that, rather than involving bats, balls, and stumps, centered on a ninety-minute video on how to avoid the threat of match fixing. Among the threats players were warned about in the session was the so-called honey trap. A honey trap refers to the use of a beautiful woman (or man, as the case may be) who uses her (or his) sex appeal to get a player in a compromising situation, which is secretly filmed and then used by match fixers to blackmail the player. A player might be told, for instance, to score less than ten runs or to let in a goal. The scenario is not so far-fetched. In Singapore, for example, several years ago a soccer referee was sentenced and jailed for trading sex for match fixing.[20]

Although documented cases of the successful use of the honey trap remain rare, the threat of match fixing is very real, and the number of players and officials found guilty of it is on the rise. For instance, a German soccer referee was jailed in 2006 for fixing games, including one in the prestigious German Cup.[21] Soon after, Italian soccer was rocked by a match-fixing scandal that included one of its most prestigious clubs, Juventus.[22] Wikipedia has a list of top-level cricket stars who have been sanctioned for match fixing that totals more than thirty names.[23] In 2016, the South African government investigated widespread allegations of match fixing.[24] Worldwide, such cases are almost always tied to organized gambling, and, in recent years, they often have occurred in Asia, where gambling is popular and unregulated.[25]

It turns out, however, that defining what is meant by match fixing, and thus developing rules and regulations in response, is more difficult than it might seem upon first impression. Furthermore, studies have shown over and over again that many people, including sports fans, just don't see match fixing as a major problem. I argue that because of the stakes involved, match fixing is typically found in lower-tier competitions, where simple economics means that athletes and officials are more easily bought off. But that's not to say that match fixing couldn't happen in the biggest sports settings, just that it is unlikely. Ultimately, however, match fixing is more a problem for the gambling industry than it is for the sports fan.

Doping: Lance Armstrong Gets the Last Laugh

Doping refers to the use of methods or substances that enhance athletic performance and are prohibited because they are unsafe or deemed unfair. One example of a *method* is the drawing of an athlete's blood for subsequent transfusion back into that same athlete just prior to competition to boost oxygen capacity, via greater blood volume, and thus endurance. An example of a *substance* that boosts performance is the anabolic steroid, which contributes to added muscle mass and strength. We can divide performance enhancement into three different categories, which I call "stronger," "longer," and "better." Some drugs can act on all three categories at the same time. In 2015, WADA included almost 300 specific chemicals and three families of methods on its prohibited list.

Sport has faced crisis after crisis related to doping. Athletes have been caught violating rules, and more recently sport organizations have been caught covering up doping and even extorting athletes. A few years ago, Lance Armstrong and cycling were at the center of this storm. More recently, international track and field, especially in Russia, China, and Kenya, has been at the center. Then Maria Sharapova and meldonium pushed athletics off center stage. Swimming, football, baseball, and even soccer and tennis have alleged doping problems. Rather than getting better, doping in sport seems to be getting worse.

There is ample evidence to suggest that doping in sport is endemic, and little evidence to indicate that antidoping efforts actually do much at all. It is time to take a good hard look at the notion of "cleanliness" in sport in favor of a more evidence-based, transparent approach to the regulation of banned performance-enhancing substances. I argue that the current approach to antidoping has been a complete and dismal failure, and that athletes most of all suffer the consequences of this failure.

Technology: Hacking the Athlete and the Games

Another edge battle surrounds what has been called the "technological augmentation" of the biological human. Beyond doping, athletes routinely take advantage of modern technologies to improve their performance. Golfers and baseball players have laser surgery on their eyes, not just to get to 20/20 vision, but to take their eyes to the limits of human visual capabilities. Ligaments and tendons are not just repaired, but improved. Athletes today run on and jump off of prosthetics that enable them to go faster and farther than human legs allow; they have surgeries after injuries that make their bodies stronger than they were previously. Some athletes go to extremes, such as fighters who have their facial skin replaced and bones shaved in order to reduce the odds that they will bleed in a fight. Cutting-edge genetic technologies offer the promise of techniques to create potential superathletes—perhaps not so far in the future.

Technologies also change the games themselves. Tennis, cricket, soccer, football, and basketball are among the sports that use technologies to aid in enforcing rules. High-definition television and ultra-slow-motion replays give spectators a way to watch games that allows for a better view than that possible for referees on the field. With such vision, referees' mistakes and on-the-field action can pose challenges to the legitimacy of sport. Consequently, new rules are invented. Some are simple to implement, like goal-line technology in soccer to help the referee determine if the ball crosses the line. Others, like video review of football catches in the NFL, force us to confront the uncomfortable fact that a "catch" is a subjective event in sport. Technology can go only so far in helping officials, and at times it can make their jobs harder and enforcing the rules impossible.

Technologies threaten the integrity of sport itself. Hydrodynamic suits in swimming, grooved wedges in golf, and sophisticated brooms in curling have all been judged to aid the athlete too much for use in those sports. Technologies also allow for new ways to cheat: in early 2016, a professional cyclist was caught with a hidden electric motor in her bike.* When put to good use, technological augmentation of sport holds the promise of making sport better; when it is used improperly or unthinkingly, the opposite is possible.

Technology provides another challenge to the idea of the "purity" of sport. Technological changes will force changes to rules governing athletes as well as to the games themselves. I argue that we are overdue to open a discussion of technology in sport. That means that sport might change. Fasten your seat belt.

Sex Testing: When Mother Nature Cheats

The final battleground centers on what might seem to be a simple question: How should sports organizations determine who is eligible to participate in women's sports and events? After all, pretty much everywhere you go has a public restroom for men and one for women. We all pick one. Easy, right?†

Biological sex is anything but simple, as scientists and sporting officials have learned. Western societies (in particular) over the past century have gone to great lengths to distinguish two genders— male and female—and to hide, erase, or gloss over any ambiguities that exist in the space between male and female. Sport has been a central part of this trend. For more than a half century, sport has

---

* A new term was coined in the process: "technological fraud." See Benoit Noel, "Cookson Confirms 'Technological Fraud' at Cyclocross Worlds," *VELONEWS* (January 31, 2016), http://velonews.competitor.com/2016/01/news/first-technological-fraud-case-rocks-cycling-world_394276.

† No so fast, you might say, based on headlines in 2016: http://money.cnn.com/2016/04/20/news/companies/target-transgender-bathroom-lgbt/.

looked to science to offer a definitive way to classify what it means to be female. Over that period, controversy after controversy has arisen showing that efforts to delineate once and for all what it means to be a woman for sporting purposes have failed again and again. The consequences have been significant for some athletes, who have been denied the right to compete or suffered public shaming. I argue that today we are in a position to end the half-century of debates over "sex testing" once and for all. Sport can serve its highest ideals by leading the way to a more just and equal world.

How to Win the War for Sport

The keys to winning the war for sport are the focus of part III. There I discuss science, governance, and how we might apply twenty-first-century values to sport.

Experts, including scientists, can be handy to have around. When an athlete is badly injured, he or she goes to a surgeon to get fixed. It is logical, therefore, that when sport is broken, we turn to relevant experts to fix things up. However, winning the war for sport will require more than simply calling on experts—it will require the ability to distinguish when experts can help and when they can't. As we will see, science has an important role to play in antidoping, but too much science can make matters worse. In sex testing, science cannot provide a unique or simple test to tell who is and who is not a woman. Asking science to answer questions like this encourages us to hide questions about gender and politics in the guise of technical issues. And that serves no one.

Science and other forms of expertise have an important role to play in winning the war for sport, but only if we put experts in their proper place. A crucial challenge for the sports world is to be able to secure independent advice from experts, especially when that advice may be uncomfortable or challenge conventional wisdom. Too often, sports organizations rely on experts who may have conflicts of interest, which in turn may compromise their advice or how it is perceived. Better advice doesn't mean that better decisions will be made, although it is likely to help.

Securing better advice is one part of the need to improve sports governance overall. For many decades, sports organizations, particularly international ones, like the Fédération Internationale de Football Association (FIFA) or the International Olympic Committee (IOC), have evolved under the principle that they should be able to govern themselves. In the language of the sports world, these organizations should have "autonomy." And for a long time, governments, sponsors, and athletes have supported this view. However, in recent years, autonomy has been used as a cover for corruption and the exploitation of athletes. Autonomy has failed sport.

We can look at recent governance failures in sport for guidance on how things might be done better. Greater accountability and transparency does not mean that sports should be taken over by the United Nations or that international sports organizations should become international corporations, although both options are well worth discussing. Rather, in whatever form sports organizations take in the twenty-first century, they should be expected to adopt the best practices of modern governance as they are applied to other national and international organizations outside of sport. It doesn't seem a lot to ask, but sports organizations have often resisted such calls.

Finally, winning the war for sport depends on articulating a new set of values to guide sport to replace those that are outdated. And athletes should be at the center of the process of identifying those values. The voices of the athletes who play sport should no longer be silenced or ignored by the people who administer sport. Only then can the rules that make sport possible be truly legitimate and broadly accepted. Winning the war for sport will require much more open debate and discussion than has been the case to date. Such a conversation may be difficult at times, it may involve strongly held opposing points of view, and it may enter uncomfortable territory. Let's get started!

Chapter 2

The Spirit of Sport

The word *sport*, according to the *Oxford English Dictionary*, derives from the Old English word *disport*, which refers to "anything which affords diversion and entertainment."[1] Writing in the 1600s, Blaise Pascal, the famous mathematician, mulled on the nature of happiness and human life. He wrote of the challenges faced by humans and how they wear on us: "We either think on the miseries we have, or on those that threaten us."[2] Yet, Pascal continued, although we may be "filled with a thousand essential causes of weariness, , as a game of billiards, suffices to divert [us]."

Sport—playing a game—does indeed divert us. Yet sport is far more than a mere diversion. Sport can be found everywhere and across time. It is no exaggeration to say that sport is fundamental to the human experience.

A few hundred years ago, the word *sport* was a euphemism for sex. In 1772, the English writer Thomas Bridges observed, "in England, if you trust report, Whether in country, town, or court, The parsons daughters make best sport."[3] Given how much people like competition, it is probably understandable that the modern usage of the word *sport* shares an etymological history with romps with the parson's daughter. Apart from sex (or maybe even more than sex), the modern understanding of sport as a competition, typically but not always athletic, offers something close to a universal human value.

This chapter takes a look at what has been called the "spirit of sport"—a phrase that comes from the modern Olympic movement and characterizes the values underlying the rules of sport. Figure

2.1 shows the frequency of the usage of the phrase "spirit of sport" in English-language books. A century ago, the spirit of sport was much discussed as the institutions and games of the modern Olympic, college, and professional sports began to take shape. The phrase fell out of favor in the second half of the twentieth century as the institutions of sport assumed their modern forms, but it has seen a remarkable resurgence in the twenty-first century.

Figure 2.1. Frequency of the Phrase "Spirit of Sport" (1860–2008)

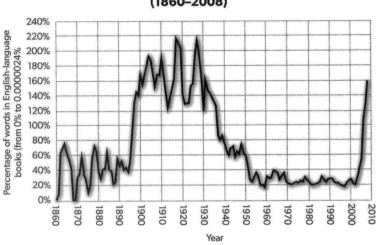

Source: Google Ngrams, https://books.google.com/ngrams.

One reason for this resurgence is the ongoing war for the soul of sport. As we fight that war, we instinctively appeal to the values that we believe underpin sport. That takes us back to the spirit of sport. But what is it? Are its underlying values the same today as they were in the past? Or are there other values that could and should define sport in the twenty-first century?

In this chapter, I argue that the spirit of sport is what we say it is—we hold the power to define the meaning of sport. It is time to use that freedom to open up the spirit of sport to renewed discussion, debate, and change. First, however, let's get closer to the heart of what we mean by the "spirit of sport." Is it something with a price tag? Where should we expect to find it? Where might we have lost it?

Money Matters, But Not That Much

A discussion of modern sport often turns to money. Baseball players get $100 million-plus contracts. FIFA has more than $1 billion in the bank. Cities gift the NFL hundreds of millions of dollars in subsidies for new stadiums. Top golfers and tennis players get tens of millions in endorsement contracts. Nike, Adidas, and Under Armor are rolling in profits. College football coaches and athletics administrators are paid millions of dollars.

But although money is the focus of a lot of discussion, in the big economic picture, sport is just not that big. One popular textbook on sports economics observes, "while sport looms large in people's minds, in economic terms it is still a small proportion of overall economic activity, at least as measured."[4] We can get a sense of the size of sports in the overall economy by taking a look at some numbers.

Table 2.1. Revenue of US Professional Sports Leagues and the NCAA, 2013

Sport organization	2013 revenue*	Average team value*	Average attendance	Total attendance
NFL	$9.2	$1.2	68,373	17,510,569
MLB	$7.1	$0.8	30,513	74,026,895
NBA	$4.6	$0.6	17,347	12,758,849
NHL	$2.6	$0.4	17,720	21,320,299
MLS	$0.5	$0.1	18,639	5,986,119
NASCAR	$0.8	$0.1	97,722	3,600,000
NCAA	$0.9	n/a	45,671	44,353,878

* In billions.

Table 2.1 shows some recent summary statistics for the major US professional sports leagues and the NCAA. The league with the most revenue is the NFL, with more than $12 billion in 2015.[5] The NFL wants to see this grow to more than $25 billion by 2027.[6] How much is $12 billion? Turkish Airlines, the world's seventh-largest international airline, has revenue of about $12 billion.[7] Another comparison of $12 billion in revenue is the entire US coffee industry.[8] To put that number in context, $12 billion was also about how much Apple earned every two weeks in the first quarter of 2016.[9] In dollars and cents, the NFL is about 4 percent of the size of Apple. Yet the Super Bowl is the most watched TV program in the United States and, apart from soccer's World Cup, maybe even the world. Money doesn't tell the whole story.

In 2014, Bloomberg Business asked how the NFL might compare if it were a "real business" rather than a nonprofit.[10] (A nonprofit! Amazing, right?)* Bloomberg suggested that the market capitalization of the NFL would be $46 billion, based on the sum of individual team valuations. Putting together revenue and market capitalization, Bloomberg concluded that "the NFL has one of the smallest revenue bases. It would rank behind seventeen of the companies in terms of the amount of money it brings in." Hypothetically, it would rank 106th in the S&P 500 in terms of market capitalization and 255th in revenue. Bloomberg also notes that the NFL commissioner made $37 million in 2013 (and more in 2014), which was more than Disney CEO Robert Iger, who made $34 million leading a company with $48 billion in revenue.[11]

The entire 2013 revenue of the major US sports (including NASCAR and the NCAA) was about $25 billion. That represented about 0.15 percent of the total US gross domestic product (GDP), a measure of the size of the nation's economy.[12] The overall sports industry, which in addition to professional sports includes things like health clubs, equipment, and apparel, was estimated to be $485 billion in 2013,[13] representing almost 3 percent of GDP. More broadly, the global sports industry was estimated to be about $1.5 trillion in 2013, or about 2 percent of global GDP.[14] No matter how you slice the data, whether looking narrowly at the professional sports or broadly at the sports industry, sport is not a very big part of the US or the global economy.

---

* In 2015, the NFL gave up its nonprofit status, which it was granted in 1942; Drew Harwell and Will Hobson, "The NFL Is Dropping Its Tax-Exempt Status. Why That Ends Up Helping Them Out," *Washington Post*, April 28, 2015, https://www.washingtonpost.com/news/business/wp/2015/04/28/the-nfl-is-dropping-its-tax-exempt-status-why-that-ends-up-helping-them-out/. The NBA and NASCAR are not nonprofits. The PGA and the NHL are nonprofits.

What about sport in Europe? Soccer (or "football" as Europeans call it) is the overwhelmingly dominant sport across the continent.[15] Table 2.2 shows some information about the biggest football leagues in Europe. The total annual revenue in 2013 for football is coincidentally quite similar to the $25 billion in revenue of the major US sports. About half of that comes from the "Big Five" domestic leagues in England, Germany, Spain, Italy, and France.* Even though the mix of games and leagues is very different in Europe compared with the United States, the magnitude and share of the economy of professional sport in Europe is similar to those in the United States.

Table 2.2. Revenue of European Soccer Leagues, 2013

Sport organization	Country	Euros*	Dollars*	Teams	Average attendance	Total attendance
Premier League	England	€2,946	$3,830	20	35,931	13,653,780
Bundesliga	Germany	€2,018	$2,623	18	41,914	12,825,684
La Liga	Spain	€1,859	$2,417	20	29,330	11,145,277
Serie A	Italy	€1,682	$2,187	20	23,300	8,854,000
Ligue 1	France	€1,297	$1,686	20	21,519	6,111,488
Rest of Europe		€9,800	$12,740		n/a	n/a

* In millions.

In contrast to the relatively small proportion of the economy that sport occupies, it takes up a large share of our collective attention. Hard numbers are difficult to come by, but a 2001 study at Northwestern University found that in the United States, the most commonly reported subject in newspapers of all sizes was sports.[16] In 2015, ESPN was the most watched US cable network, having aired eighteen of the top twenty-seven most-watched programs.[17] The largest television audience in UK history was for the final of the 1966 World Cup; in the Philippines, a 2006 boxing match between

---

*   The English second division, the Championship, had 2013 revenue of about US $560 million, making it larger in economic terms than the US Major League Soccer (MLS); Deloitte Sports Business Group Articles, "Annual Review of Football Finance 2015-Revolution," http://www2.deloitte.com/uk/en/pages/sports-business-group/articles/annual-review-of-football-finance.html.

Manny Pacquiao and Erik Morales broke the national record for TV viewers.[18]

In short, sport has an outsized presence in society when compared to its economic footprint. Money matters a great deal in sport, but sport is not defined by economics. There is something about sport not captured by economics that captivates us, that holds our attention, and doesn't let us go. What is it? For more than a century, that je ne sais quoi has been called the "spirit of sport." Let's see if we can get a sense of it.

Looking for the Spirit of Sport: Track and Field—And a Famous Flop

Track and field is characterized by its utter simplicity. Running, jumping, throwing. Athleticism at its most fundamental. Unlike most team sports, athletics offers the clear objectivity of results. We know that Usain Bolt runs faster than Jesse Owens, even though Owens died six years before Bolt was born, because they ran the same race.* As soon as children can walk, they want to run, and they want to race. How fast can I go? Am I faster than my mom, dad, brother, or sister?

The spirit of sport might be described as competition for the sake of competition, for something pure and untainted. If that is indeed what the spirit of sport is, then the best place to find it is in the most simple of all sports, track and field. But when we take a close look, we find that simplicity and purity are hard to pin down. In reality, sport is characterized by innovations—both human and technological—and by efforts to push the boundaries of the rules. Let's take a look at the high jump, which is characterized by a century-long quest to see how high humans can soar.

One of the longest-standing athletic world records for both men and women is for the high jump. Like sprinting, the sport is a sim-

---

* Ah, but it is more complicated than this. They ran on different surfaces, used different equipment, and were timed with different technology. Even in the simplest of competitions, the 100-meter race, things are not as simple as they might appear.

ple one—athletes try to get their entire body over a horizontal bar without dislodging it. The highest clearance wins.

The world record for men has been held since 1993 by Javier Sotomayor of Cuba, who cleared 2.45 meters (just under 8 feet 1 inch). To get a sense of just how mind-blowing this athletic feat is, imagine jumping as high as the crossbar of a standard soccer goal. Think about that the next time you are standing on a soccer field. It seems impossible. For women, the record is 2.09 meters (or a bit over 6 feet 10 inches) and it has been held since 1987 by Stefka Kostadinova of Bulgaria. That is like jumping over the top of Blake Griffin, the Los Angeles Clippers basketball player. Seemingly just as impossible. These records have stood for what is an eternity in sporting terms, by far the longest period since high jump records were first, kept more than a century ago, as shown in figure 2.2.

Will these records ever be broken? Have athletes jumped as high as they ever will? Is there still an edge to be gained? Questions like these drive athletes to compete against each other, and against history. They also help us to the notion of the spirit of sport.

Figure 2.2. Men's and Women's High Jump World Record Progression

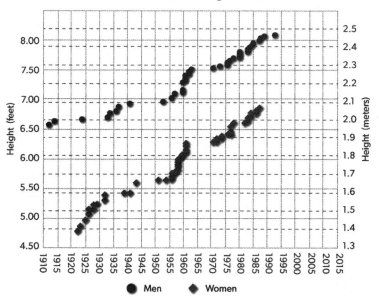

● Men ◆ Women

The high jump was not an event in the ancient Greek Olympic Games.[19] It emerged out of Germany in the late eighteenth century and, like many demonstrations of physical prowess, evolved into a competitive sport in England in the following century. Athletes first cleared the bar by jumping over it and lifting their legs. Humans are nothing if not innovative, and new techniques quickly followed. The Scissors, Eastern Cutoff, Western Roll, and Straddle were names of new techniques that offered alternative ways for the athlete to get his or her center of mass above the bar while also allowing those pesky legs to also get over the bar cleanly. The 1936 Olympics saw each of these techniques in use, but by the 1950s, athletes had mostly adopted the Straddle, which required them to roll over the bar belly-down and one leg at a time. Each innovation in technique saw greater advantages in performance, and world records were repeatedly set and broken in the first half of the twentieth century.

But it was not just technique that evolved. In 1957, Soviet Yuri Stepanov set a new world record at 2.16 meters. He cleverly used a shoe—what we might call an "elevator shoe"—with a very thick bottom, adding perhaps as much as an inch (~25 millimeters) to his height. This low-tech innovation gave him a slight edge in his leap. Because the International Amateur Athletic Federation had no rules in place for shoe sole thickness, Stepanov's jump was legal. But it was also viewed as problematic. So, soon thereafter, shoe sole thickness was regulated at a maximum of 13 millimeters, but Stepanov's thick-soled record was allowed to stand. The thick-soled shoe is an early example of how "technological augmentation" changes competition and forces us to consider and sometimes implement new rules, a subject explored in chapter 7.

The Soviets were not done innovating, however. National coach Vladimir Dyachov studied film to determine what characteristics in form led to the highest jumps. He developed a new approach called the Dive Straddle, in which the jumper cleared the bar one body segment at a time, rather than having the torso in parallel with the bar. Athletes who had mastered earlier styles sometimes faced difficulties in learning new techniques, creating ample opportunity for successful innovators to set new records.

The high jump was originally conducted entirely on a flat surface at ground level. Athletes jumped from and landed on what was typically a dirt track. This put a premium on landing on one's feet or at least in a way that would not cause injury. Sawdust or dirt piles were later introduced to facilitate landing, which furthered the ability of athletes to innovate. But it was the introduction of foam landing pads around 1960 that led to even greater innovation, because they enabled athletes to land safely upon completing their jump. Innovations that enable athletes to perform better are surely part of the spirit of sport.

In 1968, a twenty-one-year-old athlete from Oregon, Dick Fosbury, followed up his victories in the NCAA indoor and outdoor championships with a gold medal at the 1968 Olympic Games. What made Fosbury's victory so improbable was that he utilized a radically different technique than that being employed by the sport's elite. That radical technique bears his name, the Fosbury Flop. More than forty years later, Fosbury recalled that people laughed when he first exhibited the technique, which involves jumping backwards over the bar, leading with one's head, and landing on one's back—hence the name. Fosbury wasn't concerned that his jumping style was called a flop: "I wasn't offended, any athlete responds to and craves attention. . . . You feed off that attention."[20] The adulation and attention, even fame, that come with doing something no one ever has done before are perhaps also part the spirit of sport.

The Flop was born in no small part because Fosbury's high school had installed a modern landing pit, replacing the pile of wood chips that had cushioned the falls of previous, presumably bruised, Medford High School jumpers. Fosbury wasn't the first or only person to flop. A Montana high school jumper named Bruce Quande also used the technique. Quande, however, did not go on to athletic success. Another, more successful, independent invention of what we call the Fosbury Flop came out of Canada, where Debbie Brill was working on what was locally known as the Brill Bend. She went on to set an indoor world record (1.99 meters in 1979), but missed her shot at an Olympic gold medal because of the Canadian boycott of the 1980 Moscow Olympics.

Debbie Brill competing in Germany in 1972.

Today, the Fosbury Flop is well into middle age. Its use has become almost universal in elite high jumping. The men's record has stood for more than twenty years and the women's for almost thirty. Has innovation in the high jump reached a plateau? Is there no more edge to eke out of this sport?

I asked these questions of Jesus Dapena, a professor emeritus of kinesiology at the University of Indiana's School of Public Health, who is a long-time student of and one of the world's experts on the high jump. He told me that "Every person who has ever given a limit has had to wipe the egg off his face soon after when someone invariably broke the limits he had proposed!" Still, he ventured some guesses: "Of course, there are limits. Is it possible to jump 2.50 meters [8.2 feet]? I'd say, probably yes. 2.60 meters [8.5 feet]? I don't know. 3.00 [meters, or 9.8 feet]? I'd say no—and if it ever happens, I'll be long dead by then, so I'll be safe from the egg-on-face situation!"[21]

One factor that may be responsible for the slowdown in high jump record breaking may be the ubiquity of the Fosbury Flop itself. Based on his research, Dapena concludes that "ultimately, the Fosbury-flop is the best technique for some jumpers, and the straddle for others." Thus, we might expect to see both techniques employed, depending on what works best for a particular athlete. But, Dapena explains, today "only the Fosbury-flop is in use; the straddle has disappeared," due, he argues, to the fact that the Fosbury Flop is easier to learn.

If Dapena is right, that the Straddle would be better for some athletes, then there are likely elite high jumpers today utilizing the Fosbury Flop who might jump a bit higher using the Straddle. Similarly, there may be jumpers who may have never reached elite levels because they were not suited for the Fosbury Flop. Either way, the net result is to reduce the potential for higher jumps by using a less-than-optimal technique for some jumpers and, perhaps, to reduce the pool of athletes competing in the high jump. Ironically, while the Fosbury Flop once helped athletes break performance boundaries, its ubiquity today could be holding them back.

But the moral of the story of Dick Fosbury—and Yuri Stepanov and Debbie Brill and all the others who have tried to jump higher than anyone else ever has—is not about imposing limits, but about extending them, pushing to the edge and then beyond. This drive to constantly push back the limits of performance, to do what no one else has done, is surely part of the spirit of sport. So, too, is the readiness to innovate in techniques and equipment (shoes, landing areas, etc.) in order to excel in athletic prowess through competition.

So, is trying to do one's best the spirit of sport? Is it as simple as that? As simple as jumping over a bar? Regrettably, no. The issues can get complicated—very complicated, very fast.

Losing Sight of the Spirit of Sport: Scorching the Track with a Wicked Problem

"Wicked problems" are ones that, in the words of the classic 1973 article that explained the concept, "are ill-defined; and they rely upon elusive political judgment for resolution."[22] Such problems are "resolved," not solved. They are called "wicked" because "they are "malignant" (in contrast to "benign"), or "vicious" (like a circle), or "tricky" (like a leprechaun), or "aggressive" (like a lion, in contrast to the docility of a lamb). By definition, we can never really solve a wicked problem; we can only do better or worse at trying to manage it. And better or worse depends on what we think the problem is in the first place, or whether we think that there even is a problem requiring action. Wicked problems can be addressed only through negotiation, and negotiation can only make the problem better or worse; negotiation can't solve the problem. An oft-cited example of a problem of this sort is crime, which is never solved completely; we just do better or worse at tackling it, depending on the responses that we put into place through our political and social systems.

Many of the controversies facing sport today are wicked problems. Let's continue with the beauty and simplicity of track and field to illustrate how a situation can turn from simple to wicked in very short order.

Leo Tolstoy, the nineteenth-century Russian novelist, once said, "All great literature is one of two stories; a man goes on a journey or a stranger comes to town." The story of Justin Gatlin, the American sprinter and for most of 2015 the fastest man in the world, offers a bit of both stories. Out of track and field for four years during his athletic prime (a man on a journey), he returned to the sport (a stranger comes to town) at an advanced age—in terms of athletics—to achieve track and field successes that had never been witnessed before.

It would be a feel-good story of achievement following adversity but for the fact that Gatlin's four years away from track and field competition were the result of a ban that he served for doping. His return and rise to prominence thus raise thorny questions about the possible long-term benefits of banned substances, the appropriateness of bans, and what it means to excel at the highest levels of track and field. In short, Gatlin's story has tension, drama, and conflict. It also illustrates why doping in sport is a wicked problem—there are no absolute solutions, just imperfect rules and regulations (the result of negotiations) that leave many loose ends, which many people view as unsatisfactory.

The five fastest times in the 100 meters in 2015 belonged to Gatlin.[23] In the most prominent 100-meter race of 2015, at the World Championships in Beijing, Gatlin was edged out by 0.01 of a second by Usain Bolt, the photogenic Jamaican sprinter. The media had built up the race as one between good and evil—Bolt, the athlete who had achieved his successes the right way, and Gatlin, the cheater. As Bolt edged Gatlin at the finish line, a BBC commentator gushed, "He's saved his title, he's saved his reputation—he may have even saved his sport."[24]

Despite the soaring rhetoric, no one accused Gatlin outright of achieving his current success by breaking the rules. But questions remain. Ross Tucker, a South African scientist and an expert in athletic performance, explains that "Gatlin is the problem that will not go away. . . . He is a former doper, dominating a historically doped event, while running faster than his previously doped self."[25] For his part, Gatlin is aware of the talk: "There's nothing I can do," he has said, "except go out there and keep running and pushing the envelope."[26]

Justin Gatlin en route to gold in the 100 meters at a Doha Diamond League meet in 2015.

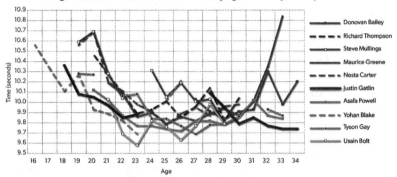

Figure 2.3. Best Annual 100-Meter Times by Age for Ten Top Male Sprinters

I was curious about how unusual Gatlin's performance is as a thirty-three-year-old man in 2015. Data can help us understand how Gatlin's performances stand up in historical context, but data cannot adjudicate between good and evil.

To better understand Gatlin's performance, the first thing I did was to gather data for the top sprinters ever at the 100 meters, and compare how their times progressed as they aged.[27] That data is shown in figure 2.3. As you look at the figure, bear in mind that lower on the chart means faster on the track.

That chart is a bit noisy, but what it shows is how exceptional Gatlin's improvement was from ages twenty-eight to thirty-three, achieving successive personal bests. Gatlin explains that his doping suspension may be the cause of his late form: "I've been away from the sport for four years—I literally didn't run for four years, so my body's been rested."[28] He does have a point, because moving his times four years to the left would make his curve much less unusual.

But Gatlin was not placed in a time capsule for four years. He aged like everyone else. If taking four years off from competition in the prime of a sprinter's career is thought to lead to record-shattering times, then we'd probably see more athletes taking long breaks. But that seems doubtful, given that the best sprint times occurred between ages of twenty-two and twenty-seven for this set of athletes. Father time is unforgiving.

Figure 2.4 presents a cleaned-up version of the data, which shows a moving three-year average of times of the fastest nine ath-

Figure 2.4. Best Annual 100-Meter Times by Age for Top Ten Male Sprinters

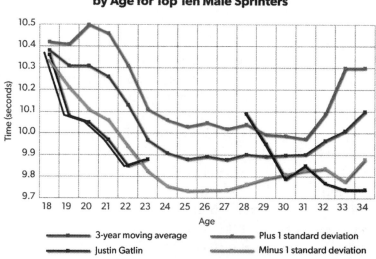

3-year moving average   Plus 1 standard deviation
Justin Gatlin   Minus 1 standard deviation

letes other than Gatlin, plus boundaries that most times of the other runners fall within (technically called the "standard deviation").*

The top ten fastest male sprinters in the world stopped improving as a group by about age twenty-five. Gatlin's times and improvement are, it is safe to say, unprecedented among this group of runners.

The longer Gatlin scorches the track, the more his incredible feats and the questions that they raise will be discussed. The data clearly show that Gatlin has been doing something remarkable, maybe even incredible. Whether those achievements would have occurred without doping is another question altogether, and one that can't be answered by looking at the numbers. In truth, the role of doping in sport can never be seen in performance numbers alone, no matter how remarkable they may seem. It is a sign of the times

---

*   The pattern is much the same for the 200 meters, which is not shown here but can be seen here: *The Least Thing*, "More on Justin Gatlin's Age-Defying Times," July 8, 2015, http://leastthing.blogspot.com/2015/07/more-on-justin-gatlins-age-defying-times.html.

that incredible performances often evoke feelings of not just awe and appreciation but also doubt and cynicism.

Here is why Gatlin—and the issue of doping more generally—presents sport with a wicked problem. Seen from one perspective, Gatlin has achieved incredible sports performance and deserves to be recognized as an unprecedented champion, because of both his age and his performance. What he is accomplishing might, under different circumstances, be an example of the spirit of sport such as described in the discussion of high jumping: the exceeding of limits, the attention that results. Yet his history of doping means that he (and indeed everyone) is cheated from celebrating those successes.

Seen from another perspective, Gatlin's successes have been achieved improperly; they are the consequence of him breaking the rules, serving his punishment, and then returning to benefit from his transgressions. From this point of view, Gatlin's competitors (and indeed everyone) are being cheated. There are no easy answers here—in fact, as we will see in chapter 6, on doping, there are no solutions at all, only different ways to manage the challenge.

For instance, some people propose lifetime bans for athletes who dope, thus removing them from the equation in future competition. In this scenario, there would be no Justin Gatlins to worry about. However, the inherently imprecise nature of the science of antidoping and the rights of athletes to due process mean that lifetime bans of this sort have been ruled impermissible.[29] There is a movement afoot to criminalize doping violations—perhaps even to throw athletes into jail.[30] Sports bodies have strongly objected to such laws, as they would create an uneven amalgam of laws around the world, which was the reason for the establishment of harmonized rules in the first place under WADA. Some people have proposed that former dopers should be able to race but not be able to hold records or win medals. This too is problematic—why have them race at all then?

Sprinting, a simple sport, becomes wickedly complex with the introduction of rules that regulate the use of performance-enhancing substances. As chapter 6 explains, there are no general solutions in response to the challenge of doping in sport. We (athletes, governments, sponsors, fans, etc.) negotiate rules to govern sport and then we must live with the consequences. If the rules are deemed unsatisfactory, we can change them. We can do better or worse, and the evidence suggests that, today, we are doing worse.

When Justin Gatlin became the personification of evil in sport in 2015, while achieving unprecedented success on the track, one thing he left in his wake was the spirit of sport. Some people complained that it was still there—with Gatlin performing remarkable athletic feats—but that it was being obscured, even suffocated, by rules and regulations. But the urge to define the spirit of sport as something apart from the rules of competition fails to recognize that sport is made possible by rules. The spirit of sport is not obscured by rules; the spirit of sport is found in the rules that govern competition.

Finding the Spirit of Sport: It's in the Rules We Make

Ultimately, our collective agreement to respect and abide by rules traces its modern history to Pierre de Coubertin and the movement he founded, the Olympic movement. Modern sport—including college sports in the United States and professional sports leagues around the world—has been deeply influenced by the philosophy of "Olympism . . . a philosophy of life which places sport at the service of humanity"[31] and that demands that athletes swear "an oath of fidelity to the rules and unselfishness." The Olympic oath of fidelity became formalized as the Olympic Oath, written by Coubertin, in the 1920 Olympic Games in Antwerp, Belgium. The oath reads: "In the name of all competitors, I promise that we shall take part in these Olympic Games, respecting and abiding by the rules that govern them, in the true spirit of sportsmanship, for the glory of sport and the honour of our teams."[32] Other sports typically have their own version of an oath of fidelity. For instance, the NFL has what it calls an "Integrity of the Game Certification," which emphasizes adherence to the rules.[33]

Does this mean that the spirit of sport is to be found in the rules that govern sport and without which there would be no sport? Maybe. But looking for the spirit in the rules is problematic, because the rules are often—perhaps usually—open to interpretation. And the scope for interpretation can be so wide that the people and institutions whose job it is to enforce those rules—from referees and umpires to sports bodies and governments—find it all but impossible to do their jobs.

Moreover, the rules that govern sport are not purely technical or legalistic lists of dos and don'ts. At their core, the rules are the practical reflections of the abstract values that we and all sport-loving individuals and societies hold dear.

Over the past century, the phrase "spirit of sport" has been subject to as much textual exegesis as any biblical passage.[34] The notion of the spirit of sport goes as far back as the Old Testament, which declares that "if anyone competes as an athlete, he does not receive the victor's crown unless he competes according to the rules."[35] It is thus no surprise that the many symbols and rites of the Olympic Games evoke the trappings of a formal religion.

Religion deals with *very* big questions (such as "Why are we here?"). The questions that sport presents aren't *that* big, but they aren't trivial either: How should we behave? What should the rules be? Who gets to decide? Sport has long upheld a value structure that provides justifications for answering questions like these. The core values in this structure have been amateurism, purity, autonomy, and uncertainty. Unfortunately, no matter how appealing these values may be in their abstract, idealized forms, they no longer serve sport particularly well in the twenty-first century. Exactly why and how they are outmoded is something that will become clearer as this book progresses, but let's take a quick look at each of these values and the battles being fought to save them or to change them.

Amateurism

The battle over amateurism has been going on for a while. The words *amateur* and *professional* came into their modern usage in the first decade of the nineteenth century.[36] The ancient Greeks are often held up as the model of amateurism in sport, but the reality is that the Greeks had no such concept, and the original Olympians were well rewarded for their sporting accomplishments. Early Olympians organized into the equivalent of modern-day trade unions to negotiate their pay, the structure of the game, and even their pension plans. The modern version of the Olympics was based on a mythological concept of amateurism. The American athlete Jim Thorpe, of Native American ancestry, was stripped of his 1912 Olympic gold medal in the decathlon because he had played minor league professional baseball in 1911, earning $60 per month.[37] It wouldn't be until the 1980s that the notion of "amateurism" in the Olympic Games was replaced by an ethos of professionalism. Today, a major battleground over amateurism focuses on college athletics in the United States, where amateurism has broken down but has yet to be fully replaced.

Purity

The notion of "purity" in sport comes up in several of the battlefields discussed in this book. Amateurism reflects a kind of purity in the sense of the love of competition untainted by the supposedly crass desire for material gain. As one scholar has written, "such commercialization debases the nobility and purity of sport as an activity and opens the road to corruption, gambling, fixing and exploitation."[38] The puritanical ideal in sport is found in the tales of nude Greek athletes. There, too, the reality is less pure than the mythology we have created. [39] Not everyone today has abandoned "a fanciful notion of purity in sport,"[40] but many of us—probably most of us—have embraced a more realistic view. Our healthy cynicism, however, is not shared (not publicly, anyway) by many sports bodies, which continue to invoke purity as the basis for policies related to doping, technological augmentation, sex testing, and even match fixing.

Uncertainty

What is sport anyway? A leading school of thought is that sports, as contrasted with other forms of entertainment, are defined by what is called "uncertainty of outcome." Ryan Rodenberg, a professor of sport management at Florida State University, explains that "uncertainty of outcome" is "what differentiates spectator sports as a form of entertainment from other (scripted) options such as books, films, musicals, and professional wrestling."[43] Uncertainty of outcome has come into focus because of heightened concerns about "match fixing"—the prearrangement of sporting outcomes, which might be wins or losses or discrete actions within a game. Usually, match fixing is associated with gambling and an effort to secure an improper edge in betting markets; sport is just a means of securing that edge. Using the notion of "uncertainty of outcome" to define sport is deeply problematic, however. Consider that competition is nothing more than efforts by opposing parties to remove uncertainty of outcome, because competition, by definition, involves different parties trying to assure themselves (and not their opponents) of victory. The fuzziness of "uncertainty of outcome" makes defining match fixing difficult, and trying to regulate it almost impossible. Sport, I argue, is more than uncertainty of outcome.

Autonomy

The notion that sports bodies should be free to govern themselves without interference from governments has a long history. The notion of "autonomy" in sports governance originates in Europe, where, "for most of the 20th century, the majority of European states allowed sports organisations to develop as bodies fully independent of the public authorities."[41] In 1955, the Olympic charter stated that "National Olympic Committees must be completely independent and autonomous and entirely removed from political, religious or commercial influence."[42] In today's era of big money sponsorships and vast governmental influence over sport, the notion of autonomy of governance may seem quaint. But even today, sports bodies, especially international ones, expect to have autonomy over decision making. In practice, autonomy has led to a lack of accountability and numerous governance failures. At the same time, many professional sports organizations, such as the NFL and the NBA, are deeply interwoven with public authorities—some would say far too tightly intertwined. Finding the right balance of self-governance and public involvement in sports bodies is a defining challenge of the contemporary sport landscape.

~ ~ ~

Throughout this book, I argue that the values of amateurism, purity, autonomy, and uncertainty no longer serve sport well and should be replaced. Traditionalists may object, protesting that we can't just cast values aside, that values aren't fashion accessories; they are enduring, even timeless, touchstones. But that's just not true. Values do change, all the time, in sports as in other aspects of life. I argue that the values underpinning sport have already changed; in most cases, we just have to realize it and deal with the consequences.

One episode in the history of US college football helps to illustrate how we tailor rules to our values, and how both values and rules can change over time. The 1960s and 1970s saw periods of racial tension in US society, and, as often occurs, societal tensions were reflected in sport. The spirit of sport meant one thing for a long time, but then values changed, and with it, so too did the spirit of sport. In the episode described below, the change to the spirit of sport was motivated by no less an authority than God himself.

In 1969, fourteen African-American football players in the highly successful program at the University of Wyoming wanted to protest the treatment of blacks in the United States.[44] The Brigham Young University (BYU) football team was coming to Laramie that week, providing Wyoming students with an opportunity to protest the policy of the Mormon Church (BYU is a bastion of Mormonism) to exclude blacks from the Mormon clergy. Such protests involving athletes were not uncommon; the year before, two American sprinters had famously raised black-gloved fists on the medal stand at the Mexico City Olympic Games. The Wyoming football coach's reaction to the protest by his fourteen players was quick—he kicked them off the team before the game.

At the BYU football game, some Wyoming students displayed a Confederate flag, perhaps to emphasize their belief that African Americans needed to be careful about kicking up a fuss. *Sports Illustrated* weighed in, perhaps a bit tongue in cheek: "Good riddance, and never mind a lot of talk about civil rights, because this is Wyoming, and out here we do things our way. Like Coach [Lloyd] Eaton told those athletes: Boys, if you don't like the way we run things around here then you better go play at Grambling or Morgan

State.""* The issue quickly rose to national prominence. A lawsuit was filed by some of the athletes.

Over time, tensions subsided. Many of the fourteen players transferred to other institutions, the lawsuit fizzled out, and Eaton allowed three of the players to return to play football for him the following year. Several went on to play in the NFL, with one, Joe Williams, winning a Super Bowl with the Dallas Cowboys. Eaton was "promoted" into administration, and later left to take a minor position in the NFL.[45] The controversy had lasting effects, however. Wyoming "was marked as a racist institution" and suffered consequences in recruiting, securing only one winning season in the 1970s and losing twenty-six of thirty-eight games following the dismissal of the players.[46] The more lasting consequence, however, was to draw national attention to the discriminatory policies of the Mormon Church.

In the years that followed, pressure built. The University of Arizona opened an investigation of BYU to determine if it was a racist institution.[47] Upon arriving in Tucson for a college football game, the BYU squad faced protesters. Not long after, Stanford and San Jose State decide to boycott BYU in every sport. Pressure on BYU had been amplified by the "Wyoming Fourteen" and had reached a crisis point for BYU. Tom Hudspeth, BYU head football coach in 1969, "was 'made aware' that [Mormon] Church leadership wanted him to add African-Americans to his team, and fast."[48] And he did, but it wasn't enough.

That is when God stepped in. In June 1978, the president of the Mormon Church revealed that God had "heard our prayers, and by revelation has confirmed that the long-promised day has come [in which] all worthy male members of the Church may be ordained to the priesthood without regard for race or color."[49] In the ten years prior to the revelation from God, BYU had won 57 out of 110 football games; in the ten years after, 103 out of 127.[50] Chang-

---

* It is not clear to me whether *Sports Illustrated* was mocking the folks in Wyoming or agreeing with them. The writing is inscrutable enough to permit both interpretations: Pat Putnam, "No Defeats, Loads of Trouble," *Sports Illustrated*, November 3, 1969, http://www.si.com/vault/1969/11/03/611044/no-defeats-loads-of-trouble.

ing perceptions of the values espoused by BYU enabled it to draw from a larger pool of athletes, helping to improve the team on the field. BYU was at the center of changing social values, which in turn helped to change the fortunes of BYU football. As Michael Oriard writes, "fourteen young black football players at the University of Wyoming helped change Mormon theology."[51] In 2002, the University of Wyoming erected a statue to the Wyoming Fourteen.

This episode shows that values shape sport and that sport, in turn, shapes values. There was a time when racism and segregation were part of the spirit of sport in the United States. As values and practices changed, sport had to change also. As in the case of the Wyoming Fourteen, sport played a role in ushering along changes in both sport and society.

~   ~   ~

The central conclusion of this book is that sport and those charged with developing and enforcing the rules that govern it need to recognize a new set of values as the basis for its governance in the twenty-first century. These new values are professionalism, pragmatism, accountability, and transparency.

Professionalism is not actually a new value; it has been emerging within sport for decades, if not longer. Accountability and transparency have become more important in sport with each new revelation of a failure in sports governance—and those revelations are growing more numerous and more shocking. Pragmatism has always been a defining feature of how we govern sport, and it's time to recognize and embrace that reality more fully.

We can change and improve the rules that define sport because sport is what we make it. If values have changed, or need to change, then sport should change accordingly. Defining the spirit of sport in the twenty-first century does not require an act of God. It does, however, require that we openly discuss and debate sport, what it is, why we value it, and how we wish it to be governed. Such discussions will benefit from a vocabulary that permits nuance and differences of opinions to be clearly identified. And a vocabulary for talking about the edge is where we turn next.

Chapter 3

Cheating, Gamesmanship, and Going over the Edge

In discussions of sport, the word *cheating* is used in blunt fashion to refer to a wide range of actions. For instance, in 2016, tennis star Maria Sharapova failed a drug test at the Australian Open for taking a substance called meldonium, which had been added to the list of prohibited substances just a couple of weeks earlier. Sharapova revealed that she had been taking meldonium for a decade, leading former top-ten professional tennis player Jennifer Capriati to label Sharapova a cheater over those ten years: "I didn't have the high priced team of drs [sic] that found a way for me to cheat and get around the system and wait for science to catch up."[1] In stark contrast, another former professional, John McEnroe, said that Sharapova's use of the drug before it was added to the prohibited list was fair game: "If a drug is legal? That is like a no-brainer. I mean, are you kidding? People have been looking since the beginning of time for an edge, and you're constantly looking for these things in any way, shape or form."[2]

To productively debate the point of contention between Capriati and McEnroe, we need a clear conception of what it means to cheat in sport, as well as a clear idea of those other activities that might go right up to the edge but don't quite make it to the other side. In other words, we need a palette of shades of gray rather than black and white. This chapter develops a vocabulary for discussions about the edge. It offers a definition of cheating and related behaviors, and thus it sets the stage for consideration of the five battlegrounds in the next part of this book.

Rules and Norms

In the semifinals of the 2013 Australian Open, Belarusian tennis star Victoria Azarenka's game was falling apart. Playing against American Sloane Stephens, Azarenka was winning in the final set by five games to three, and she was about to start serving what could have been the final game. She lost five match points and eventually the game.[3] She was on the verge of a complete breakdown. Azarenka then caused a stir when she then took a ten-minute injury time-out to regain her composure. Her composure regained, Azarenka returned from the "injury timeout" and promptly won the match.

Afterwards, David Nainkin, Stephens's coach said, "I thought it was very unfair—cheating within the rules. It was unsportsmanlike. . . . I think there's a gray area in the rule book that shouldn't be allowed. End of story."[4] Chris Fowler, a tennis commentator for ESPN, tweeted about the episode: "Ever heard a player basically admit she/ he was nervous and thus invented 2 injuries to get a 10 minute time-out? Rule change needed."[5] Cheating or not? McEnroe and Capriati raised the same question about Sharapova and meldonium.

We can start to make some sense of this debate by asking what, if anything, did Azarenka do wrong?

According to the Australian Open tournament director, nothing: "Everything was within the rules of the game." Azarenka's behavior provides an opportunity to make an important distinction when it comes to rules. There are rules *of* the game and rules *for* the game. This is a fundamental distinction, not just for sport, but also for society as a whole.

For instance, the US Constitution sets forth rules *of* the political "game" in the United States; the Constitution lays down *how* the United States is to be governed, including defining the branches of government, their respective powers, how they can use those powers, what rights ordinary citizens have, what rights individual states have, and so forth. With these rules in place, the US Congress, the president, and the court system can make and enforce the rules *for* the political game; these three branches of government create the rules that govern the nation from day to day, such as how fast you can drive on a federal highway, how much tax you must pay to the federal government, how much pollution power plants can emit, and so forth. Changing laws happens all the time, but changing the US Constitution happens only rarely because it is a big deal to change the rules of the political system.

In more formal terms, the distinction is between *constitutive* and *regulatory* rules. *Constitutive rules* refer to the establishment of fundamental rules of making decisions; they are rules about the rules. This distinction has been around since at least the eighteenth century, when it was explained by the very clever but often hard to understand philosopher Immanuel Kant.[6] Mercifully, John Searle, a professor at the University of California, Berkeley, explains the concept more clearly: "Constitutive rules do not merely regulate playing football or chess, but, as it were, *they create the very possibility* of playing such games."[7] Searle continues: "Regulative rules regulate a pre-existing activity." In other words, you can't apply the rules of tennis until you first figure out what those rules are.

Like most sporting bodies, the International Tennis Federation (ITF) has a constitution, a 138-page document that explains how decisions about tennis, including the rules of the game, are to be made and who is to make them.[8] The ITF constitution also explains the rules that tennis is to follow for antidoping and anticorruption, in both of these cases referring to other institutions (and even more constitutive rules). It is often the case that the constitutive rules *for* a particular sport require far more pages to explain than the rules *of* that sport.

For instance, under the provisions of the ITF constitution, the regulatory rules of tennis are codified in a comparatively pithy forty-three-page document.[9] The regulatory rules include such things as the dimensions of the court, how scoring is to take place, and when to change sides. When players compete together in an annual set of competitions, more regulatory rules are needed, such as how rankings are determined, how seedings are organized, what tournaments players must play, and so on. Constitutive rules set the stage for creating and managing competition; once these rules are in place, regulatory rules created under them define a particular game.

Regulatory rules govern what happens in the playing of a game. When the rules of the game are violated, then there typically is some sanction for the offender or a reward for his or her opponent. For instance, if Azarenka hits the ball out, Stephens gets a point. If players or officials want to change the rules of tennis, such as by allowing instant replay, then they have to follow the guidelines of the ITF constitution, which explains how those rules are to be changed.

In principle, the rules that govern play within a sport are designed to create a closed system, meaning that every possible contingency is expected to be covered by the rules of the game—no one wants referees (or players) making up rules as a game is being played. In practice, this is not always the case; people are clever and the world is complicated, even in sports. Sometimes in sports we find a "rules hole" that needs fixing, just as Congress may find a loophole in the laws that needs plugging.[10] We will return to these concepts later in this chapter.

Victoria Azarenka's injury timeout during the 2013 Australian Open semifinals.

Now back to Azarenka and her injury timeout. According to the Australian Open tournament director, "Everything was within the rules of the game." Azarenka's behavior was within the boundaries of the regulatory rules of tennis, but Fowler (and others) suggested that changes to those rules are needed, which requires making changes as allowed under the constitution of tennis. Sometimes, the changes that are deemed necessary go beyond making changes to the rules of the game and involve changing the constitution itself, such as when tennis (like most other international sports) agreed to follow the provisions of the WADA after its creation in 1999.

This brings us to another distinction—that between *rules* and *norms*. Regulatory rules are formal guidelines for play. Norms are expectations for what constitutes appropriate behavior in play.[11] Rules are written down; norms generally are not. Some norms are specific to a sport, but others involve more general considerations reflecting broader social and cultural factors. As you might guess, because rules are written down, they are easier to reach agreement on than are norms. Making such a distinction helps us understand why people such as Capriati and McEnroe can see the same behavior and come to diametrically opposed views on whether that behavior is cheating. McEnroe and Capriati are reflecting different norms for what constitutes appropriate behavior.

So when Sloane Stephens's coach accused Azarenka of "cheating within the rules," he meant that although her behavior was not formally illegal under the rules, it violated the generally held expectations of the tennis community for what constitutes appropriate behavior. Azarenka, he claimed, had violated the tennis community's norms.

If the tennis community feels strongly enough, as indicated by Fowler's tweet, then it can engage the constitutive rule-making process to change the rules of play to address violations of what are held as norms. Alternatively, it can hope that the social pressure associated with violating a community norm is sufficient to compel the desired behavior. Think about the practice of "flopping" in the NBA—the simulation of contact between players in order to sway the referee into calling a foul. Once upon a time, social pressure was strong enough to encourage players not to flop—or at least not often and not flagrantly. Times change, however, and when social pressure was deemed insufficient to stop players from trying to trick referees by simulating fouls, the rules of basketball were changed to try to reduce the incidence of such simulation through postgame video review and the levying of sanctions on players who were judged to have broken the new rule.[12]

Rules can be enforced by governing bodies using penalties for on-the-field violations and sanctions for breaking constitutive rules beyond the field of play.[13] If a National Football League (NFL) player is caught illegally holding another player in a game, the referee will throw a yellow flag and enforce a ten-yard penalty. But if an NFL player is taking human growth hormone—which is prohibited—he will not be caught by a referee in a striped shirt. Officials who govern what happens off the field of play determine whether a constitutive rule has been violated. Norms are typically enforced by player conduct or in the court of public opinion. If a baseball pitcher hits a batter with a pitch, you can expect the pitcher from the hit batter's team to throw some inside pitches in retaliation. That is norm enforcement in action. There is a fine line between a pitcher throwing some "chin music" designed to secure tactical advantage in the encounter with a batter, and a pitcher throwing at the batter with intent to cause bodily harm. A "brush back" pitch is well within the rules and norms of Major League Baseball (MLB), but throwing at a batter violates the rules and can be cause for the pitcher to be ejected from the game by the umpire. Throwing at a batter is a fine edge between following an accepted norm and violating formal rules.

Norms can be turned into formal rules. Consider a 2012 suspension that the Union of European Football Associations (UEFA, soccer's governing body in Europe) gave to Luiz Adriano of the Ukrainian soccer team Shakhtar Donetsk.[14] In soccer, the game clock runs continuously. There are no timeouts, no injury stoppages, and (thankfully) no commercial breaks. But play does occasionally stop, such as when a player is down on the field and the referee decides that the player may need some medical attention. The referee has discretion to add on a bit of time at the end of each half to compensate for such stoppages.

When a player is down on the soccer field, a team customarily kicks the ball out of bounds or the referee stops play.* There is no rule saying that this is so, but that is how the game is played. After the injured player recovers or hobbles off the field, play is restarted by returning the ball to the team that had the ball when play was stopped. This usually occurs in the form of a kick back to the goalie, so that play can restart without either team gaining any advantage from the stoppage.

This exact situation developed midway through the first half of Shakhtar's 2012 European Champions League match with Danish club Nordsjaelland. A Nordsjaelland player was injured and play was halted so that he could be tended to by a trainer. He quickly recovered and the referee restarted play with a drop ball in Shakhtar's end of the field. As is customary, Nordsjaelland did not contest the drop ball, and allowed the Shakhtar player to kick it toward the Nordsjaelland goalie, where play would restart from a neutral position.

Then things took a strange turn. Luiz Adriano sprinted after the back pass from his position at forward, easily catching up to the ball. He was uncontested—everyone expected the ball to make its way to the Nordsjaelland goalie for play to restart. Adriano easily went around the baffled goalie and put the ball into the net for a goal to tie the match. The Fox Sports announcers were flabbergasted: "That is not in the spirit of the game . . . Shame on you Luiz Adriano . . . You do not do that!"[15]

But he did. And the goal stood. Of course it did; there is no rule in soccer about playing the ball back to an opponent after a stoppage of play. Once the referee conducted the uncontested drop kick, the game was on.

In this instance, although no formal rule was broken, a strongly held norm was violated. UEFA sanctioned Adriano, under the organization's general conduct policy, suspending him for one game and requiring that he perform one day of football-related community

---

* Even this norm may be changing. Today, it seems that players often are skeptical of their peers, and sometimes continue play, rather than kicking the ball out of bounds, when they are in a good offensive position or the down player is away from the action.

service.[16] In doing so, UEFA created a new rule from a norm. It established a precedent under which future violators of the pass-back-to-restart norm would be expected to be sanctioned in exactly the same way.

Norm violations need not become formal rules. A violation of a norm might be responded to with another norm. In 1999, a similar pass-back-to-the-goalie situation occurred in the English FA Cup when Arsenal, accidently it seems, scored off a back pass in a match against Sheffield United, which ultimately helped Arsenal to a 2–1 victory. The Arsenal manager, Arsene Wenger, realized the error and offered to replay the match ten days later. This gentleman's agreement, well outside any formal rules, was allowed by the English Football Association. Wenger's offer helped to solidify the norm, but it did not elevate it to a formal rule.*

The relationship between rules and norms is highly contextual, varying according to sport, league, and even nation, and developing an appreciation for the subtleties of behavior in different contexts can be challenging. The degree of enforcement of rules can be shaped by norms; some rules will be strongly enforced (e.g., offside in soccer), others less so (e.g., traveling in the NBA). That makes understanding the application of rules in sport a complicated, nuanced, and contextual affair. No one will get a sophisticated understanding of baseball or cricket solely by reading rule books.

Rules for sports can also interact with norms from outside sport, as in the case of Wyoming and BYU football. Here is a more recent example: In 2012, the Miami Marlin's baseball manager Ozzie Guillen was suspended for five games. What was his offense? He publicly expressed admiration for Cuban leader Fidel Castro. The Marlin's organization explained the suspension: "The pain and suffering caused by Fidel Castro cannot be minimized, especially in a community filled with victims of the dictatorship."[17]

What does baseball have to do with Fidel Castro? In South Florida, apparently a lot. Of course, similar questions could be asked

---

* As the favorite, Arsenal may have found it easy to act so magnanimously. Arsenal won the replay as well. See "Arsenal 2-1 Sheffield United (1998–99) FA Cup—Result Void," https://www.youtube.com/watch?t=71&v=whO5GAFBp30.

about the relationship of domestic violence and players in the NFL, about the relationship between tax fraud by FC Barcelona's superstar Lionel Messi and Spanish soccer, and about the arrest of USA goalie Hope Solo on charges (later dismissed) of assault and US women's soccer. Although rules can be created to oversee what happens in competition, sport and the world outside sport tend to intermix when it comes to the enforcement of broadly held social norms.

These examples highlight why it is so important to establish some intellectual and linguistic order when we discuss cheating in sport. As sport becomes more complex, so too must our ability to discuss and debate what happens at the edge. We are free to shape sports rules however we'd like, but to reach agreement on satisfactory rules, we need a language suitable to the task.

Let's find a language we can use.

What Is Cheating?

The concepts of rules and norms give us tools with which to create a framework for discussing what happens in sporting competition. To put it in fewer words, let's use rules and norms to create a simple taxonomy of cheating. Figure 3.1 depicts some things that can happen during a game or match—three of which involve combinations of rules and norm violations:

- *Ordinary play* occurs when no rules and no norms are violated. Ordinary play is what happens most of the time during a match or game.

- A *penalty* occurs when a rule is broken and a sanction is imposed, but no norm is violated. Penalties for rule breaking are part of the essential fabric of games. The offender pays some sort of cost when a rule is broken. For instance, a tennis player loses a point or a football team has to move back ten yards. When a penalty occurs but is not seen or called by the officials, it is a "blown call."*

- *Gamesmanship* occurs when a rule is not broken but a norm

---

* Of course, such calls often require a degree of judgment, so there is inevitably a gray area between a penalty and a blown call.

is violated. For instance, a tennis player takes an injury time-out even though she is not injured.

- *Cynical play* occurs when a rule is broken and a norm is violated. For instance, a soccer player deliberately kicks another player but then screams and falls to the ground, pretending that he is the victim. When an official misses the call, it compounds the cynicism, because the player may be seen as getting away with something that fellow competitors or fans will view to be unfair. Cynical play is the closest thing to cheating within game play, and an area in which much debate over cheating occurs.

Figure 3.1. A Taxonomy of Cheating

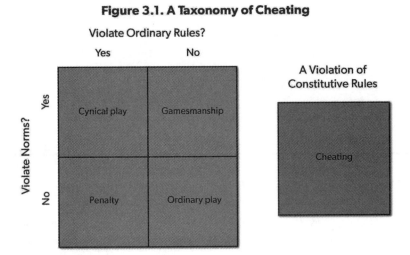

"Cheating" is used a lot in discussions of sport, but it is rarely defined precisely. We'll need a precise definition of cheating in sport in order to explain why I've chosen to focus on the five battlefields that take up the next section of the book.

In sport, some rules are meant to be broken. Breaking rules is in fact often part of the game. Athletes calculate costs and benefits of breaking rules and the chance that a penalty will be enforced. Should a cornerback on a football field commit pass interference on a long pass down the field? Should a centerback on a soccer field foul a striker heading toward her team's goal? Should a basketball team start fouling at the end of a game to try to catch up? The breaking of rules is an essential part of the fabric of sport norms and rules. So the act of breaking the rules, even intentionally, is not by itself enough to qualify as "cheating."

To understand what cheating is, we need to recall the difference between regulative rules and constitutive rules, because that difference provides a clear basis for defining cheating. Here I define cheating to be *the violation of the constitutive rules of a game*. Cheating thus threatens the possibility of sport itself. It is far more serious than breaking the regulatory rules of a game, even intentionally or cynically, and more serious than violating widely held norms. Cheating strikes at the "very possibility" of sport, at the very legitimacy of the games that we play. That is why cheating is so important.

Fifty Shades of Gamesmanship

This simple five-part categorization (cheating, cynical play, gamesmanship, penalty, and ordinary play) gives us some conceptual clarity and a language for discussing efforts by athletes, coaches, and others to secure an edge in competitive sport. Because the issues that arise are colored in shades of gray rather than in sharp back and whites, having a language can help clarify the issues and identify where people may agree and where they may disagree. In sport, the rules are what we make them, and interpretations as to what is over the edge will always be based on subjective human judgment. Thus, it is crucial to be able to communicate with one another, even if we may disagree with one another.

Using this five-part vocabulary, Azarenka was guilty of gamesmanship. She broke no rule of tennis, but her use of the injury timeout for competitive advantage violated some strongly held norms. Is the strongly voiced disapproval of fellow players and sports commentators a sufficient penalty for gamesmanship? Or are rule changes needed, as suggested by Chris Fowler? Because the spirit of sport is about adherence to rules, and rules are our inventions, the only way to resolve such issues is to discuss them, debate them, negotiate them (if things get that far), and come to some practical agreement on how to change them if they can be changed. In the

Azarenka case, the tennis world moved on after many people expressed their outrage, and rule changes were not made. Azarenka's gamesmanship (and that of others using the same strategy) was apparently not enough of a motivation to change the rules.

Gamesmanship is complex because it encompasses a spectrum from the accepted (and expected) to the offensive. And what constitutes gamesmanship is not universally shared—far from it. Local context matters enormously.

Consider a 2013 soccer match in the Copa Libertadores (the South American version of the UEFA Champions League) between Atlético Mineiro and São Paolo. During a pause in play, as a result of the ball being kicked out of bounds near midfield, Atlético's star player, Ronaldinho, wandered over to the opposing goalie to ask for a swig from his water bottle. The goalie obliged. Ronaldinho took a long sip, spat it out, and wandered over to the sideline, where he was wide open as play restarted. He received the throw-in, made a quick pass, and a goal resulted. Ricardo, a former student of mine and a Brazilian, e-mailed me to ask, "Genius or morally reprehensible?"*

Ricardo noted that Brazilian Portuguese has a phrase to describe such behavior—*jetinho brasileiro*,[18] which he describes as "both a reproach and praise, nuanced and complex." South American Spanish has a similar phrase—*viveza criolla*. Daniel Rosa, a journalist, explains: "There's an expression in Uruguay about how you want to win. If it's in the last minute and with a moment that enrages your opponent, all the better. That is *viveza*: knowing how to gain any advantage."[19]

Gamesmanship is contextual. What is acceptable in Brazil might not be acceptable in Denmark, and vice versa. In the Brazilian league match, Ronaldinho's ploy was viewed by many as clever gamesmanship. Yet, Adriano's similar behavior in the Champions League match was formally sanctioned. Both actions were well within the formal rules. But only one violated a well-established, local norm.†

---

* See Ronaldinho's trickery here: Chilean Football League, "Controversial Goal Because of Ronaldinho the Liberators," https://www.youtube.com/watch?v=7daGFe8Q3kc.

† For a case of a restart in a soccer match between Liverpool and Sunderland where the proper application of a norm was contested because of the

Debates about gamesmanship and where lines governing behavior might be drawn are thus as much about the context of a culture as they are about the game itself. We can start to get a sense of this contextuality by creating a spectrum of acceptability in sports gamesmanship. I'll start by suggesting two end points, which I suspect very few people will find controversial. One end point is behavior that I'd guess is universally deemed acceptable; at the other end is behavior that I'd guess is universally deplorable.

At the acceptable end of the spectrum let's place the practice of framing a pitch by a catcher in baseball. Balls and strikes are called by a human umpire, and catchers often try to catch the ball in such a way as to suggest that the pitch was in the strike zone rather than just outside.* The catcher might limit movement or pause ever so slightly after catching the ball. The catcher is trying to influence the umpire's call of ball or strike through his behavior, not unlike diving in soccer or flopping in the NBA.

The framing of a pitch is not just an aesthetic matter. It can affect outcomes. Steve Yeager, who played MLB for fifteen years and coaches catching for the Los Angeles Dodgers, explained to *Grantland*, "If a catcher can perfect a great way of receiving the ball, and he gets the ball maybe a half a ball outside—or even a ball outside— off the corners consistently, I think he's worth his weight in gold." Numbers back this up. Take Jose Molina, who catches for the Tampa Bay Rays. After taking into account various confounding factors, one model of the impact of pitch framing finds that Molina "saved his teams 111 runs—or, using the standard 10-runs-to-a-win conversion, about 11 wins—because of framing from 2008 to 2013."[20] *Grantland* concluded, based on these numbers, that Molina's value to the Rays was actually worth well in excess of his actual weight in 24-karat gold.

Pitch framing is gamesmanship. But it is also an accepted and meaningful part of the game of baseball.

---

ambiguity of its status as a norm rather than a formal rule: Steve Busfield, see "Should Liverpool's Goal against Sunderland Have Stood?" *Guardian*, September 27, 2010, http://www.guardian.co.uk/football/blog/2010/sep/27/liverpool-sunderland-stuart-attwell.

* Chapter 7 discusses human versus nonhuman baseball umpires.

At the other end of the gamesmanship spectrum—the deplorable end—we can place the Harlequins rugby club. In April 2009, the Harlequins faced Leinster in a quarterfinal playoff match. Late in the match, a wing, Tom Williams, had to be substituted because blood was pouring from his mouth. Poor guy. The substitution was fortuitous, because it would not have been allowed except for the apparent injury, and Williams was replaced by a goal-kicker, Nick Evans, who would be more likely than Williams to score, and Harlequins needed points. Unfortunately for the Harlequins, the substitution did not work out in their favor, as Evans missed a late kick and Leinster held on for a close 6-5 victory.[21]

It was soon revealed that Williams had manufactured the supposed injury by biting into a "blood capsule" in his mouth to release fake blood and earn the substitution. *Sky News* had captured Williams winking to teammates as he was being substituted. An inquiry followed. The affair became known as "Bloodgate" and resulted in numerous penalties and suspensions.[22]

The behavior in Bloodgate shares a few similarities with efforts to frame pitches (in baseball) and to simulate tackles (soccer) and charges (basketball). Players use the means at their disposal to convince a game official that what he or she is seeing is actually something else. A ball is a strike. A healthy player is injured. The similarities don't go much further, however. The use of blood capsules was universally viewed as a form of gamesmanship that went too far, way too far. In fact, it went so far that it was no longer appropriate to call it gamesmanship. Instead, it was a clear-cut case of cheating. It was a violation of the constitutive rules of rugby, because it was judged to be "misconduct," defined as "prejudicial to the interests of the Union or the Game." The committee that reviewed the case concluded that "just like taking a banned substance to enhance one's performance, fabricating a blood injury to alter the course of the game was also cheating."*

---

* It was misconduct as defined under the regulations of the International Rugby Boards (IRB), as explained here: http://www.epcrugby. com/images/content/Tom_Williams_and_Harlequins_Independent_ Disciplinary_Committee_Decision.PDF. The most recent version of the

Even though the sport of rugby had no specific rules against the use of blood capsules, gamesmanship deemed sufficiently unacceptable can be defined as cheating under the constitutive laws of the game. But a large gray area exists between pitch framing and blood capsules.

Ultimately, the decision to define an activity as against the rules *of a game* versus the rules *for a game* is the result of a negotiation among those who have a stake in the game, along with those with authority to make changes. Sport is a constant negotiation between fans, administrators, athletes, and others. We change rules all the time, both rules *for* sport and rules *of* sport. Sometimes we even move rules from one category to the other. Cheating is thus a moving target rather than something to be defined once and for all.

Rule Making and Its Limits

If rules are indeed the defining feature of sport and central to what it means to cheat or not, then there is nothing more important to the integrity of sport than the making and enforcing of rules. If you think about it, most discussion and debate over sports is about exactly these topics. Was the soccer player really offside? Did the football player really catch the ball? How should we deal with blood capsules? How should we deal with the player who scores on a soccer restart? If cheating is defined as a violation of the constitutive rules of sport, then it is important to understand how rules *for* the game and *of* the game change over time.

Rules are not fixed. We can change them. And we often do. For instance, the offside rule in soccer has been changed many times since the laws of "association football" were first drawn up in 1863.[23] The offside rule was changed as recently as 2015.[24] Changes have been introduced to clarify rules and to improve the perceived quality of the game, such as by giving a greater advantage to offenses rather than defenses. Changes in rules often face opposition from those who value the norms of consistency and tradition.

---

regulations governing rugby can be found at http://www.englandrugby.com/governance/regulations/#.

Sometimes, factors external to the game forces rules changes. The NFL has changed its definition of what it means to catch a ball multiple times in recent years. These changes have been motivated by the widespread availability of televised high-definition replays, which allow an unprecedented look at game play that far exceeds the ability of referees in real time. Instant replay was introduced to assist referees, but as the clarity of the replays has improved, the meaning of "catch the ball" has grown murkier, and the NFL has struggled to cope with this muddiness in its rule making, arguably making the job of referees much more difficult.

The scholarly literature on rules and norms is vast and spans many disciplines. In this section, I highlight three overarching lessons that will be helpful in thinking about rule making in sport (and indeed more broadly) when we turn to the five battlefields in the war against cheating in sports.

Lesson 1: People Respond to Incentives

In February 1994, two Caribbean nations were facing off in the preliminary group stages of the Caribbean Cup soccer tournament.[25] The rules of the tournament meant that, based on the matches played previously, Barbados needed to defeat Grenada by at least two goals to advance to the final stage of the tournament.[26] Otherwise Grenada would advance. Deep into the second half, Barbados was leading by 2–0 and looking set to advance.

But then Grenada scored in the eighty-third minute, making it 2–1 in favor of Barbados. Had the match ended with this score, Grenada would have advanced despite losing the match. Here is where things got tricky. The tournament rules specified that if a match were tied at the end of regular time, then the teams would play a sudden-death extra time, with the first team to score not just winning, but recorded as a two-goal winner. These rules created some unique incentives within the game.

Under these rules and with this score line, Barbados now had two chances to advance to the final. It could score another goal in regulation and win 3–1, restoring that necessary two-goal advantage, or it could score a single goal in an overtime period and secure a two-goal victory. Ian Preston and Stefan Szymanski explain what happened next: "The Barbados players realized with 3 minutes to play that they were unlikely to score again in the time remaining and deliberately kicked the ball into their own goal to tie the match at 2–2 and force an overtime period."[27] The thinking was that if they needed one goal to advance, they'd have better chances during extra time. But to get to overtime, they needed to score on themselves. So they did.

Under these tournament rules, Grenada would advance with a one-goal loss, so after Barbados tied up the match by scoring on themselves, the Grenada players immediately tried to do the same. For Grenada, losing by one goal meant winning. Preston and Szymanski described the farcical results: "The two teams then spent the remaining few minutes with Barbados defending both ends of the field as Grenada tried to put the ball into either goal, but time expired with the score still tied."* In the end, Barbados scored in extra time and advanced to the finals of the tournament, where perhaps Karma proved the ultimate winner. Barbados did not win any of their three games in the final group stage.[28]

After losing to Barbados, the Granada manager complained: "I feel cheated. The person who came up with these rules must be a candidate for a madhouse. . . . Our players did not even know which direction to attack: our goal or their goal. I have never seen this happen before. In football, you are supposed to score against the opponents to win, not for them."[29] The consequence of the scoring rules and tournament design changed the incentive structure for the players in the tournament and fundamentally changed the nature of the game.

The lesson here is that players will respond to incentives. Expecting athletes and others in sport not to respond to the incentives created for them goes against both human instinct and common sense. Tournament design is a particularly vexing problem in terms of aligning incentives with outcomes in a way that preserves the integrity of competition. For instance, in the 2012 London Olym-

---

* Watch a video showing a bit of this farce here: Barbados vs. Grenada (Shell Caribbean Cup, 1994), https://www.youtube.com/watch?v=ThpYsN-4p7w.

pics, eight badminton players were sent home for intentionally losing matches in order to be better positioned in later rounds. At the time, Andreas Selliaas observed that Usain Bolt rarely gave his best effort in early rounds of qualifying, much like the badminton players, yet he went unsanctioned: "Is this okay? Yes, because he wants to win and save his strength for when it really counts."[30]

As the following chapters make abundantly clear, rules create incentives, and people respond to incentives. We need to think very carefully about situations where players respond to the incentives provided by rules. How can it be cheating when a player follows the rules of a game?

Lesson 2: Rules Have Unintended Consequences

One of the enduring realties of making decisions is the so-called law of unintended consequences.[31] No matter how many experts we consult or how much analysis we devote to making decisions, the outcomes of those decisions often turn out to be unexpected, and sometimes undesired. Thus, how we respond to unintended consequences is just as important as what rules we established in the first place.

It is not clear how much thinking went into the design of the 1994 Caribbean Cup soccer tournament, but the spectacle of one team trying to score on both goals and the other defending both was probably not considered when the rules were put together. By contrast, strategic positioning in an Olympic badminton tournament was surely foreseeable based on experience.

The unintended consequences of rule making can occur far from the field of play. Women's elite gymnastics provides an example of how rules for the sport create incentives leading to undesired outcomes, necessitating further constitutive rule making and opening the door to cheating.

When Michael Phelps, the decorated American swimmer, earned his fourth medal (of a total of seven medals) at the 2012 London Olympics, he raised his lifetime tally of Olympic medals to twenty-two and moved into first place among Olympic medal winners. The person he passed on the medals table was Larisa Latynina, a Soviet gymnast who had won eighteen medals in the years from 1956 to 1964.[32]

Latynina's medal haul is not the only thing that captures our attention today. She won her first Olympic medal when she was twenty-one years old and her final one when she was twenty-nine. Remarkably, she won gold in every individual event (save one) at the 1957 European and World Championships at age twenty-two while pregnant.[33] Today, most gymnasts are out of the sport by the time they reach their twenties. No Olympic all-around gold medalist has been older than Latynina since Věra Čáslavská of Czechoslovakia in 1968.

Woman gymnasts have become significantly younger over the past fifty years because of scoring rules that have increasingly rewarded the skills of younger, more flexible athletes. Yet, over the same time, the Fédération Internationale de Gymnastique (FIG) has steadily increased the minimum age requirement -- from fourteen to fifteen years old in 1981, and then to sixteen years old in 1997.[34] Under today's rules, Nadia Comăneci, who dazzled the world in the 1976 Olympic Games, would be too young to participate.

Jackie Fie, who worked for almost thirty years on the FIG Women's Technical Committee and is a member of the International Gymnastics Hall of Fame, explained that increasing the minimum age was "prompted by many concerns, including the musculoskeletal development of young competitors, lengthening gymnastics careers, preventing burnout, and in order to redirect the image of the sport positively for the public, spectators and media."[35]

Yet, coincident with the changes to the minimum age have been changes to the FIG "code of points" (which sets rules for the scoring of routines) that prioritize the kinds of physical capabilities more likely to be found among younger athletes.[36] The *Economist* observes that "these changes have rewarded acrobatics more highly. So what was a common tumbling pass on the floor forty years ago would today be expected of a gymnast at a more junior level. At the top of the sport, gymnasts perform routines made up almost exclusively of combinations of intricate full body rotations in order to maximise their score."[37] In other words, women's gymnastics has become more about acrobatics than about ballet.

These rule changes favor younger athletes. A 2003 study of the biomechanics of young elite gymnasts found that "the smaller gymnast, with a high strength to mass ratio, has greater potential for performing skills involving whole-body rotations."[38] A 2014 review of changes to the FIG code of points found "the tendency of using more gymnastic and choreography elements is obvious, mainly to the leading athletes who are adequately prepared to execute faultlessly both, high-risk acrobatic skills and difficult gymnastics elements."[39]

Rules that emphasize younger athletes and rules regulating age create differing incentives: "Women's gymnastics thus point in two directions at once."[40] Hindsight is always 20/20, but one unanticipated consequence of the incentive structure was that at least one nation sought to evade the minimum age rules of the FIG. The *New York Times* observed that at the 2008 Beijing Olympics, China's gold medal winning women's gymnastics team "didn't just look young. They looked childlike." One member of the team was even missing a baby tooth.[41]

Two years later, following an investigation by the FIG, one Chinese gymnast was stripped of her medal from Sydney 2000 for violating the minimum-age requirement. The 2008 results were allowed to stand, despite much skepticism. Steve Penny, the president of USA Gymnastics observed: "There still is what I believe to be unanswered questions about this issue, but there is only so much you can prove when it comes to falsified documents."[42]

One consequence of the controversy was the creation of new rules for how the ages of gymnasts are validated. Beginning in 2009, FIG no longer relies solely on state documents, such as birth certificates or even passports, both of which can be forged, especially if state officials are involved. Instead, FIG initiated an internal licensing system that is detailed in a 213-page rule book.*

For gymnastics, the unintended consequence of changes to rules governing minimum age and criteria for scoring within competitions was a new opportunity for cheating. That unanticipated opportunity was apparently taken, necessitating the creation of an

---

* You can see the rule book at http://www.fig-gymnastics.com/site/rules/main.

entirely new framework of constitutive rules to oversee the regulation of age among competitors.

What else might FIG have done? Logically the possibilities are limited. FIG could have relaxed the minimum-age requirement, or it could have changed the scoring rules to reflect the skill sets of older athletes. The trade-offs between simplicity and a perceived need for more constitutive rules usually involves a tolerance for unintended consequences, as more rules almost always mean more unintended consequences. But unintended consequences can, in turn, mean more rules. Here is yet another example of a wicked problem in action.

Lesson 3: Rules Are Always Imperfect

Rules can never cover every possible contingency. Thus, how we set up rules and regulations has profound significance for the outcomes that we observe. Sometimes the consequences are to the game—such as the farcical Caribbean soccer game—and sometimes to athletes themselves—such as young girls pressed into elite competitions.

One of the distinctive features of sport is that action on the field is governed by a set of laws or rules that are expected to cover every contingency. This is certainly not the case for the governance of sport off the field, nor in broader society. In both sport governance and society, we create systems of *jurisprudence* to judge how rules should be applied. In society, these are typically judicial systems of courts; in sport governance, this often takes the form of arbitration. But even on the field of play, rules have to be interpreted and applied. What about when something happens in competition that is not covered by the rules?

In June 2012, a "rules hole" was revealed in the procedures of USA Track & Field (USATF), the national governing body that has responsibility for overseeing the track and field athletes who represent the United States in the Olympics. In the finals of the 100 meters, Allyson Felix and Jeneba Tarmoh tied for third place.* A photo

---

* This was not the first instance of a tie in Olympics track and field qualification; it happened in 1984; see Julie Cart, "Play It Again: Turner, Fitzgerald-Brown, Page and Hightower to Have Rematch Saturday," *Los Angeles Times,* June 7, 1985, http://articles.latimes.com/1985-06-07/sports/sp-16199_1_stephanie-hightower.

of their finish couldn't settle who had finished ahead of the other. With the top three finishers advancing to the Olympics, a third place tie is problematic. The USATF had no procedure for resolving a third place tie, and needed to come up with one quickly.[43]

The day after the race, officials closed the rules hole by implementing a new rule.[44] The new rule allows the athletes to settle the race by a coin toss or by a second race a week later. Tarmoh eventually dropped out, while Felix finished in fifth place at London 2012.[45] The fact that the rule had to be made after the fact, leading one runner to walk away from the event, led some observers to complain. One lamented that "the only amateurs left in Olympic sports are the officials running them."[46] As we all learned in the 2000 presidential election between George W. Bush and Al Gore, creating rules (in that case for counting Florida ballots) after a race is likely to make no one happy other than the beneficiaries of the ad hoc rule making.

There are many other examples of rules holes and subsequent decisions to fill those holes. In 1999, the NFL implemented a new rule that said that once a quarterback started throwing a pass by moving his arm forward, the pass would be ruled incomplete even if the quarterback changed his mind midthrow and tried to "tuck" the ball "back towards his body."[47] This so-called tuck rule caused more problems than it solved.

During a playoff game in 2002 between the New England Patriots and the Oakland Raiders, in a snowstorm, with less than two minutes left on the clock, Patriots quarterback Tom Brady started a motion to pass the ball, decided not to, and apparently fumbled the ball as he tried to tuck it away. Oakland recovered the ball, but after consulting instant replay and conferring with other officials, the referee gave the ball back to the Patriots.[48] The call not only decided the game but also sparked controversy, as it depended not on the video evidence but on what it meant to throw or fumble a football. The rule survived for fourteen years. In 2013, the NFL voted to get rid of the tuck rule, eliminating uncertainty in referee judgments not via technology but via procedure.[49]

Rules holes show us that even in the most highly regulated situations, unforeseen contingencies arise. If rules cannot be created to cover every possible occurrence in a sporting context, then there is no hope for comprehensive rule making in broader society. Science, technology, and changing values all contribute to a perceived need for rules to change. How we deal with rules holes is a hallmark of good governance in sport, because rule making is always going to be imperfect, always subject to revision, and always in need of close attention.

~   ~   ~

We now have a vocabulary that can help us understand what's at stake in the war against cheating and how that war is being fought. To summarize, here are the key terms:

- *Constitutive rules:* Rules about rules
- *Regulatory rules:* Rules that govern game play
- *Norms:* Broadly held societal expectations for behavior
- *Cheating:* The violation of constitutive rules
- *Ordinary play:* A competition in practice
- *Penalty:* A sanction imposed for the violation of regulatory rules
- *Cynical play:* A violation of both regulatory rules and norms
- *Gamesmanship:* A violation of norms but not of regulatory rules
- *Rules hole:* A contingency not covered by existing rules

The next part of this book takes a close look at five battlegrounds in that war: amateurism in college sports, doping, match fixing, technology in sport, and sex testing. On each battleground, constitutive rules are being violated—or, to put it bluntly, people are accused of cheating. And their cheating doesn't just affect the outcome of a particular game or match; it could also strike at the very existence of sport as we know it. These battlegrounds are where going over the edge can threaten the possibility of sport itself.

PART II

THE BATTLEGROUNDS

Chapter 4

Amateurs: Who Is Being Cheated?

"Right now the NCAA is like a dictatorship. No one represents us in negotiations. The only way things are going to change is if players have a union."[1] With these words in early 2014, Northwestern University's Cain Kolter, the starting quarterback on its football team, announced that he was leading an effort to unionize the school's football players. Football players at Northwestern, and indeed college athletes generally, don't have the right to unionize because under US law they are not considered employees. Instead, they are considered students who pursue athletics as an extracurricular activity. In recent years, the notion of the college athlete participating in sports as a side activity to university education has come under intense pressure.

Big-time college sports in the United States are dependent on amateurism as the basis for a vast suite of rules and regulations. "Big-time" typically refers to men's football and basketball programs—multibillion-dollar enterprises with far more in common with professional leagues than with other intercollegiate sports.

I argue in this chapter that big-time college sports are unsustainable in their current form and that changes in how college sports are run are inevitable. What those changes might be and how they might affect universities and sports is highly uncertain, but I do have some ideas about how college athletics might adapt to the realities of the twenty-first century while preserving much of what makes college athletics so beloved. It is possible to replace an out-dated reliance on a romantic myth of amateurism with a pragmatic approach to professionalism that preserves the essence of college sports. But first, before looking forward, let's take a look back at how college sport found itself at the current fork in the road.

When Cain Kolter and his fellow teammates sought to unionize, the NCAA responded with strong opposition: "This union-backed attempt to turn student-athletes into employees undermines the purpose of college: an education. Student-athletes are not employees, and their participation in college sports is voluntary."[2] The idea of college athletes as employees would undercut the entire premise of the NCAA, which is based on the notion that "student-athletes" are students first, athletes second.

Kolter and his fellow players took their request to unionize to the National Labor Relations Board (NLRB), the governmental body responsible for protecting the rights of labor. In a move that surprised many, the regional arm of the NLRB ruled in favor of the athletes, concluding, "that players receiving scholarships from [Northwestern University] are 'employees.'"[3] The decision marked a watershed moment in the evolution of college sports. For the first time, some college athletes were judged under US law to be employees of the university that granted them scholarships and other benefits in exchange for participation in their sports.

The NLRB decision attracted attention at the highest levels of American politics. The US House of Representatives Committee on Education and the Workforce held a hearing on unionization, in which opinions sorted on predictable political lines. Representative John Kline, a Minnesota Republican, invoked President Franklin Roosevelt in expressing his opposition to the NLRB decision: "It's hard to imagine President Roosevelt thought the [National Labor Relations Act] would one day apply to the relationship between student athletes and academic institutions, yet that is precisely where we are."[4] On the other side of the aisle, Representative George Miller, a union-friendly Democrat from California, applauded the verdict: "In the end, this is a classic labor dispute. The NCAA empire is holding all the cards, making all the rules, and capturing all the profits."[5]

The NLRB decision was not the only blow to the NCAA in 2014. Later that year, a US district court ruled that the NCAA could not prohibit men's football and basketball players from being compensated for the commercial use of their names, images, or likenesses.[6] Former UCLA star basketball player Ed O'Bannon spearheaded the lawsuit. O'Bannon was motivated originally by the use of virtual representations of former college athletes—specifically himself—in the very popular and highly successful video games produced by EA Sports.[7] O'Bannon saw himself in the video game and realized that he wasn't being compensated in any way and decided to do something.

The O'Bannon ruling did not allow college athletes to receive payments as individuals, such as those associated with the sale of a jersey with specific names on the back. The ruling did allow colleges to create a trust for each athlete, with royalty payments made to athletes after their college eligibility is used up.

The two decisions suggested that a dam had apparently been broken. But in the increasingly litigious world of college sports, the breach did not last long. The NLRB decision was overturned at the national level in August 2015.[8] The NLRB did not actually weigh in on the question of whether or not the Northwestern players were employees. Instead, the NLRB declined to assert jurisdiction over the issue, noting an "absence of explicit congressional direction."[9] In the language of college sports, the NLRB decided to "punt." Even so, the NLRB said that its decision "does not preclude a reconsideration of this issue in the future." The Northwestern athletes had lost this battle, but the war was far from over.

In September 2015, a US appeals court ruled that paying students a name, image, or likeness would turn college athletics into professional leagues with "minor league status."[10] The court explained: "The difference between offering student-athletes education-related compensation and offering them cash sums untethered to educational expenses is not minor; it is a quantum leap."[11] Rather, the court ruled that colleges could offer students the full cost of attendance, which it defined as an education-related expense. The NCAA quickly adopted "cost of attendance" payments which led to college athletes receiving more than $160 million in additional benefits, according to an analysis by *USA Today*, as universities added this new benefit to their scholarship packages.[12] Of course, regulating the "cost of attendance" necessitated more layers of rules and enforcement by the NCAA.[13]

I'm sure that we have not heard the last of the O'Bannon case. And it is far from the only lawsuit that the NCAA is facing on issues related to compensation of athletes. The NCAA has, like the little boy in the Dutch story, plugged the holes in the dike, keeping back the flood waters of change. But despite the momentary respite for the NCAA, what should be clear from the Northwestern and O'Bannon judgments is that the model of college sports that has existed for more than a century that holds that college athletes are amateurs is changing. Whether the NCAA admits it or not, what is happening is a labor negotiation, with the athletes holding considerable untapped power. To understand the nature of that change, and where things might be headed, requires a journey back in time.

The Origins of the NCAA

Children like to play games and they like to compete against each other. This goes especially for college kids—young adults—and this seems to have been the case almost as far back as American universities have existed.

If a date can be put on the start of modern American collegiate sports, that would be August 3, 1852.[14] That summer day saw the first intercollegiate sporting event: a crew race between Harvard and Yale sponsored by a railroad company.[15] Foreshadowing the next 150 years of college sports, in pursuit of an advantage over their rivals, Harvard (allegedly) recruited a local coxswain to lead their boat who was not a student, but who could row like a beast.[16]

Organized games between schools followed in a variety of sports. The first intercollegiate baseball game was Amherst versus Williams in 1859; the first intercollegiate football game was Rutgers versus Princeton in 1869.[17] Sports grew rapidly on and between campuses. In the 1890s, the president of MIT worried that if sports continued to attract interest in universities, "it will soon be fairly a question whether the letters B.A. stand more for Bachelor of Arts or Bachelor of Athletics."[18]

The growth of college sports created the demand for an organization to oversee the competitions in a manner more formalized than students could provide. One key challenge was to standardize the rules of the games and their application. Interscholastic competition would not get very far if teams played baseball or football by different rules. So in 1895, seven university presidents from Midwest schools met in Chicago "to adopt rules and regulations for student participation in intercollegiate sports."[19] That coalition would later become the Big Ten Conference.

The early years of college sports were not all fun and games. Far from it. In 1905, 19 football players were killed in intercollegiate games and 137 more were seriously injured. Over the previous five years, 26 players had died as a result of playing football.[20] There were calls to ban the sport as too dangerous, too brutal. Columbia University outlawed football, and Harvard considered a ban.[21] Even as sport grew in popularity, the fate of sport hung in the balance.

Enter President Theodore Roosevelt.

In 1876, Roosevelt was a small, asthmatic freshman at Harvard. He attended the second football game ever player between Harvard and Yale and immediately became a fan of the game and of sport more generally.[22] In a speech made in 1900, one year before becoming US president, Roosevelt expressed his views on the importance of sport:

> The great growth in the love of athletic sports, for instance, while fraught with danger if it becomes one-sided and unhealthy, has beyond all question had an excellent effect in increased manliness. . . . In short, in life, as in a football game, the principle to follow is: Hit the line hard; don't foul and don't shirk, but hit the line hard![23]

In 1905, as the casualty toll mounted on football fields, Roosevelt used his "bully pulpit" to bring together representatives of Harvard, Yale, and Princeton to fix football. The universities agreed to take steps to reduce the brutality of the game. One historian called this resulting agreement "probably the most important event in the history of intercollegiate sport."[24]

Yet, the agreement did not eliminate the brutality of the game. Ronald Smith, a professor at Penn State, recounts one particularly nasty episode in 1905 involving Penn against Harvard, one of the schools that had agreed a few months previously to help clean up the game: "During the game the Harvard center was kicked in the groin several times by a Penn player. After having complained to the umpire with no satisfaction, the Harvard man belted the Penn player in the face and was banished from the game."[25] Hearing of the episode, President Roosevelt contacted the Harvard coach and asked for an explanation. In a subsequent game between Harvard and Yale, another violent incident occurred, this time prompting President Roosevelt to contact the lead game official. The fact that Harvard had shut out Yale probably helped motivate Roosevelt, a Harvard alum.[26]

A US president taking an interest in the governance of college sports is not a quirk of the early twentieth century. It also happens today. In 2013, President Barack Obama expressed concerns about the violence of football, both professional and college, specifically related to concussions:

> I'm a big football fan, but I have to tell you if I had a son, I'd have to think long and hard before I let him play football. And I think that those of us who love the sport are going to have to wrestle with the fact that it will probably change gradually to try to reduce some of the violence . . .

A 1905 game between the Harvard Crimson and the Yale Bulldogs.

That's something that I'd like to see the NCAA think about.[27]

One year later, the NCAA settled a lawsuit over concussions among football players.[28] In early 2015, President Obama was reported to be considering creating a "commission" on college athletics.[29] In some ways, little had changed in the course of more than a century. College sports are of such national and cultural significance that the US president gets involved in its governance.

And when a president speaks, people tend to listen. With President Roosevelt applying pressure, the carnage on the field and calls for the sport to be outlawed led to the creation of the Intercollegiate Athletic Association of the United States in 1906, which became the National Collegiate Athletic Association in 1910.[30] The NCAA began with sixty-two members; today it has more than 1,200.[31] President Roosevelt "should properly be viewed as one of the founding fathers" of the NCAA.[32]

The NCAA took quick action to standardize the rules of the game of football and other sports. With rules in place, the NCAA organized competitions between schools. By 1941, it oversaw national championships in only two sports.[33] By 2016, this had grown to ninety national championships in twenty-three sports (across divisions and for men and women) involving more than 54,000 athletes.[34]

Off the field, the NCAA's governance focus shifted from standardizing games to defining what it meant in practice for elite athletics to take place on the campuses of US colleges and universities. But securing compliance to NCAA rules on the part of institutions that are known for their decentralized and sometimes haphazard governance was problematic. For decades, the NCAA was a weak organization. Its oversight powers had little bite until after World War II when, motivated by the dramatic postwar expansion of college athletics thanks to the GI Bill, the NCAA developed stricter guidelines and more effective ways of ensuring compliance.

During recent decades, the NCAA has seen one scandal after another as member institutions broke its many rules, often to gain a competitive advantage in competition but sometimes for personal gain. The NCAA meted out punishments while observers expressed shock and demands for something more to be done. Then the cycle would repeat.

Here are just a few notable examples:

- In the early 1950s, the NCAA took on the Kentucky basketball program and its legendary coach Adolph Rupp. Players in the program had accepted payment to fix the outcome of games, what is called point shaving (and today is often called match fixing). The NCAA recommended that the program be banned for one year, prompting the university's president to cancel the university's participation in the upcoming season.[35]

- In the 1980s, the Southern Methodist University (SMU) football program was given the "death penalty" by the NCAA. An investigation revealed that, during 1985–86, thirteen football players had been paid more than $60,000 by boosters of the program, organized by SMU football officials.[36] The SMU football program was eliminated for two years before being reinstated. (It was a short death.)

- In the 2010s, the University of North Carolina found that some of its scholarship athletes had been enrolled in "paper classes"—courses they never attended but for which they received high grades. The allegations of academic misconduct involved both the football team and its storied basketball program. A professor, the football coach, and the university chancellor all resigned or lost their jobs as a result of the scandal, which continues to unfold.[37]

These controversies barely scratch the surface of NCAA rule violations. An analysis by *Inside Higher Ed* in 2011 found that 53 of the 120 NCAA members that participated in its highest football division had committed "major rules violations" between 2001 and 2010.[38] During the 1990s, the number was 54 out of 120 members, and in the 1980s, it was 57 of 106. For the half decade from 2011 to 2016, it was 34 of 128 members.[39] It was not just universities with big-time athletics programs that ran afoul of NCAA rules and regulations, either. MacMurray College in Florida, with about 600 students, was given the NCAA death penalty for its tennis program in 2005. The head tennis coach had arranged for tuition to be paid for ten foreign tennis players, in contravention of NCAA rules for Division III schools.[40]

One reason for the numerous violations may be the dramatic expansion of NCAA rules and regulations. Figure 4.1 shows the number of pages in the NCAA rule book at different points in time. In 2016, these rules took up more than 1,100 pages.[41] My university (the University of Colorado) has five full-time staff with responsibility for ensuring that the university follows NCAA rules. The rules cover a wide range of activities. In 2014, the University of South Carolina reported twenty-two minor violations of NCAA rules, including a recruit who took a picture at a spring practice with a former South Carolina player who was playing in the NFL and "impermissible iced decorations on a cookie cakes given to prospects."[42]

NCAA rules have their origins in the long-standing belief that college athletes should be amateurs who play the game for the love of sport as a side activity while getting an education, their primary reason for being at the college or university. Today, that belief is formalized in almost 500 pages of NCAA rules and regulations that discuss what is required for an athlete to maintain his or her amateur status, governing everything from what an athlete can eat to whom he or she can speak with and when.[43]

The rejection of the notion of amateurism lies at the core of the challenges to the NCAA by Kain Colter and his fellow teammates at Northwestern University and by Ed O'Bannon and others behind

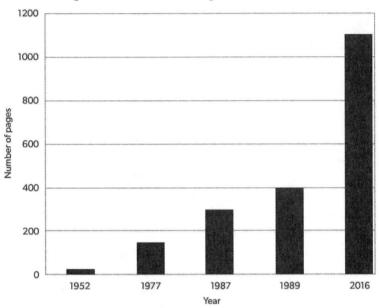

Figure 4.1. Number of Pages of NCAA Rules

their lawsuit against the NCAA. Remarkably, the ideal of amateurism that lies at the center of today's debates over college athletics is based on a historical myth. The NCAA is implementing a fairy tale.

The Fairy Tale: College Athletes Are Amateurs

At the core of debates about the role of sport on American college campuses lies the notion of "amateurism." The NCAA explains that "Amateur competition is a bedrock principle of college athletics and the NCAA."[44] The word *amateur* is French in its origin, "indicating action or consumption arising from taste rather than instrumental self interest."[45] It certainly sounds romantic. In theory, amateurs pursue sport primarily because they love competition. In practice, such romanticism gives way to the real world.

The Olympics provide a good example of the path that college sports appear to be on. Amateurism used to be the hallmark of the Olympic movement. I say "used to be" because Olympic athletes are no longer expected to be amateurs in any sense of the concept. Rather, virtually all Olympic athletes are professional athletes. They have to be, because attaining world-class skill in any sport is a full-time job. By the late 1980s, the amateur ideal in the Olympics had been "replaced by an unqualified intensity for competition, commercial interests, focus on winning, and full-time professional dedication to the sport."[46]

Ironically, the evolution of the Olympics to allowing full-time professional athletes to compete did not represent a move away from the highly mythologized practices of ancient Greece, but rather toward what really occurred in ancient Greece.

The original Olympians did not practice amateurism in sport. Greeks back then didn't even have a word for "amateur." David Young, author of a book on the myth of Olympic amateurism, says that the notion was "a far-flung and amazingly successful deception, a kind of historical hoax, in which scholar[s] joined hands with sportsm[e]n and administrator[s] so as to mislead the public and influence modern sporting life."[47] The idea of ancient Greeks as amateurs served as an effective rationalization for a modern amateurism.

In the 1970s and 1980s, Olympic sports parted ways with the ideal of amateurism, but this idea persists in US college sports. That ideal has less to do with romanticized views of ancient Greeks than it does with British class distinctions of the nineteenth century. Kenneth Shropshire, a law professor at the University of Pennsylvania, explains that "the dominant view in the latter half of the nineteenth century [was] that . . . those who competed for money [were] basically inferior in nature."[48] A distinction based on amateurism prevented upper-class gentlemen from having to compete with men who labored for a living, lest the workingmen win all the sports competitions. Thus, "it is from these antiquated rules that the modern eligibility rules of the NCAA evolved." It is easy to be an amateur when you are rich. As if to underscore the point, the Ivy League of the nation's wealthiest universities still does not offer athletic scholarships, even in programs that participate at the highest levels of NCAA competition.[49]

Walter Byers served as the executive director of the NCAA from 1951 to 1988 and helped to oversee its enormous growth during that period. Writing in 1995 and looking back over the organization that he had helped mold, Byers had harsh words: "The management of intercollegiate athletics stays in place committed to an outmoded code of amateurism drawn, quite frankly, with many of the same words that they had drawn in 1956."

The year 1956 is significant because that is when a college scholarship in exchange for athletics participation was put into place as a way to formalize amateurism on college campuses. Byers attributed an atmosphere of exploitation to "the neo-plantation mentality that exists on the campuses of our country and in the conference offices and in the NCAA that the rewards belong to the overseers and the supervisors."[50] These are harsh words, evocative of the history of slavery in the United States, and made more significant by the significant participation of African-American athletes in college sports.[51]

The prohibition against athletes profiting from participation in college sports predates the invention of the college athletic scholarship. During the controversial period for football at the beginning of the twentieth century, Harvard's president Charles Eliot explained that it was not just the violence of the game that was troublesome: "Deaths and injuries are not the strongest arguments against football. That cheating and brutality are profitable is the main evil."[52] Today, as college sports draw ever more money, the amateur ideal seems increasingly untenable, regardless of whether it is grounded in a historical fiction, class divisions, or something else. Profits (for some), revenue (in large amounts), and expenditures (everywhere) are as fundamental to big-time college sports as are tailgating and basketball tournament brackets.

Prior to the creation of the NCAA, there was little concern or interest in formalizing a distinction between amateur and professional. For instance, here is a description of the benefits provided to one Yale athlete in the 1890s: "[He] had a suite of rooms in the dorm, free meals at the university club, a one-hundred-dollar scholarship, he could sell programs and keep the profit, and was made an agent of the American Tobacco Company, receiving a commission on cigarettes sold in New Haven, plus a ten-day paid vacation to Cuba."[53] Shropshire, the University of Pennsylvania professor, observes that at the beginning of the twentieth century, "amateurism, at least as historically conceived, was largely absent from college sports."[54]

However, the NCAA adopted an eligibility code as part of its first constitution that mandated that participants be full-time students who were prohibited compensation for playing.[55] There was also to be no "proselytizing," or what we call today the recruiting of athletes.[56] Because the NCAA had little in the way of enforcement powers, the code was often ignored in the early years, and athletes received compensation despite the rules.

One early case of documented compensation for college athletes occurred in 1899: the manager of Columbia University made improper payments to five players.[57] More than a half century of informal compensation of athletes followed, a practice that stopped only when the athletic scholarship was created, accompanied by NCAA rules and enforcement capabilities. Prior to that time, college athletes were prohibited from being paid by universities for participation in sports, but many had on-campus jobs or were "subsidized or employed by generous alumni and boosters."[58]

One of the first battlegrounds over amateurism in college sports was baseball, which developed a burgeoning professional presence in the early 1900s. In 1909, Amos Alonzo Stagg, the football, basketball, and baseball coach at the University of Chicago, justified the importance of keeping college sports for amateurs on the grounds of protecting both the emerging professional leagues and amateurism: "The American loves to win and we are willing to pay the price. This creates a wide demand for good baseball players and a certain type of college player sooner or later gets involved." Stagg foresaw that the mixing of college and professional athletes would expand to other sports: "It is my prophecy that in a few years you will find that many of our large cities will be supporting professional football teams composed of ex-college players. . . . The passing of [less restrictive amateurism rules] would be an unceasing catastrophe."[59] The mixing of professionals and amateurs would be "anarchy"—thus, they had to be rigorously kept apart. More than a century later, the efforts to enforce amateurism are showing their age.

Big-Time College Athletics at a Crossroads

It is little surprise that the main factor behind the breakdown in the college sports amateur ideal today is money. Lots of money. Money in college sports is big and getting bigger. It has led to vast inequities among colleges that seek to compete with each other, reinforcing a division between the have and have-nots.

Where you find piles of money, politics is not far away. In the discussion of college athletics, people debate issues such as whether college athletes are employees or not, whether they are exploited or not, whether coaches are paid too much, and so on. But the reality is that as long as athletes are involved in a system that generates huge amounts of money, they will hold incredible power. Just consider the University of Missouri in 2015, where football players upset over racial tensions on campus announced a boycott of an upcoming game unless the university's president was fired.[60] The president announced his resignation a few days later.

If college athletes wish to demand greater compensation (or anything else), then they can readily do so. Imagine a team refusing to take the court in the NCAA Final Four game or a college football team striking on the eve of the national championship. There is a lot of latent political power in college sports—how it is deployed is another issue altogether.

Thus, the political power of the collegiate athletic system will exist so long as there is big money in athletics. In 2009, institutional spending per athlete at the schools that compete in the highest NCAA football division totaled more than $105,000, as compared to spending about $13,000 per student overall.[61] University spending per athlete increased by about 50 percent over four years, but only 22 percent per student overall. The costs of maintaining a big-time college sports program are increasing dramatically.

Only 12 of the top 231 NCAA athletics programs, by revenue, were financially self-sufficient in 2015.[62] Texas A&M, whose revenue exceeded expenses by more than $80 million, was at the top. At the other end of the scale was James Madison University, where $36 million of its $45 million athletics budget was subsidized by university funds from outside the athletics department. Of the top 231 schools, 176 require a subsidy of greater than 30 percent of their total athletics budget. In benefit-cost terms, just about every university raises external funds for athletics that far exceed whatever subsidy the university provides.

But perhaps the "subsidy" should be called an "investment." For instance, at the University of Colorado, Boulder, where I work, the university provides about $10 million per year to athletics, but the athletics department generates an additional $60 million, bringing its budget up to about $70 million.* That means that for every dollar that the university invests in athletics, the program provides a return of about $6. Some universities, like the University of Michigan, provide a much larger return on university investment; others provide a lower return. Whether a 6-to-1 benefit-cost ratio is acceptable or desirable is of course a judgment call based on how one values college athletics in the first place. Even calling university support of athletics a "subsidy" (i.e., a negative to be avoided) versus an "investment" (i.e., a positive, with potential for a large return) involves a choice with implications for how athletics are framed as an activity on campus. Debates over money in college athletics are often merely a stalking horse for more fundamental disagreements about how college athletics are valued in the first place.

Language Matters

The choice to call university spending on athletics a "subsidy" versus an "investment" is not the only place where language reflects what is valued. In a course I teach on sports governance at the University of Colorado, Boulder, students (including scholarship athletes) often express surprise at the origins of the phrase "student-athlete"—a phrase that they hear on an almost daily basis with little awareness of its origins or significance.

The origins and use of "student-athlete" by the NCAA illustrates the tensions brought on by money and the efforts to prevent college athletes from sharing in the spoils. At the same time the

---

*   These are round numbers. The university subsidy includes direct support plus student fees of about $1 million.

athletic scholarship was invented, Walter Byers, the head of the NCAA, coined the phrase "student-athlete" to designate the recipients of these benefits. Byers later explained, "We crafted the term student-athlete and soon it was embedded in all NCAA rules and interpretations."[63]

One important motivation for the usage of "student-athlete" in the 1950s was the filing of a worker's compensation claim against Fort Lewis College in Colorado for death benefits by the widow of a football player who died as a result of injuries sustained in a game. The Colorado Supreme Court ruled against the widow because the college was "not in the football business."[64] Taylor Branch, in his book *The Cartel*, observes that "Using the 'student-athlete' defense, colleges have compiled a string of victories in liability cases." The language that we use to discuss the NCAA and college athletics is not value-free. Even how we commonly describe the athletes on campus reflects history and practice.

Television and Money

The NCAA's growth is largely a consequence of the marriage of college sports and television broadcasting. The NCAA got into the business of televising college sports in the early 1950s, when it negotiated its first TV contract, worth $1 million.[65] How quaint.

The March Madness spring postseason basketball tournament operates under a fourteen-year, $10.8 billion television agreement, almost $800 million per year.[66] This total will rise to $1.1 billion per year from 2025 to 2032.[67] Figure 4.2 shows how quickly TV revenue for the NCAA tournament has grown, exceeding that of the NFL, the NBA, and MLB.[68]

Another example of the influence of money on college sports is football: in 2014, ESPN paid $7.3 billion for the rights to host college football playoff and championship games.[69]

The numbers show every sign of continuing to grow. The 2016 March Madness championship game between Villanova and North Carolina had the second-largest TV audience ever for a college basketball game on a cable TV channel.* The 2015 and 2016 college football championship games had 33.4 and 25.7 million viewers, respectively, making them the most-watched and the sixth-most-watched cable television shows in history.†

The financial numbers are large not only for TV contracts. They are also significant for individual teams and athletes. It 2012, the University of Louisville basketball team generated more than $35 million in profits—$1.35 million per home game—with the team playing in the KFC Yum Center (named after a restaurant chain),

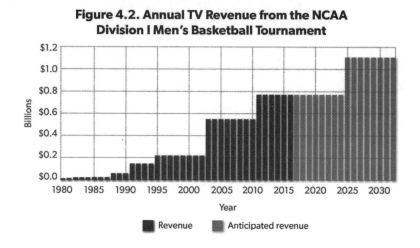

Figure 4.2. Annual TV Revenue from the NCAA Division I Men's Basketball Tournament

an arena that was publicly funded to the tune of $238 million.[70] Individual athletes have significant economic value as well. Johnny Manziel, the Texas A&M quarterback who won the Heisman Trophy in 2013, generated an estimated $37 million worth of publicity for his university that season.[71]

---

*   It trailed only the Kentucky-Wisconsin semifinal from 2015; see http://variety.com/2016/tv/news/ncaa-mens-basketball-title-game-ratings-tumble-on-cable-1201745947/.

†   The top eight such shows are all college football games; see *The Least Thing*, "How Big Will College Football Get?" January 12, 2015, http://leastthing.blogspot.com/2015/01/how-big-will-college-football-get.html.

A CBS camera at a Kansas Jayhawks practice in the opening round of March Madness 2016. TV companies pay about $800 million each year to cover the tournament.

With tens of billions of dollars in revenue via TV contracts and coaches making tens of millions of dollars, it is no surprise that college athletes and observers are pressing for change. And changes have occurred. The NCAA has begrudgingly started to increase the compensation of college athletes by allowing universities to expand the definition of a "scholarship" to include incidental costs and personal expenses.[72] The NCAA also recently changed its rules to allow unrestricted meals and snacks and travel for athletes' families to football and basketball championships.

Such small changes in the direction of greater compensation for college athletes represent an effort by the NCAA to engage in labor negotiations without using negotiation language or even acknowledging what it is doing. It is hard to see how these concessions will do anything more than embolden college athletes and their representatives to demand more. The NCAA has begun a long journey down a slippery slope.

Possible Reforms: Professionalization and Realpolitik

How might the unsettled state of college athletics be resolved? I suggest two possible reforms. One is to treat college athletes like universities treat other students and professors when it comes to intellectual property. The second is to treat college athletics like colleges treat other areas of vocation valued on campus and to give out degrees in sport. Both ideas are radical, but they might help to preserve college sport in a way that is fair and workable.

Compensating Athletes Like Others on Campus

In 1956, the NCAA decided that athletes should be compensated in the form of a scholarship to attend college; in recent years, the NCAA has been increasing the value of such compensation. A college scholarship has considerable economic value. For instance, the head basketball coach at the University of Colorado, Tad Boyle, explained to me and my students that he tells potential recruits and their families that a scholarship to Colorado is worth about $250,000 for an out-of-state player over five years. So the issue is not whether college athletes should be compensated, but how much.

Paying college athletes a salary, like universities pay professors and coaches, is conceivable, at least in theory. Graduate students (and some undergraduates) receive stipends in addition to tuition scholarships for working on campus. How much these students can be paid is closely regulated by funding agencies. These assistantships (as they are typically called) are analogous to the athletic scholarships (plus minimal stipends) that the NCAA now allows athletes to be provided. Athletics departments could hire athletes in the same way that research labs hire graduate students.* Of course, this would not address the fact that some athletes have considerably more economic value than others.

As in the case of Johnny Manziel, it is clear that many college athletes have considerable, unexploited earnings potential. Is there

---

* I describe a plan for compensating college athletes in more detail in chapter 11.

a way to facilitate athletes who wish to capitalize on their economic value while avoiding fully professionalizing college sports? I think so. The answer may lie in treating athletes like universities treat professors.

In 1980, the US Congress passed what the *Economist* called "possibly the most inspired piece of legislation to be enacted in America over the past half-century."[73] The Bayh-Dole Act changed property rights with respect to discoveries made in universities as a result of federally funded research. Prior to 1980, the US government retained ownership of intellectual property associated with discoveries that resulted from federal research and development. Few of the patents owned by the federal government were being been commercialized, and policy makers sought a way to capitalize on the billions of dollars in federal R&D taking place at universities.

Under the Bayh-Dole Act, professors and other university researchers who create intellectual property gain a share in its rewards, thereby creating strong incentives both to discover and to commercialize. In the two decades following the passage of the law, US universities increased their patents by 1,000 percent and added an estimated $40 billion annually to the economy. At the same time, the law ensured that technology transfer activities on campus would be closely monitored to ensure that the mission of universities was not compromised by financial conflicts of interest.

So what does Bayh-Dole tell us about college athletics? Several years ago, former senator Birch Bayh explained why the Bayh-Dole Act works: "It aligns the interests of the taxpaying public, the federal government, research universities, their departments, inventors, and private sector developers transforming government supported research into usable products."[74] The NCAA and universities might explore aligning the interests of scholarship athletes, university campuses, the NCAA, and the sports public with the incredible revenue potential of college sports.

Assigning to universities the intellectual property rights of athletes who play under their names while creating a revenue-sharing model with those athletes would meet this need. Such an approach would encourage the further generation of revenue from sports, creating a windfall for some college athletics programs, and deliver deserved rewards to the scholarship athletes who play the games.

Create Athletics Majors

In contrast to proposals that make athletes more like professors, coaches, and other employees, it is possible to tackle the issue in a different direction by considering how to make college athletes more like the students that they are. One way to do this would be to create degree programs in sport.

This idea is not new and it comes with a considerable amount of baggage. In 2004, the *Washington Post* reported that of the 117 universities that fielded Division I football teams, "nearly three dozen universities award academic credit for participation on intercollegiate sports teams."[75] Such courses are largely viewed as a substitute for real coursework and a way to keep football players (mostly) eligible. At Kansas State, for instance, football players enrolled in ATHM 104, Varsity Football, with letter grades that were given out by head coach Bill Snyder.

Such courses are generally seen as illegitimate. The head football coach at the University of Virginia, Al Groh, laughed off the practice: "I'm sure there are a few kids on this team that would like to substitute something like 'Sophisticated Blitz Tactics' for advanced physics. But I don't see the possibility of that happening at Virginia." A law professor at the University of Nebraska expressed a similar view in 2015: "There comes a point when you are turning higher education into a pretzel to accommodate the high-revenue, fan attention-grabbing two sports" of men's football and basketball.[76] In 2012, Cardale Jones, a quarterback at Ohio State University, stated in a quickly deleted tweet: "Why should we have to go to class if we came here to play football? We ain't come to play school. Classes are pointless."[77]

Attending classes and playing sports have not always been considered separate activities. US universities have a long history of awarding college credit for physical education, although in recent years, physical education has fallen out of favor. In the 1920s, almost all universities awarded physical education credits; by 1970, the number had dropped to below 90 percent; and by 2010, it was down to less than 40 percent of schools.[78] Part of this trend is no doubt the changing nature of the economy, where physical labor is no longer an important qualification for most jobs. But in 1950, when this wasn't the case, Harvard explained why PE was necessary in its curriculum: "The school will be concerned with the health of its pupils, both physical and mental. The human body must be healthy, fit for work, able to carry out the purposes of the mind."[79]

Although physical education is no longer as prevalent as it once was, there are compelling arguments for opening a discussion about creating athletics majors on campus. Universities routinely give degrees in vocations and the arts, notably music, dance, and theater, in which performances are often given to the public.[80] What is the difference between a Shakespeare play, a jazz ensemble, and a basketball game? A Florida State University professor of educational psychology argued the case for sport degrees, "Kids come to universities to play basketball and football professionally. Why don't we legitimize that effort?"[81]

Any proposal to create a degree in "athletics" comparable to degrees in music or theater would have to surmount a number of obstacles. One is the widespread prejudice against sport in the modern American university. Another is the legacy of academic fraud that has followed athletics for decades, such as the "paper class" scandal at the University of North Carolina or the various schemes of giving class credit and even grades for participating in football. Another obstacle is the institutionalized division between academics and athletics on most college campuses. Bridges between the two would have to be built.

John V. Lombardi, former president of Louisiana State University and the University of Florida, has made the case for degrees in athletics. He cites music as a model:

> If a student wants to receive a performance degree, they not only must perform at the highest skill level (and be recruited and selected based on auditions that demonstrate the talent and commitment required to succeed), but they must also take a range of academic courses related to their profession. Music theory, composition, mu-

sic history for the musician, for example. In addition, of course, they must fulfill the university's general education requirements.[82]

He further argues that universities would need to offer a "structured curriculum" in areas such as "sports history, sports law, [and] sports finance." Such degree programs would need to ensure academic integrity and focus, as many other programs do, on a transition from the university to the job market. Could such a program be successfully implemented? As a college professor, I have no doubt that it could. What is standing in the way? Lombardi explains: "What we need now is a courageous university president with a strong athletics program to launch this process and mobilize the support and enthusiasm of like-minded innovators."

A gap has opened up between the concept of college athletics as a supposed extracurricular activity enjoyed by amateurs and the realities of big money and wide exposure. This gap is seen as an opportunity by those bringing challenges in the legal and policy environment. This gap will have to close. We can make college sports more professional or more academic. We are at a fork in the road, and eventually, college athletics will either choose its future or have change forced upon it.

Chapter 5

Cheating to Lose

On February 15, 2013, the sky over southern Russia was lit up by a massive explosion. Windows in thousands of buildings were shattered due to the shock wave, which sent more than fifteen hundred people to the hospital. The explosion was the result of a meteor, estimated to be more than sixty feet in diameter. Most of the power of the explosion, at about 100,000 feet above the Earth's surface, did not reach the ground. If it had, damage and injuries would surely have been far greater, as the total energy released was equivalent to dozens of atomic bombs.[1]

The Chelyabinsk meteor was the largest to enter the Earth's atmosphere since 1908 and served as a dramatic reminder that the Earth is at some risk of catastrophe from a rogue meteoroid. But how big is that risk? And, correspondingly, how much should the public pay to monitor the threat and prepare for its consequences? These are difficult questions made more important by the fact that the answers venture into the territory of existential threats. A big space rock could end all life on earth. So it's not a risk to dismiss cavalierly.

The threat of space rocks to life on Earth offers a useful paradigm for contemplating match fixing in sport. Match fixing refers to efforts to prearrange sporting outcomes, including who wins and who loses. Such arrangements are often linked to ploys to capitalize on foreknowledge through gambling. If you know in advance who is going to win a competition but no one else does, you can make a lot of money by making the correct bet. It is easy to imagine how match fixing might pose an existential threat to sport, but no one really knows how big the threat is—just like the threat to Earth posed by massive rocks careening through space.

This chapter explores the territory of match fixing and reports good news and bad news. The good news is that match fixing is less of a threat among athletes at the highest levels of competition due to the simple math of costs and benefits. Global superstars make far too much money playing it straight to risk their careers on fixing matches. More good news is that fans don't appear to be too worried about match fixing, at least those who aren't betting on sports contests.

The bad news is that match fixing is a real problem in lower tiers of sport, especially those that combine an unstable mixture of low compensation for athletes with opportunities for high stakes wagers on the contests. Here the cost-and-benefit calculus works in the direction of creating incentives for fixing. At all levels of sport, referees are also vulnerable to fixing schemes. Like the other battlegrounds we visit in this book, match fixing is an example of a "wicked problem"—we can never eliminate the threat, but we can do better or worse at coping with it.

The most significant efforts to combat match fixing come from the European Union, where an array of bodies, public and private, has sought to address the manipulation of sport competitions. As we will see, these organizations have struggled to come up with a practical definition of match fixing, ultimately choosing to focus on "uncertainty" in sports outcomes. For reasons I'll discuss, these approaches are unlikely to work very well. I argue that a better approach is to think about match fixing through the lens of financial conflicts of interest.

Like the threat of asteroids and meteors whizzing around the solar system, the threat of match fixing is real. To deal with it effectively requires understanding the nature of the threat and then determining what success looks like. As on the other battlegrounds, success lies in greater accountability and transparency among athletes, referees, and governing bodies.

BOOM! A Meteor Explodes over the NBA

In the 2002 NBA playoffs, the Los Angeles Lakers, led by superstars Kobe Bryant and Shaquille O'Neill, found themselves down three games to two against the Sacramento Kings, a team that hadn't won a championship since 1951, when they were the Rochester Royals. One more victory and the Kings would advance to the finals.

With twelve seconds left in the sixth game, the Kings were losing by just one point and the Lakers had possession of the ball, which they were inbounding from under the basket. Bryant, one of the greatest basketball players of all time, was being closely guarded by Mike Bibby, who was having a breakout series for the Kings. It was a pivotal moment in the game, and in the series.

Bryant was standing on the free-throw line, facing the end line. Bibby was facing Bryant. In fact, Bryant and Bibby were chest to chest, with their arms gently around each other, like you might see in a 1980s-era junior high school slow dance. The moment did not last long: Bryant broke the embrace using his left arm to nudge Bibby to his left while lifting his right arm across Bibby's body in an effort to get around him and (he hoped) be open for the inbound pass. Unfortunately for Bibby, Bryant's right elbow did not come cleanly across his body, and instead it encountered Bibby's face. Ouch.

As Bibby reached for his face and fell back on the floor, Bryant broke free for an instant, only to be pulled down by Bibby, when the referee's whistle blew. FOUL!

The referee's call went against Bibby, who lay on the floor for a few minutes stunned by Bryant's sharp elbow. He later recalled his shock at learning that he was being called for the foul: "It pissed me off because when I got up, I thought they called a foul on him. I didn't know what happened. I remember saying, 'You called a foul on me?' And my nose was bleeding, and I blew some of my blood out onto the court just to show them."[2]

Bob Delaney, one of the three NBA referees who officiated the game, later acknowledged that he should have done things differently, explaining that, with the advantage of hindsight, he should have called Bibby for holding Bryant before the play started and then called a parallel technical on Bryant for the elbow to the face: "I would've called the away-from-the-play foul, which means the Lakers would've shot one and retained possession, and called a technical on Kobe. Sacramento shoots one technical foul, LA does the same, and they inbound the ball from the same spot."[3] Even-steven.

Instead, the Lakers benefitted from the call. In fact, the Lakers benefitted from a lot of calls. In the pivotal fourth quarter, the Lakers shot twenty-seven free throws to the Kings' nine. Roland Beech of 82games.com evaluated the performance of the referees and concluded that their decision making led to a six-point advantage for the Lakers over the course of the game.[4]

The Lakers won, 106–102.

Michael Wilbon, a sports columnist and ESPN personality, explained that he has the utmost respect for the work of game officials as "the most honest people in sports," but, even so, "that game was an abomination." Well, referees are part of the game, and like players, they have good games and bad games; sometimes luck favors one team rather than another. For instance, in one 2016 NBA playoff game, the NBA reported that its officials blew five calls in the final 13.5 seconds alone.[5] It happens.

Win some, lose some, right?

Not so fast.

In the summer of 2007, a federal grand jury indicted NBA referee Tim Donaghy, a thirteen-year veteran of the league, for betting on games and then officiating to influence the outcome in collusion with organized crime.[6] Donaghy admitted to accepting money from people with a betting interest to share inside information about teams and players. He even admitted to officiating games that he himself had bet on, although he denied actually "fixing" game results.[7] Donaghy ended up serving a fifteen-month prison sentence.

One allegation from Donaghy in particular rocked the sports world. He claimed that the NBA had ordered referees to fix the outcomes of certain playoff matches, including the infamous 2002 Lakers-Kings game. Donaghy explained: "It was in the NBA's interest to add another game to the series."[8] David Stern, the president of the NBA, called the allegations "baseless."

The 2002 Lakers-Kings game has become a bit like the assassination of President John F. Kennedy. There are enough conspiracy theories to sustain many hours of sports talk radio, and there are plenty of shady suspects on the NBA's version of the grassy knoll. Everyone can agree that it was a very poorly officiated game. Whether it was a bad day for the refs or something more sinister will be debated among NBA aficionados for a long time.

Tim Donaghy's mug-shot from 2010.

What is not in dispute is that NBA games have been influenced by at least one crooked referee. Such influence goes far beyond wins and losses. Brandon Lang, who handicaps games for a living and was played by Matthew McConaughey in *Two for the Money,* a movie about sports gambling, explains that the large number of betting options in sport offers an opportunity for fixing many aspects of a game: "You can bet on who's going to win, by how many points. You can bet whether it's going to be a high-scoring or low-scoring game with the over/under. You can bet the first, second, third, or fourth quarter. You can bet the first-half and second-half winner or loser."[9]

Sports betting has been around as long as there have been sports. The global sports betting market can be divided into a regulated sector, which is overseen by governments, and an unregulated, often illegal sector. The European Betting and Gaming Association estimated that the total size of the regulated sports gambling sector in 2016 is $70 billion.* To put that into context, recall that the total size of the professional sports market in the United States and Europe is about $50 billion. There aren't solid numbers on the size of unregulated gambling, but it is widely assumed to be many times larger than the regulated sector. One expert suggests that its mag-

---

* The entire sector of regulated gambling (including lotteries, casinos, etc.) is estimated to be more than $500 billion, so sport is just a small fraction of that total; see European Gaming and Betting Association (EGBA), "Sports Betting: Commercial and Integrity Issues: Final Report," http://www.egba.eu/media/Sports-Betting-Report-FINAL.pdf.

nitude should be measured in the trillions of dollars, with much of that being wagered in Asia, where gambling is enormously popular.[10]

Whatever the size of the global sports betting market, it is safe to conclude that it is larger in magnitude than the size of the global professional sports economy. The huge amount of money at stake provides both opportunity and motivation for the fixing of sporting events. The data that are available suggest that, internationally, the most popular sports to wager on are soccer, cricket, and tennis, and in the United States, it's football (both college and NFL) and basketball, especially the annual March Madness NCAA tournament.[11] Not surprisingly, the most popular sports to wager on are also typically those that are most popular in a given region—cricket in India, soccer in Europe, football in the United States. In the United States, the latest battleground over sports betting involves so-called daily fantasy sports, which allow people to make bets on individual players in a sport who are assembled together in a virtual team. Bets placed on an individual's performance within a team sport context create new opportunities for fixing. In addition, modern technology increasingly allows for wagers to be made far afield from where the games are played, offering new opportunities for fixing to take place.

For instance, in early 2016, the International Tennis Federation suspended several tennis umpires for their role in a gambling scheme.[12] The umpires oversaw matches on the ITF Futures Tour, the lowest tier of professional tennis, where prize money for winning tournaments is generally around $10,000.[13] The umpires keep the official match score on a tablet at courtside. In some cases, they would delay entering the score by about a minute, giving enough time for someone in on the scheme sitting courtside to text the score to colleagues in advance of the point being posted. In the world of gambling, one minute of advance knowledge can translate into a winning bet.* "Courtsiding," as the practice is known, doesn't require a corrupt umpire, just an ability to get scores to gamblers before those scores are officially posted.[14]

---

* It was also alleged that in some cases the umpires texted the score to coconspirators before entering them into their tablets.

Referees have a lot of control over sporting events, but so do the players. Concerns about fixing often center on athletes. When wins and losses are fixed, it is often called "match fixing." When the point spread is being manipulated, it's called "point shaving." And when some other aspect of the game is being influenced, which may or may not have to do with who wins or by how much, it is called "spot fixing." As wagering has become more complex, so too have the opportunities to manipulate sporting events to secure an advantage in the betting markets.

In recent years, sport has seen frequent allegations of match fixing around the world and across sports. Soccer in Italy, Turkey, Norway, and elsewhere. Cricket in India, Pakistan, and South Africa. Even sumo wrestling in Japan and NASCAR in the United States.[15] The various allegations suggest that match fixing could be a huge problem. Chris Eaton, analyst for the International Centre for Sport Security and former head of security for FIFA, argues that match fixing is "far more insidious and deeply rooted in sport than doping."[16] Similarly, then president of the International Olympic Committee (IOC), Jacques Rogge warned before London 2012 that match fixing was a "cancer" on sport and that sports betting could prove "crippling."[17] Such claims, and others like them, present match fixing as an existential threat to sport itself.

But are such worries well grounded? Getting a good understanding of the threat posed by match fixing is important to putting the risk into proper context, and thus to developing proportional responses. As UK sports law expert Kevin Carpenter has written: "The perception of a problem of match fixing can be as serious a threat as the actual problem itself."[18] In the remainder of this chapter, I take a closer look at match fixing and argue that although the threat is real and won't be going away, it can be somewhat contained. Even so, improved responses to the threat are well justified. Let's start by looking at efforts to define match fixing, which turns out to be about as easy as nailing Jello to a wall.

What Is Match Fixing?

The frequent match fixing scandals and the serious concerns expressed at the highest levels of sport have led to efforts to coordinate a response. The European Union, as it so often does in the world of sport, has provided leadership in trying to coordinate a common approach to dealing with the threat of match fixing. The European Commission, which implements the decisions of the European Union's governing bodies, looked at responses to match fixing around the world and found that match fixing is not against the law in many countries or even prohibited at the international level: "International conventions on corruption do not impose the criminalisation of acts related to the manipulation of sport results."[19] Within the twenty-eight nations of the European Union, the survey found that there has been a "lack of a coherent and comparable legal basis between Member States and no consensus on what match fixing is or what kind of problem it represents." Without a clear definition of what match fixing actually is, it will be hard to regulate.

Unfortunately, the leading operational definition of match fixing is problematic. The Council of Europe, an international body that has taken the lead in responding to the threat of corruption in sport, has proposed an international convention on the manipulation of sporting competitions.[20] This type of agreement, if ratified, could form the basis for a broader UN agreement, much as occurred with doping in sport.[21] The proposed convention is thus a critically important document in how governments and sports bodies are preparing to respond to the threat of match fixing.

The convention defines match fixing as the "manipulation of sports competitions." That means "any intentional and improper alteration of the course or result of a sports competition in order to remove all or some of the uncertainty associated with this competition, with a view to obtaining an undue advantage for oneself or for others."[22] The council notes that much of the incentive for match fixing comes from efforts to win money in sports gambling by prearranging events or outcomes in sport.

The convention's definition is problematic for several reasons. First, competition is nothing more than an attempt to remove uncertainty. Sport is a battle over uncertainty. A pitcher wants to make an out, a batter wants to get on base. Both are trying to eliminate uncertainty. Teams compete to secure victory, to eliminate the chances that their opponent emerges victorious (and thus to eliminate the uncertainty associated with the competition). At the start of a fair match, opposing sides wish to reduce the uncertainty of the outcome such that certain outcomes are ruled out (e.g., the opponent proving victorious) and others are inevitable (e.g., a victory for themselves). A definition of corruption as an effort to rob sport of uncertainty has the unhelpful effect of defining the actions of would-be corruptors in the same manner that we define the actions of fair competitors: Both would-be corruptors of and fair-minded participants in sport seek to reduce the uncertainty of the outcome.

Consequently, it is not the effort to reduce uncertainty or its consequential reduction that is problematic; it is the means employed. The council's definition replaces one undefined term with several: "improper alteration" and "undue advantage" to "remove uncertainty." But that leaves us still needing to define "improper" and "undue."

Consider the case of Matt Le Tissier, who played soccer for Southampton in the English Premier League in the 1990s. Le Tissier noted in his autobiography that he had prearranged a bet on the timing of the first throw-in, something that a player on the pitch had direct control over. He explained:

> I couldn't see a problem with making a few quid on the time of the first throw-in. Spread betting had just started to become popular. It was a new idea that allowed punters to back anything from the final score to the first throw-in. There was a lot of money to be made by exploiting it, we stood to win well into four figures.[23]

Le Tissier botched the scam, however, by failing to kick the ball hard enough to make it out of bounds, sending it instead to a teammate who was not in on the fix. Years later, Le Tissier explained that the longer the ball stayed in play, the more money he would lose: "Suddenly it was no longer a question of winning money. We stood to lose a lot of cash if it went much longer than 75 seconds before the ball went out. I had visions of a guy coming to kneecap me."

Le Tissier wound up breaking even on the bet and scored a goal in that game, which Southampton won 2–0. So was the scheme an example of the "manipulation of sports competitions"? Common sense says yes. But under the Council of Europe's definition of match fixing, it is hard to come to the same conclusion. No advantage was gained by Le Tissier. Balls go out of bounds many times in a game, and one out-of-bounds ball in the first minutes of the game could have no discernible effect on the match. And Southampton even won the match, making it hard to say that the plan had any relevance to the uncertainty of the outcome of the match.*

Let's take a step back and ask, What is uncertainty, anyway? In my 2007 book on science and decision making, *The Honest Broker*, I define uncertainty to mean that in a particular situation more than one outcome is consistent with our expectations. An "outcome" simply refers to an actual situation (i.e., some realized or true condition) in the past, present, or future, such as the number of whales in the ocean, the current temperature you feel on your skin as you read this sentence, or the roll of a die.[24] Or an outcome could refer to the timing of the first throw-in of a soccer match. The uncertainty associated with the throw-in has nothing to do with the outcome of the match.†

In sports, the outcome that people generally care about most is wins and losses. Match fixing is often called "cheating to lose" because it involves prearranging a loss (or a closer score than that which bookies have taken bets on) in order to make money.

But there are plenty of events in a sporting contest that might be prearranged that have little or nothing to do with the competition itself. As the Le Tissier incident suggests, in sport, an outcome can refer to any number of things beyond wins and losses. It could

---

* Le Tissier was indeed cleared of any wrongdoing: "Matt Le Tissier in the Clear over Failed Spread-Betting Sting at Southampton," *Guardian*, September 22, 2009, http://www.theguardian.com/football/2009/sep/22/matt-le-tissier-betting-scam.

† And for observers, whether Le Tissier kicks the ball out on purpose or not, the timing of the first throw in is still *subjectively* uncertain to us, even if there is no *objective* uncertainty. When you dig into it, uncertainty turns out to be a fascinating and complex subject. For more, see Pielke, *The Honest Broker*.

be the result of individual events within a game (a serve, a pitch, a corner kick, a field goal attempt, the timing of a ball kicked out of bounds, etc.), the result of a series of contests (a league winner or tournament champion), or something else. Some of these events are related to uncertainty in the outcome of competition, but many are not. Some are not even related to competition,

A better definition of match fixing would emphasize the unscripted nature of sport. When allegations of match fixing in tennis surfaced in 2016, prior to the Australian Open, former US professional James Blake said, "The greatest thing about tennis and sports in general is the unscripted nature of it, the fact that anything can happen."[25] When Serena Williams, the world's top women's player, takes on a qualifier in the first round of a tournament, let's be honest—there is not a whole lot of uncertainty surrounding who is going to win. However, how the match occurs is unscripted and it evolves with both players trying to win, rather than putting on a staged performance. Thinking of match fixing not in terms of influencing uncertainty but in terms of altering the unscripted nature of sport offers some advantages for thinking through possible responses to the risks posted by match fixing. Later in this chapter, we'll return to how we might deal with match fixing when it is viewed in terms of the scripting of unscripted sport.

The Economics of Match Fixing

The economics of competition suggest that, in general, match fixing of any sport is not a significant threat at the highest levels of elite sport because the economics just don't work out. This doesn't mean that match fixing is not a problem; it means that economics shapes where match fixing is most likely to occur. At the highest levels of professional sport, the top players don't feel that it's worth the risk to fix.* For instance, the tennis player Novak Djokovic claims that in 2007, his team was approached with an offer of $200,000 to fix a match.[26] But Djokovic made about $4 million a year in tournament

---

* It is worth noting that a similar calculus for doping, the subject of the next chapter, leads many athletes to conclude that doping is worth the risks.

winnings alone, not counting endorsements.[27] Over his career he has made in excess of $100 million on the court.[28] Unless he is irrationally greedy or just dumb (both of which he is clearly not), it is unfathomable that he would risk such earnings potential to be involved in fixing, or that would-be fixers could ever make it worth his while to participate in their schemes even if he wanted to. However, the incentives work differently at lower levels of competition, where match fixing is (and will always be) a wicked problem.

In 2014, analysts at the Harvard Sports Analysis Collective took a look at income inequality in the major US sports leagues.[29] They used a measure called a "Gini coefficient" to compare the degree of inequality across different professional leagues. The Gini coefficient is a measure of inequality, with zero representing perfect equality and 1.0 representing perfect inequality. The measure was first presented in 1912 by Corrado Gini, an Italian social scientist, and is widely used in academic studies of equality within and between nations.[30] It can also be applied to sport.

Harvard analysts found that among US sports leagues, the NHL is the most equitable and MLB is the most inequitable. They found that salary caps help limit income inequality. In the study, a Gini coefficient of 0.0 means that every player has the same income—perfect equality—and a Gini coefficient of 1.0 means that one player takes home all the income—perfect inequality. Here are their results:

- NHL: 0.42
- NBA: 0.52
- MLS: 0.54
- NFL: 0.57
- MLB: 0.62

For comparison, according to the Organisation for Economic Co-operation and Development (OECD), in 2010, the United States had a Gini coefficient of 0.38, Sweden was 0.27, and Mexico was 0.47 (after taxes and transfers).[31] In other words, Mexico was more unequal than the United States, and a lot more unequal than Sweden.* The professional sports leagues are characterized by a few really big earners, but there is a lot of money being spread around, making it difficult to buy off players.

But that's not the case in all sports. Ryan Rodenberg, an assistant professor of sports law analytics at Florida State University, conducted an analysis in 2012 of the top-100-ranked tennis players on the Association of Tennis Professionals, or ATP (men's), and World Tennis Association, or WTA (women's), tours. Rodenberg found a Gini coefficient of 0.44 for men and 0.48 for women.[32] Since 1990, the women's tour has had greater income inequality than the men's tour, but in recent years, the gap has closed considerably, with the men's Gini coefficient rising by 0.11 points, likely due in part to the overwhelming dominance of a small number of male players.[33]

Jeff Sackman, who blogs at TennisAbstract.com, sought to quantify the expected value of tennis matches to professional tennis players at various levels of competition. He calculated the probabilities of victory for each match and then multiplied that by the prize money available in each tournament.[34] He found that more than half of the matches on the ATP Tour had an expected value of less than $10,000. That puts us in the ballpark of what it might cost to fix a match.† Sackman found that the median expected winnings for a first-round match at the majors is only $6,200. At the challenger level of tennis—sort of a minor league tour—the median expected value of winning a match was only about $600. These numbers help to explain why match fixing in tennis is a concern at the lower tiers of the profession—the costs and benefits favor fixing when it costs less to fix, and when the rewards to the player are higher.

Increasing tournament winnings or making them more equitable may make sense for a lot of reasons, but won't do much to address match fixing. From 2007 to 2011, Novak Djokovic, Rafael Nadal, and Roger Federer took home between 20 percent and 26 percent of all ATP World Tour winnings. In response to concern from players, both the ATP and the WTA have dramatically increased the amount

---

*   The kinds of inequality that the OECD measures includes inequalities in income and access to education and health care.

†   Of course, any fixer is taking a risk, so the actual cost would reflect a risk premium.

of tournament winnings paid out to early-round losers. Wimbledon, for instance, increased the purse awarded to losers in the first three rounds by 90 percent from 2012 to 2014.[35] As Sackman notes, doubling prize money (a huge increase) would not do much to change the economics of match fixing, because the prize money would still be quite small in comparison to the costs of fixing.

Table 5.1 shows that, with the possible exception of Major League Soccer, the salaries within the major professional sports are very high, making match fixing an extremely costly proposition for would-be schemers.[36] This helps explain why the most high-profile match fixing scandals in the United States in recent years have occurred at the college level, where athletes are not paid salaries. The University of Toledo (football) and the University of San Diego (basketball) both found themselves in point shaving scandals in recent years: athletes took money to influence games to the benefit of gamblers.[37] As long as there is an economic value to fixing that exceeds the benefits (and risks) of not-fixing, then simple economics tells us that match fixing will stay with us to some degree.

How Big a Problem Is Match Fixing?

As economist David Butler notes, the economics of match fixing encourage fixers to focus on lower-tier competitions. "The benefits of a fixed match in the betting market can be the same regardless of

Table 5.1. Salary Statistics for Five Professional US Sports Leagues (in Millions of Dollars)

2014	NBA	NFL	NHL	MLB	MLS
Gini	0.52	0.61	0.41	0.63	0.49
Highest	$24.8	$27.8	$10.5	$31.0	$7.2
Lowest	$0.2	$0.4	$0.6	$0.4	$0.04
Median	$2.8	$0.7	$2.1	$1.3	$0.09
Average	$4.7	$2.2	$2.7	$4.0	$0.23
Total payroll	$2,083	$3,988	$2,189	$3,931	$130
% of league revenues to salaries	55%	37%	71%	47%	17%
# of salaries	438	1,798	800	989	571
# of teams	30	32	30	30	20

who is playing (i.e., a 2–1 [top-tier] Arsenal win pay-offs the same as a 2/1 [fourth tier] Northampton win), match fixers have a far greater incentive to target lower tier fixtures where costs are lower as compensation for the players would not have to be as great."[38] The economics and scrutiny of top-level sport makes it more likely that match fixing will occur at lower levels of sport. And, with all due respect to teams like Albion Sports FC of the Northern Counties East Football League in England and their supporters, match fixing in lower-tier competitions, far from the public eye and media spotlight, is not going to keep most sports fans and officials awake at night.[39]

Academics have tried to quantify the prevalence of match fixing across competitions, but they have produced little evidence of a widespread crisis.

A decade ago, one set of studies did claim that match fixing was endemic in basketball. In 2006 and 2007, economists Justin Wolfers and Jonathan Gibbs published separate papers alleging widespread point shaving in NCAA and NBA basketball games. They did this through what is called "forensic economics." They looked at a lot of data on basketball games and the betting spreads for those games to see if they could detect unusual patterns. Both Wolfers and Gibbs found patterns in scores as compared to spreads that they could not explain, and determined that point shaving was the best explanation. They concluded that about 6 percent of NCAA games with large point spreads showed evidence of having been fixed. With more than 5,000 games per year in Division I, this would imply that more than 300 games were being fixed, a huge number. The claim was "the subject of feature articles in 14 newspapers, including the *New York Times*, the *Chicago Tribune*, *USA Today*, *Sports Illustrated*, and *Barron's*, as well as National Public Radio and CNBC TV."[40] But these fantastic claims did not stand up. When other researchers looked at the same data they concluded that there were better, and far less sinister, explanations for the data patterns. Perhaps more convincingly, over the past ten years, if 300 NCAA games per year were being fixed, then it is logical to assume that there would have been more than just a few point-shaving controversies.

The balance of evidence today is that point shaving in US sports is rare and isolated.[41] After looking at events like the Tim Donaghy episode in the NBA and the Toledo point-shaving scandal in the NCAA, one set of researchers declared that "our analysis reveals that such incidents do not reflect widespread corruption and that costly significant changes in policy—fanned by past and likely future media alarm—would be unwarranted."[42] Even in international tennis, where match fixing has occupied considerable attention, the incidence does not appear large. Richard Ings, former chief executive of the Australian Sports Anti-Doping Authority and vice president of the ATP, who umpired more than 2,000 professional tennis matches, told me that the scale of match fixing in professional tennis is in his judgment about 20 out of the top 100,000 professional matches played each year.[43] That is something to be concerned about, and is suggestive of a need for continued vigilance, but it does not imply a crisis.

The European Sports Security Association (ESSA), a group that monitors betting patterns for the European gambling industry, reported in 2015 that across sports, tennis had the most suspicious betting activity, with seventy-three reported incidents. Of course, not all suspicious betting patterns are the result of match fixing (e.g., some could be due to inside information or other factors). Soccer was next on the list, with eighteen suspicious events. The ESSA tally for 2015 is shown in figure 5.1. But none of the suspicious betting on soccer events was in the United Kingdom, Germany, Italy, France, or Spain—where the world's biggest teams play—or in the United States, Mexico, or the Netherlands.[44] Even so, there are some leagues—in Turkey and Italy for instance—where allegations of match fixing are commonplace.[45] Such scandals have been confined to their idiosyncratic national settings and have not metastasized across borders. The evidence suggests that match fixing, at least in terms of its role in suspicious betting patterns, is a limited phenomenon—at least in the biggest leagues in Europe and North America.

In Asia, the story is a bit different because of the prevalence of unregulated gambling. In the early 2010s, a Singapore-based crime syndicate sought to influence mainly lower-tier matches in leagues around the world. It had some degree of success, as convictions were

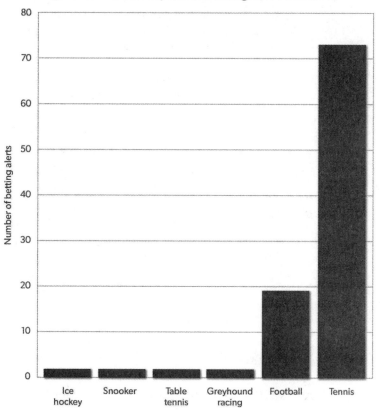

Figure 5.1. ESSA Suspicious Betting Alerts for 2015

Source: ESSA (Sports Betting Integrity), "ESSA Q4 2015 Integrity Report," http://www.eu-ssa.org/wp-content/uploads/QR4-BROCHURE-WEB.pdf.

reached for match fixing in Finland, Hungary, Slovenia, and Austria.[46] The highest level that the fixing is alleged to have reached was allegedly a European Champions League match between English giant Liverpool and Hungarian minnow Debrecan. Liverpool won the match 1–0, and no proceedings were brought against players or the clubs.[47] Like so much in the world of match fixing, there is more smoke here than fire.

Match fixing has proved to be endemic in Indian and Pakistan cricket. Wikipedia lists more than thirty top-level cricketers, most from India and Pakistan, who have been banned for match fixing

Pakistani cricket Mohammed Amir was sentenced to six months in 2011 for conspiracy to cheat at gambling. In a spot-fixing scandal, he had bowled planned "no balls" in a match against England in 2010.

by the International Cricket Council.[48] Shantanu Guha Ray, author of *Fixed!: Cash and Corruption in Cricket*, says of Indian cricket in 2016 that "fixing is routine" and "no one cares."[49] Despite the various allegations and scandals that have rocked cricket, fans keep coming back. Data gathered by Nick Harris, editor of, show that in 2014, following numerous match-fixing scandals, the Indian Premier League was the sixth most-attended (per match) professional league in the world. Italian soccer was just behind at number seven.[50]

All this evidence paints a nuanced picture. Match fixing is undoubtedly a real phenomenon. It has been documented in many sports around the world. But at the same time, most alleged and actual fixing has been seen at the lower levels of competition or in specific national leagues in regions where corruption is more common throughout society. Despite the evidence, the existential threat posed to sport that some have worried about has not materialized. How much does the sporting public actually care about fixing? The answer may surprise you.

Do Fans Care About Fixing?

Let's consider an empirical question. If match fixing is to be defined as an effort to improperly reduce uncertainty in sport, do sports spectators actually value uncertainty as the defining characteristic of sport? If this value is strong, one could make an argument against efforts to reduce uncertainty, based on the subjective perceptions of stakeholders in sporting events. If fans don't really value uncertainty, why worry about defining what it means, much less trying to regulate it? After all, audiences routinely turn out to see performances of *Romeo and Juliet* and reruns of *Star Wars,* knowing that there is no uncertainty in the outcome or the events within the story. Perhaps, however, sports are different?

In a 2003 paper, Stefan Szymanski looked at academic studies that sought to quantify how much fans valued uncertainty in sport. He found that the evidence was indeed mixed:

> Overall, of the 22 cases cited here, ten offer clear support for the uncertainty of outcome hypothesis, seven offer weak support, and five contradict it. Given that even supportive studies on the issue of match uncertainty seem to imply that attendance is maximized when the home team is about twice as likely to win as the visiting team, the empirical evidence in this area seems far from unambiguous.[51]

Fans, it seems, are happiest when there is about a two-thirds chance that their team will win. In 2016, I repeated Szymanski's review to see if more recent literature said anything different. It did not. I found five studies that argued that uncertainty of outcome matters, six that said it does not, and another five that said, "It depends."

Interestingly, where studies appear to agree is that in cases where fans do value uncertainty of outcome, they prefer about a two-to-one chance that their side will win. Uncertainty is good, just not too much.[52] Szymanski writes of the dissonance between the ambiguity that fans of sport place on "uncertainty of outcome" and the significance of the concept in various aspects of the governance of sport: "This is remarkable given the weight that is placed on this argument in policy making and in antitrust cases. Given that even quite unbalanced matches, championships, and leagues can be attractive to consumers, a more nuanced approach is called for." A focus on uncertainty in sporting outcomes does not provide a clear basis for identifying corruption or regulating it. To identify a more practical approach to match fixing, we need look no further than the NFL.

Fixing Fixing: The Lessons of Bountygate

The NFL prohibits teams from offering bonuses to players for on-the-field successes, whether making a tackle or scoring a touchdown. One reason for this prohibition is to prevent teams from circumventing the league's salary cap regulations, but also to avoid creating mixed incentives for players on the field. Despite these rules, the NFL was tipped off in 2010 that the New Orleans Saints were operating a "bounty" program focused on rewards for injuring opposing players.

The NFL's subsequent investigation concluded that "the total amount of funds in the pool may have reached $50,000 or more at its height during the 2009 playoffs. The program paid players $1,500 for a 'knockout' and $1,000 for a 'cart-off' with payouts doubling or tripling during the playoffs."[53] A "knockout" referred to knocking a player out of the game via an injury; a "cart-off" referred to an injury so severe that it required the player to be taken off the field on a cart. Football is a brutal sport, and knockouts and cart-offs are fairly common occurrences in the course of ordinary competition.

Let's face it, playing football by its rules means trying to achieve total physical domination over the opponent, often through brutal hits. Former all-pro running back Tony Dorsett explains:

> If it was me, and I'm a defensive player, and I'm playing against the Dallas Cowboys, and Tony Dorsett happens to be one of their best players, it would be to our best advantage to get him out of the game. If it's within the rules of tackling and contact, so be it. I don't think it's that big of a deal. . . . They're not telling a guy to mangle somebody or kill somebody. It's "Get him out of the game."[54]

But there can be a gray area between gamesmanship and cheating. Former New York Jets linebacker Bart Scott told the *New York Times*: "Knocking someone out doesn't mean you're doing something dirty. It's no different than when the Detroit Pistons played Michael Jordan and every time he went to the hole, they were physical with him. No one was literally trying to hurt him." Former Denver Bronco Trevor Pryce said something similar: "A big hit is different. Getting rewarded for a big hit, they do that in college. You get a sticker on your helmet."[55]

In recent years, the NFL has cracked down on certain hard hits, especially those involving the head. In doing so, the NFL is taking some of the raw brutality out of the game, a response to both modern sensitivities and the risks of legal liability from players exposed to serious injuries.

The *Wall Street Journal* conducted an empirical investigation of game films from the New Orleans Saints to catalog their track record of defensive hits that led to a player leaving the field injured.[56] What did they find? Well, not very much: "Seldom did a Saints-inflicted injury force an opponent to leave the field." In forty-eight regular-season and six postseason games, such incidents occurred only eighteen times. The Saints player involved in the largest number of those cases (four) was safety Roman Harper. The *Wall Street Journal* explains what that might have meant to him under the bounty system that the Saints had in place:

> Exactly who received what on the Saints roster isn't clear, including whether Harper received any money at all. But under that formula, the total payout during those three seasons would have been about $19,000. And of that, based on the review of those seasons, Harper could have pocketed a grand total of about $4,500—peanuts for a player earning more than $7 million a year.

Given these numbers, it is unlikely that financial inducement motivated Harper, but perhaps it was pride, the "sticker on the helmet." Whatever the motivation, the bounty program was against NFL rules.

The NFL announced severe sanctions of the New Orleans Saints for operating a bounty program.[57] The punishment focused not on the knockouts and cart-offs but on the bonus program—and lying about it. The NFL explained: "Payments were made for plays such as interceptions or fumble recoveries. All such payments are against league rules." Teams are not allowed to make payments for trying to knock players out of a game, but neither are they allowed to offer incentives for perfectly legal, high-quality plays. This is explained in the NFL by-laws, where it says that

> no player or coach may receive any bonus, money, or thing of value, for winning any game played in the League. No club or any representative thereof, shall offer to pay, directly or indirectly, to a player, and no player shall receive, any bonus of any kind unless such bonus provision is attached to and/or incorporated in the contract of such player.[58]

The precedent here offers some lessons for top-level sports generally. Player contracts could explicitly prohibit receiving money for on-the-field performances of any kind, as is the case with the NFL. In this manner, match fixing could be turned from a violation of an abstract value—reducing uncertainty in sport—to a procedural matter of accountability and transparency. Taking money to "script" an unscripted sporting event should be against the rules. Players, coaches, administrators, and referees might be required to follow conflict of interest guidelines and disclose (to their governing body, not necessarily the public) their sources of income and other financial stakes. Match fixing would thus be considered a violation of conflict of interest guidelines, with which governments and businesses have lots of experience. The New Orleans Saints were sanctioned for their role in Bountygate not because uncertainty was alerted in any measurable sense, but because the team and its players violated the league's rules.

Of course, such an approach would not alter the basic economics of match fixing at lower levels of competition. Nor would it address nonfinancial types of match fixing, like the "honey pot" scheme. So some degree of match fixing will always be with us. Such is the nature of a wicked problem. What this approach would provide is a clear guideline as to what constitutes match fixing—taking money to script (part of) a sporting event. Such an approach, focused on transparency and accountability, would contribute to trust that fans have in the integrity of sport. If individual countries wish to criminalize match fixing, and some already have, then they could do so in parallel with the efforts of sports bodies to hold players and referees accountable. Putting match fixing into the framework of conflict of interest won't make it go away, but it might help us tame a part of this wicked problem.

The response to match fixing has one big difference from preparation for a meteor strike, but lots of similarities as well. In principle, we can take actions that increase or decrease the threat of match fixing. We can't do much to change the threat posed by rocks in space. By increasing transparency and accountability among athletes, referees, and other officials, however, we might reduce incentives to fix matches. Efforts by sports organizations and governments to improve responses to match fixing will be more practical if they define match fixing as a matter of financial conflict of interest rather than as a matter of uncertainty in sports outcomes. It is much easier to address a problem when it is unambiguously defined.

No matter what steps are taken, some degree of threat will always remain. Thus, programs that monitor suspicious movements in the betting market will continue to be valuable to focus attention on possible scripted competitions. Bookies, regulated and unregulated, also have some responsibility for creating incentives to fix matches through the products that they offer, especially when offering high stakes on competitions with low rewards to the competitors. Government regulation of gambling can address the regulated sector, but not gambling that occurs in the shadows. Match fixing will always be with us, but by better defining the problem and taking practical steps, it is an issue that sport can manage even if it can never eliminate it.

Chapter 6

Lance Armstrong
Gets the Last Laugh

"**Y**ou are not worth the chair that you are sitting on." This is how Lance Armstrong characterized journalist and former professional cyclist Paul Kimmage in an uncomfortable exchange at a 2009 press conference at the Amgen Tour of California.* Kimmage had stoked Armstrong's ire not only by asking him a question about doping, but also because he had previously likened Armstrong's return to cycling to a cancer out of remission. In the late 1990s, Armstrong recovered from testicular cancer and went on to win seven Tours de France. The 2009 Tour of California marked Armstrong's return to cycling from a brief retirement. It was supposed to be a feel-good sort of event, and Kimmage was crashing the party.

Armstrong's rebuke of Kimmage is but one example of why many people believe that Armstrong deserves whatever consequences he gets from sporting bodies and the law. By most accounts, and there are a lot of them, including his own, Armstrong was a first-class asshole. He was a vicious opponent; he destroyed people's careers; and he cheated his way to becoming one of the top athletes in the world.† But assholes have rights, too. Can sporting justice go too far? Arm-

---

* You can see the Kimmage-Armstrong exchange at https://www.youtube.com/watch?v=nZgns7CXeUI.

† Armstrong paid a visit to one of my classes in early 2016, and he was both generous and gracious.

strong sure thinks so: "I'm that guy everybody wants to pretend never lived. But it happened, everything happened. We know what happened."[1] Armstrong says that his punishments have gone too far: "Now it's swung so far the other way. . . . Who's that character in Harry Potter they can't talk about? Voldemort?"

But whether or not you think Armstrong deserves his fate, he raises an important issue when he argues that antidoping efforts have largely failed. In early 2016, he told me that "antidoping agencies only sanction about 1 percent of athletes, but we know that many more are doping. Yet, antidoping agencies receive tens of millions of dollars. They needed my case to prove their effectiveness."[2] Does Armstrong have a point? Is his plummet from the top of the sports world evidence not of antidoping's successes, but of its failures? It seems so. Rather than proving the effectiveness of antidoping efforts, Armstrong's case—and others—only serve to distract us from the fact that antidoping institutions and regulations are, with few exceptions, failures. This conclusion is backed by anecdotes and evidence, and won't be welcomed by many. However, given the frequent and very public scandals in antidoping over the past several years, the time may be right for opening up this difficult subject.

There has always been an element of denial in the sports world with respect to the prevalence of doping and the weakness of antidoping regulations. In an interview the day after that tense 2009 press conference, Kimmage justified his questioning about Armstrong's denial of engaging in any doping: "I find it very difficult to believe that [Armstrong] is as credible as he makes out."[3] With the perspective granted by hindsight, it is hard to believe that Kimmage's views were not widely shared by his colleagues in the media. After dressing Kimmage down at the press conference, Armstrong made a wry remark about returning to a discussion of the Tour of California that was met by laughter and applause from the assembled reporters.

The reporters should have known better. Over many years, Kimmage, David Walsh, and other investigative journalists had uncovered and reported ample evidence of doping violations by Armstrong and other cyclists. But no one needed to take their word for it or even know much about the history of the sport, in which doping

Lance Armstrong racing in the Grand Prix Midi Libre in France in 2002.

had a long legacy. Even without the rumors, the leaks, and the investigative reports, data on performances in the Tour de France provided a strong indication that something fishy was going on in the world of cycling starting in the early 1990s.

Figure 6.1 shows winning times for one of the iconic climbs in the Tour de France, L'Alpe d'Huez.* With the advantage of hindsight, we can clearly see the effects of the availability of synthetic erythropoietin, better known as EPO, a prohibited performance-enhancing drug. When the drug became widely available to cyclists in the early 1990s, climb times dropped quickly and by a large amount. The drug worked. From 1994 to 2008, the fastest time each year averaged four and a half minutes faster than the average winning time from 1977 to 1993, a huge decrease for a climb that traditionally had taken over forty minutes from bottom to top. One might think that such a remarkable and sudden increase in speed would have raised some eyebrows—or at least made plausible the claims levied by the investigative journalists.

As we now know, Kimmage and several other reporters were vindicated when the US Anti-Doping Agency (USADA) released its "reasoned decision" in 2011 detailing years of doping and a massive cover-up by Armstrong, his fellow riders, and their supporters. The cover-up was exposed by the media and whistleblowers, but became

---

*   The climb is not part of the tour every year; see "Nairo Quintana Sets a Great Time on Alpe d'Huez," Climbing-Records.com, July 13, 2013, http://www.climbing-records.com/2013/07/nairo-quintana-sets-great-time-on-alpe.html.

Figure 6.1. L'Alpe d'Huez Fastest Climb Times in the Tour De France: 1977–2013

widely known through the dogged efforts of Travis Tygart, the head of USADA, and his colleagues.

But did the pursuit and eventual ensnaring of Armstrong indicate the success of antidoping efforts? Or is the lesson here exactly the opposite: that antidoping efforts have been incredible failures? Let's look at some anecdotes and some evidence.

Erik Tysse and the Abuse of Scientific Authority

In July 2010, Norwegian race walker Erik Tysse learned that he had failed an antidoping test following a race in Sesto San Giovanni, Italy, two months earlier, in which he had finished second.[4] The substance for which he failed the test was related to EPO, and used as an indicator of EPO use. At a press conference, a tearful Tysse vehemently protested his innocence. They all do, don't they? Despite his protests, Tysse was found guilty by the Norwegian Athletics Association in a decision that was later upheld by the Court of Arbitration for Sport (CAS).[5] The rejection of Tysse's appeal was based on scientific analyses performed by a World Anti-Doping Agency

(WADA)-accredited laboratory in Rome, Italy. Tysse served a two-year suspension, returning before the 2012 London Olympics, where he placed fourteenth in the 20-kilometer race walk.[6]

From afar, Tysse's case looks like countless others in sport. Athlete is caught doping. Athlete denies doping. Antidoping agencies use science to counter the denial. Athlete is suspended. If athlete chooses to challenge the suspension, suspension is upheld. Athlete returns to sport, forever tarnished. Life goes on.

But a closer look at Tysse's case, which has been discussed in depth in Norway but not much beyond, reveals some troubling details that call into question the capabilities and integrity of WADA itself, the very agency that is supposed to be upholding the rights of athletes.

In 2013, well after Tysse's case had been decided and he had served his doping punishment, a team of four Norwegian academics published a paper in the journal *Lab Times* with some incredible claims.[7] Jon Nissen-Meyer of the University of Oslo and his colleagues alleged that WADA scientists had, among other scientific misdeeds, manipulated the evidence that purportedly indicated

Erik Tysse (left) racing in Spain in May 2015.

that Tysse had failed the doping test. Several of these scientists had testified on Tysse's behalf before CAS, and they decided to publish their concerns about the case after Tysse had served his suspension. Specifically, the Norwegian scientists alleged that officials from the WADA lab in Rome had dressed up evidence in a way so as to make Tysse's guilt appear more compelling and his innocence appear less likely. If true, this would be incredibly troubling, because scientific labs of WADA are supposed to play things straight. The organization's motto, after all, is "play true."

The Norwegian scientists argued that "to support their interpretation," the WADA scientists "presented to the CAS an altered version of [the] results." Specifically, Tysse's drug test data, presented as a series of darkened bands in a laboratory image, showed alignment between Tysse's results and the bands that would indicate doping. However, "in order to achieve this alignment, the bands in the athlete's [part of the image] were moved upwards and expanded 40%," the result of which was to more strongly suggest that Tysse's drug test indicated doping. The scientists did not hold back in their judgment of the appropriateness of such methods: "The use of such a cut-and-paste method is a deviant and unreliable way of treating and presenting data."

They alleged that the CAS arbitrators who upheld Tysse's suspension had been bamboozled by the complexities of the underlying science: "Only those not acquainted with the relevant techniques, such as arbitrators in the CAS, are likely to be deceived" by such methods. Instead, the researchers argued, the arbiters relied on their trust of WADA. The Norwegian scientists found other problems with the WADA analysis and concluded: "We do not know whether the athlete has taken any illegal drugs . . . [but given the analysis presented] the athlete should therefore be considered innocent." Dozens of independent scientists, including a Nobel Prize winner, agreed and signed a letter critical of WADA and CAS.[8]

Nissen-Meyer and his colleagues also identified other manipulations of images. One key image of Tysse's urine test results was displayed upside-down and reversed. Nissen-Meyer explained to me that as "a consequence of the inversion, it is more difficult to discover that the laboratory decreased the staining intensity of the negative control lanes and simultaneously increased the staining intensity of the lane that contained Tysse's sample."[9] In plain English, this means that the images were altered to make Tysse's sample (originally shaded fairly lightly, and then processed to look darker) look more like what would be expected in the "negative control lane," (which was processed to go from darker to lighter) had he been guilty of doping. The processed images were then used as evidence of doping, but presented as an upside-down mirror image in the drug test report, making these alterations harder to detect.*

The same image was further altered into a 3-D image for presentation in the CAS arbitration involving Tysse. This additional alteration raised even more questions. Werner Franke, Helmholtz professor of cell biology at the German Cancer Research Center, and Hans Heid, a senior scientist at the center, wrote in a letter to CAS alleging that this 3-D image of the same data provided as a supplement to CAS testimony "can only be explained by manipulation, i.e. falsification of a document used in a 'court case.'"[10] Lots of questions, but few answers.

If the issues raised about the two images weren't enough to generate troubling questions, the Norwegian scientists identified a third image that they thought looked suspicious, although they couldn't pin down exactly what was wrong with it. I shared that image with experts at the National Center for Media Forensics at the University of Colorado, Denver. They concluded that "the evidence image contains inconsistencies, [certain] regions do not naturally belong to the background image, the original images/photos should be provided for more analysis." Working with a colleague in the media, we were unsuccessful in obtaining a substantive response from WADA, much less the original image for further analysis. WADA simply pointed us back to the CAS decision on Tysse.

The questions about the various images used in the case were raised long after the case had been decided. Even so, the case is no-

---

* I asked Peter Van Eenoo, a WADA lab director familiar with the case, specifically about this image, and his answer was nonresponsive: "Of course for privacy law reasons, results of other athletes, analyzed during the same batch during the screening were 'blackened' during processing. This is a normal procedure and should be clear to anyone."

table because WADA was asked to serve as an authoritative arbitrator of science in a situation where the scientific competencies of one of its labs were at issue. The team of Norwegian scientists noted this clear conflict of interest. Sport law expert Natalie St. Cyr Clarke explains that for athletes who come before CAS, the conflict of interest among WADA-affiliated experts means that "the athlete is at an inherent disadvantage in mounting a scientific defence against anti-doping charges."[11] Other independent scientific observers remarked that the chairman of the committee passing judgment on Tysse "said quite frankly during the verbal proceedings that much of the discussion that took place was over his head."* They asked, "Is it acceptable adherence to due process of law that the Adjudication Committee, lacking its own expertise, blindly accepts WADA's procedures?"[12]

That same year, more evidence emerged that makes the Tysse case even more intriguing. The *New York Times* reported that Giuseppe Fischetto, who served both as the medical director for Italy's track and field federation and as a member of the International Association of Athletics Federations (IAAF) antidoping commission, had covered up evidence of doping by Alex Schwazer, Italy's top race walker. Schwazer had finished first in the same May 2010 race that Tysse had finished second in, and in which Tysse been identified as doping. Schwazer had also won a gold medal in Beijing in 2008.

The *Times* reported that "authorities obtained e-mail messages indicating that as early as April 2012, officials for track and field's world governing body, known as the IAAF, were aware of abnormal doping test results for" Schwazer.[13] The Italian prosecutor explained that "This circumstance can only be explained by the desire to 'preserve' a national track and field star for the 2012 London Olympic Games, in the expectation that he would perform well for Italy both

---

* Complex? You be the judge. This excerpt is from Nissen-Meyer et al.: "Cleavage of almost any of the glycosidic bonds in the carbohydrate chains attached to the protein moiety of EPO will remove one or more negatively charged sialic acid units that decorate the ends of most of the carbohydrate chains." For its part, WADA officials responded that proper procedures had been followed; see P. Hemmersbach, M. Drange, O. Rabin, F. Botre, and Y. Dehnes, "Doping Analysis on Solid Ground," *Journal of the Norwegian Medical Association*, January 24, 2012, http://tidsskriftet .no/article/2206299/en_GB.

in the 20 and the 50 kilometer walk race." The alleged cover-up appears to have some elements in common with the 2015 scandal that rocked the IAAF and Russia's track and field program. In both cases, it appears that national interest conflicted with antidoping regulations, and when the former won out, the IAAF helped to cover it up.

In a follow-up article in *Lab Times* in 2015, Nissen-Meyer and his colleagues suggested that because of the continuing difficulties that they faced in obtaining information from the WADA Rome laboratory in the case of Tysse, "one might suspect that the irregularities we have described in this case are the result of a cover-up action, taken to protect Schwazer, who delivered a urine sample for doping analysis in the same race as Tysse."[14] In May 2016, German TV channel ZDF shared data suggestive of irregular blood values for Schwazer in May 2010, offering some support for the Norwegians' theory.[15] Rome's antidoping laboratories have a well-documented history of allegations of complicity in doping scandals, dating back long before WADA accreditation, according to a whistle-blower.[16] Whether the Norwegian scientists' speculations on motivations are correct or not, there is plenty information to suggest that evidence in the Tysse case was not treated with the utmost scientific integrity and that WADA acted as a partisan in the case rather than as a neutral arbiter of evidence.

The story gets even stranger. The editors of *Lab Times* revealed in November 2015 that Peter van Eenoo, the president of a group representing the WADA-accredited laboratories, had a month earlier sent a letter on behalf of WADA laboratories to companies that had advertised with *Lab Times*. The letter complained about the Nissen-Meyer article that *Lab Times* had published: "Your company is one of the companies . . . which has supplied us with instruments for many years. As you are an important sponsor of 'Lab Times,' we want to inform you that we consider that the article and behavior of 'Lab Times' reflects badly on your company."[17] One of the companies that received the letter shared it with the editors at *Lab Times*, who wasted no time in publishing an excerpt as part of an editorial commentary about van Eenoo and his colleagues' tactics.

The *Lab Times* editors described the message that they thought the letter was carrying:

The malicious intent and undercover nature of this letter is a clear attack on press freedom. In addition, it may inflict serious damage on the business of our publishers. Van Eenoo stopped short of open threats, of course. But his heavily implied message is clear: The 35 accredited WADA labs will no longer do business with companies that advertise in *Lab Times*.[18]

Finding this incredibly unusual, I asked van Eenoo about the letter and his motivation for writing it. He explained that WADA's ethical code prohibited him and his colleagues from responding to the *Lab Times* articles in the scientific literature and that any such response would have called attention to the claims: "As a lab, we are bound by WADA's ethical code and cannot respond in such cases. In these cases all the other party wants is as much publicity as possible. By responding to this, they would have gotten exactly what they want."*

Setting aside the issue of doping, in terms of scientific integrity, the behavior of the WADA lab directors is troubling on several levels. First, if true, the allegations related to the manipulation of images used as evidence by WADA's Rome laboratory rise to the level of research misconduct. Unfortunately, such allegations are not isolated. Since WADA was created, twelve of its thirty-five accredited laboratories have been suspended or lost their accreditation due to producing "sub-optimal work."[19] The Rome lab's activities in the Tysse case, if true, are clearly suboptimal. Perhaps more troubling, when faced with evidence assembled by a team of independent academics in a popular German journal, the WADA lab directors responded with a thinly veiled threat to the companies that advertise in that journal. An independent investigation of the allegations would have been a far better response.

---

* Peter van Eenoo, personal correspondence, February 4, 2016. He further explained: "Moreover, I have full respect for freedom of speech, which is a cornerstone of our society's values, but any respectable journalist will always contact an 'accused.' Something they did not do. Additionally, they used an image from our website without asking for permission and they attacked one of my colleagues personally, not his scientific work. Science is based upon objective debate, not on personal attacks. Therefore this journal lost all credibility to me for an open scientific discussion."

Did Tysse dope? The only person who really knows the answer to that question is Tysse (and perhaps his close companions). I correspond with a number of Norwegians who have followed the case, and there are passionate and smart people on both sides of this question. Whether he did or did not dope, Tysse served his suspension and is back racing. What does appear clear is that the body responsible for enforcing antidoping rules and regulations engaged in unambiguously questionable practices for the presentation of scientific evidence. Had Tysse been better served by his representatives during his CAS case, more attention might have been paid to these issues, which have come to light only in the fullness of time. The aggressive behavior of WADA toward scientists raising questions about WADA's practices raises questions about the ability of the organization to implement a robust scientific approach to antidoping. CAS arbitrators may trust WADA, but based on how WADA treated evidence and criticism in the Tysse case, is it not clear that anyone else should.

From Anecdote to Evidence

Armstrong, the Tour de France, Tysse, Schwazer . . . these are but anecdotes. And, as the saying goes, anecdotes aren't evidence. So let's look at some evidence and history. Doping is endemic in sport, and it always has been. For a long time, sport operated under a fiction that doping was well regulated, punctuated by the occasional high-profile scandal—Johnson, Jones, Rodriguez, Armstrong. The reality is much more complex. When we look back at the history of doping in sport, we can see that performance-enhancing substances, whether allowed under the rules or not, have been around as long as people have competed against each other. Efforts to regulate their use have, according to the best evidence available, achieved only partial success and, arguably, more systemic failures.

When did the use of medicines and chemicals to gain a performance advantage in sport first begin? That might be the wrong question to ask. There has never been a time when athletes did not look to artificial means to boost their athletic prowess. One review of the history of doping concludes that "the use of drugs to enhance physical performance has been a feature of human competition since the beginning of recorded history."[20]

There are many tales of competitors who ate hearts and testicular extract in ancient times, but let's fast forward to a slightly more recent era. In the 1860s and 1870s, before baseball and football (American or soccer) became popular spectator sports, pedestrianism—long-distance walking—was the most popular spectator sport in the United States and Great Britain.[21]

American Edward Payson Weston was pedestrianism's first great champion. Competitions evolved from walking from city to city to walking systematically around a track over and over to see how fast a distance, such as 500 miles, could be covered. At the height of Weston's popularity, more than 20,000 people turned out in London in 1876 to watch him walk around a track in a six-day race in which he took on all comers. Watching someone walk around an oval track doesn't sound like the most engaging spectacle, but it garnered great attention.

Weston was known for his stamina and his remarkable powers of recovery with little or no sleep. During Weston's first visit to the United Kingdom, the *British Medical Journal* reported that he was chewing coca leaf, from which cocaine is distilled, while he walked. The negative reaction and quick denials by Weston of more general usage illustrates that even at this time the notion of doping—a word that had yet to be invented—was a concern in sport. Weston's use of the drug led to a dispute among experts on the pages of the *British Medical Journal*, leading the journal to opine presciently:

> Pushed to excess, coca is said to become a narcotic; and we shall, no doubt, hear a great deal about its use and abuse. Possibly we may be indebted to Mr. Weston for the introduction of a new stimulant and a new narcotic: two forms of novelty in excitement which our modern civilization is likely to highly esteem.[22]

Weston was no fool, and the controversy within the medical establishment helped prompt him to embrace science as a route to legitimacy. He presented himself as a subject for scientific research, later extolling the virtues of walking for health. He became one of the first antismoking advocates, long before smoking was generally viewed as a hazard to health.

The debate surrounding Weston's use of a performance-enhancing substance was minor at the time. Rather than being viewed negatively, "doping in sport blossomed during the latter part of the nineteenth century, it was viewed as standard practice, out in the open, until after World War I."[23] Cycling was one of the sports that displaced pedestrianism in terms of popularity, and doping followed along. Early racers used caffeine, alcohol, cocaine, strychnine, nitroglycerine, and ether.[24] The first

The famed pedestrian, Edward Payson Weston, in 1909, when he was seventy. He would live to be ninety.

reported death from doping in an athletic event was allegedly Arthur Linton in 1886 in a cycling race between Bordeaux and Paris.[25] It would not be the last.

The word "doping" entered the English lexicon in the early twentieth century. According to one version of its origins, the word derives from the Dutch word *dop,* "the name of an alcoholic beverage made of grape skins used by Zulu warriors in order to enhance their prowess in battle."[26] The term was first used in the context of horse racing. Today we also use the term "PEDs," or performance-enhancing drugs. Because many substances offer a route to performance enhancement, in sport, a distinction is made between allowed and prohibited performance-enhancing substances.

In 1928, the IAAF became the first international sports organization to prohibit the use of stimulants in competition.[27] Five years later, Otto Reiser, a physician, offered a prophetic perspective: "Sportive competitions are often more a matter of doping than training. It is highly regrettable that those who are in charge of supervising sport seem to lack the energy for the campaign against this evil, and that a lax, and fateful, attitude is spreading."[28] Reiser's words both about doping and about those in charge of supervising sport have a contemporary ring.

Yet it would be a long time before those in charge of supervising sport got around to developing formal guidelines to govern the use of performance-enhancing substances. The Olympics first implemented drug testing in 1968, and the NFL in 1982 (and 1987 for steroids). The NBA implemented an antidoping policy in 1983, and MLB, long troubled by doping and doping allegations, not until 2003.[29]

The evidence of the pervasive use of performance-enhancing drugs in sport has long been overwhelming. In 1969, *Sports Illustrated* published a three-part exposé by Bill Gilbert on drugs in sport. Some of the vignettes that he shared are remarkable from today's perspective:[30]

- "We occasionally use Dexamyl and Dexedrine [amphetamines] . . . we also use barbituates, Seconal, Tuinal, Nembutal . . . we also use some anti-depressants, Triavil, Tofranil, Valium . . ."—Team doctor for the St. Louis Cardinals baseball team
- "On October 24, 1968 in Grenoble, France, Jean-Louis Quadri, eighteen, a soccer player, dribbled toward the opposing goal. However, before he could get off this shot, he collapsed on the field. He was dead on arrival at the Grenoble hospital. An autopsy indicated he was heavily drugged with amphetamines."
- "All of the weight men on the [1968 US] Olympic team had to take steroids. Otherwise they would not have been in the running."—A physician in charge of medical services, 1968 US Olympic high-altitude training camp

Gilbert explained that not all uses of drugs were for performance enhancement; some were to blunt the effects of injury (which certainly could be counted as a way to enhance performance).

Bobby Braun, a hockey player for the Toronto Maple Leafs, left the sixth game of the 1964 Stanley Cup finals on a stretcher after getting hit on his leg by the puck off a shot by Detroit's Gordie Howe. Braun received a shot of novocaine, a powerful pain killer; his leg was taped up; and he returned to the ice to score the winning goal in overtime. Toronto went on to win game seven and the Stanley Cup, with Braun returning to the ice. It turned out that Braun's leg had been broken by Howe's Game six slap shot. The drugs allowed him to play on, however.

Sports lore is full of stories of injured athletes who return to the game, fighting off pain to achieve athletic success. Before the fifth game of the 1997 NBA finals between the Chicago Bulls and Utah Jazz, Michael Jordan awoke with nasty flu-like symptoms.* His teammate Scottie Pippen later said, "The way he looked, there's no way I thought he could even put on his uniform."[31] Jordan wound up playing forty-four minutes and scoring thirty-eight points, carrying the team to a two-point victory.[32] The picture of Jordan being helped off the court in a seeming daze became iconic—and part of his legacy as one of the greatest ever to play the game.

Bulls coach Phil Jackson said of the performance, "Because of the circumstances, with this being a critical game in the Finals, I'd have to say this is the greatest game I've seen Michael play."[33] Before the game, Jordan was hooked up to an IV to receive treatment to reduce his symptoms. Like Bobby Braun in the 1964 Stanley Cup, Jordan received treatment that allowed him to play the game, without which he may have been unable to perform.

What is the difference between painkillers for a broken leg and an IV infusion for flu-like symptoms? Under today's regulations governing Olympic sports (which both hockey and basketball are, although the NBA and the NHL have their own drug policies), there is a significant difference. Novocaine to dull pain would be allowed but an intravenous infusion of the sort administered to Jordan

---

* Or maybe it was food poisoning by the pizza delivery guys, depending on your appetite for conspiracy theories. See Chris Chase, "Michael Jordan Was Poisoned Before Flu Game, Says Trainer," *USA Today*, April 18, 2013, http://www.usatoday.com/story/gameon/2013/04/18/michael-jordan-food-poisoning-flu-game-chicago-bulls/2093631/.

would likely not be.* More generally, what is the difference between these interventions and, say, caffeine, steroids, or Erythropoietin (EPO)? These are vexing questions at the heart of the debate over doping in sport. But I am getting ahead of myself. We'll return to those questions in a few pages.

By the 1960s, it had become clear that doping was present in sport, but there was little consensus that doping was a problem or that any actions to stem doping were needed. But a consensus would soon emerge. In the 1960 Olympic Games in Rome, Danish cyclist Knud Jensen crashed, fracturing his skull, and soon thereafter died of his injuries. His untimely death provided an opportunity for sports bodies to highlight the perils of doping in sport. In a PhD dissertation on the history of doping in the Olympics, Thomas Hunt observes that "Olympic officials knew about the use of performance-enhancing drugs in their competitions for at least a decade prior to Knud Jensen's death." Paul Dimeo, a professor at the University of Stirling University in Scotland, has established that Jensen's death was unlikely to have been due to doping; rather, his death provided a convenient way for the burgeoning antidoping movement to establish a mythology.[34] Dimeo does not shy back from the ironic implications of the myth: "Any movement becomes compromised if its acolytes come to imagine the cause to be greater than the individuals and when they are prepared to undermine their own ideals in order to make a point."

The use of a prominent figure to illustrate the risks of doping would become a repeating pattern in sport: the presence of doping is acknowledged within sporting circles, a public tragedy or a scandal leads to calls for action, then sporting officials take some kind of action. Often, those actions are only small steps and thus set the stage for the dynamic to repeat itself. Some of the most influential figures at the center of this dynamic in recent decades include Ca-

---

*   The WADA IV policy is discussed here: "Is It Prohibited for Athletes to Use IV Infusions for Rehydration and Recovery?" USADA, http://www.usada.org/is-it-prohibited-or-dangerous-for-athletes-using-iv-infusions-for-re-hydration-and-recovery/. Whether Jordan's IV would have run afoul of today's IOC rules is an interesting question, but ultimately irrelevant because the NBA does not fall under WADA regulations.

nadian sprinter Ben Johnson, who failed a drug test in 1984 after winning the Olympic 100 meters in Los Angeles; US sprinter Marion Jones and baseball player Barry Bonds, who in the 2000s were implicated in the so-called BALCO scandal; and, of course, Lance Armstrong and other cyclists in the Tour de France.

Motivations for doping in sport often have political origins. International sports became a battleground between East and West during the Cold War, and doping was a key weapon on that battlefield. Based on historical records that became available only after the fall of the Berlin Wall, the *New York Times* reported that "East Germany operated a state-sponsored system of providing performance-enhancing drugs to as many as 10,000 athletes from 1968 to 1988."[35]

Doping was pervasive in Eastern bloc sports. To take just one example, figure 6.2 shows the winning times in swimming for the women's 400-meter individual medley race. The rapid drop in times from 1964 to 1980 has been attributed to the effects of doping. In 1976, for instance, East Germany won eleven of thirteen possible gold medals in the Montreal Olympics. In 1976, East Germany won the gold in the women's 400-meter individual medley (four 100-meter legs of back stroke, breast stroke, butterfly, and freestyle) by more than five seconds, and in 1980 by more than ten seconds.[36] The stunning performance was not unique to swimming. Internal files from the East German government revealed that in 1977, "anabolic steroids [were] applied in all Olympic sporting events . . . and by all national teams."[37] The results showed, and not just at the medals table.

At the 1976 Olympics, American athletes complained. Rod Strachan, an Olympic swimmer, said that the East German women's swimmers were "quite a bit bigger than most of the men on the American team. They could go out for football at USC." Willye White, a long jumper, said that the Americans had to catch up: "If we're going to compete, it's best that the USOC understands sports medicine. If we are going to compete against synthetic athletes, we must become synthetic athletes."[38]

Despite the evidence available at the time, "the overwhelming feature of the policy response to the emerging problem of doping

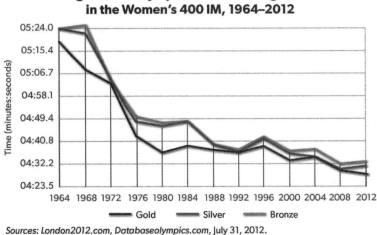

Figure 6.2. Olympic Medal-Winning Times in the Women's 400 IM, 1964–2012

Sources: *London2012.com, Databaseolympics.com*, July 31, 2012.

was one of lassitude and often willful incomprehension."[39] For instance, the 1980 Moscow Olympics took place with zero positive drug tests, a result that was treated by the IOC "as evidence of the effectiveness of existing policy rather than suspicious."[40] The Cold War had brought nations and global geopolitics into sport, along with a commitment to performance enhancement as a source of national prestige. Long after the Cold War, global geopolitics still play a role in doping. In 2016, Russia was accused of a state-sponsored scheme to evade drug tests at the Sochi Winter Olympics of 2014. The scheme involved swapping out urine samples in the dark of night to protect heavily doped Russian athletes. The FSB—the new version of the KGB, the Russian spy agency that was so busy during the Cold War—was supposedly involved.[41]

Not only are nations willing to take on the doping arms race, so too are athletes. A 2012 survey found that about 12 percent of athletes surveyed would dope if it were illegal and there were no consequences. Perhaps surprisingly, more than 5 percent said that they would dope if it were legal and it would guarantee them an Olympic gold medal, but it would also mean that they would die within five years.[42] Although these numbers represent a snapshot in time, it's easy to imagine that athletes of earlier eras harbored similar views.

The willingness of athletes to go over an ethical edge by breaking the rules in pursuit of a sporting edge helps to explain why doping is a wicked problem.

Estimates of the prevalence of doping based on hypothetical questions are actually lower than the proportion of athletes who have admitted to doping. In an anonymous survey of more than two thousand elite track and field athletes, 29 percent at the 2011 World Championships and 45 percent at the 2011 Pan-Arab Games admitted to the use of prohibited performance-enhancing drugs.[43] A 2015 study published in *Sports Medicine* estimated that between 14 and 39 percent of elite athletes dope.

By contrast, the drug tests administered by WADA detect the use of prohibited substances in only about 1 to 2 percent of samples. Similar tests given by the USADA routinely result in a detection rate of less than 1 percent.[44] The stark difference between estimates of the prevalence of doping among elite athletes and the small number who are actually sanctioned for doping violations led a Dutch antidoping official to conclude that "calls for more clarity in this area that were made more than 25 years ago have not yet yielded much progress."[45]

Whatever the actual incidence of doping in sport, clearly more than just a few percent of athletes dope. The reasons for seeking to enhance performance go well beyond sport and are deeply cultural. Writing in *Sports Illustrated* in 1969, Bill Gilbert observed that "these days it is a cultural reflex to reach for a vial, an atomizer, a capsule or a needle if you suffer from fever, chills, aches, pains, nausea, nasal congestion, irritability, the doldrums, sluggishness, body odor, obesity, emaciation, too many kids, not enough kids, nagging backache."[46] We enhance our performance because we can, and we like the results.

Not much has changed in the almost half century since Gilbert wrote those words, except perhaps the lengthening of the list of conditions that can be improved on by modern medical science. Gilbert further noted that athletes are "flaming faddists" because "the reputation and salary of an athlete depends on luck, a puddle of water, a gust of wind, a bounce of a ball." The money in sport has become larger and the competition more intense. So if there is an edge to be gained, and the chances of getting caught are pretty small, then many athletes must think, Why not apply modern medical science to sports performance?

Cracking the Code

In theory, if not in practice, the answer to this question can be found in the WADA code. The code explains how antidoping rules should be implemented in the Olympic and other sports that fall under its provisions. At the core of the code is a list that includes all substances (and procedures) considered to be prohibited. To get on the list, a substance must meet two of three criteria:[47]

- Evidence must indicate that the substance "has the potential to enhance or enhances sport performance."

- Evidence must show "that the Use of the substance or method represents an actual or potential health risk to the Athlete."

- "WADA's determination that the Use of the substance or method violates the spirit of sport."

WADA explains what it means by the "spirit of sport" in a circular fashion:

> Anti-doping programs seek to preserve what is intrinsically valuable about sport. This intrinsic value is often referred to as "the spirit of sport," it is the essence of Olympism; it is how we play true. The spirit of sport is the celebration of the human spirit, body and mind. . . . Doping is fundamentally contrary to the spirit of sport."

The spirit of sport thus refers to fidelity to rules. In the case of doping, the rules are justified in terms of fulfilling the spirit of sport. This circularity is not what the Olympics rings represent, but it does get to what lies at the heart of debates over doping. Doping rules are arbitrary and procedural because there is no agreed-upon scientific or moral basis for what constitutes legitimate performance enhancement and what does not.

Lacking the equivalent of an infallible pope, or, better yet, stone tablets brought down from a mountaintop, the modern Olympic movement has adopted a fractured and haphazard approach to doping that is replicated in the various professional sports leagues around the world that sit outside of the Olympic movement. The result is that no one really knows how many athletes dope or how effective antidoping programs are. This reality has set the stage for only one certainty: scandal after scandal after scandal.

A serious effort to fix the fractured and haphazard approach to doping occurred in the 1990s with the process that ultimately led to the creation of WADA. An international oversight organization was created for four reasons, according to Barrie Houlihan. First, some national governments were interested in stemming the "growing arrogance" of many international sporting associations, such as the IOC, by becoming involved in the oversight of sport. Second, the "near collapse" in 1998 of the Tour de France over the so-called Festina doping scandal dramatically showed the failures of current approaches. Third, international sports organizations were reeling from bribery scandals associated with the 1996 and 2002 Olympic Games site selections. Finally, the European Union showed leadership in international sport as a matter of public policy.[48]

Do Antidoping Rules and Regulations Actually Work?

Because no one really knows how effective antidoping programs are, it is impossible to know how far to go in trying to rid sport of athletes who seek an improper edge through doping. Sometimes, antidoping efforts can appear to go too far. For instance, in 2009, WADA introduced a rule requiring thousands of athletes to give testers three months' advance notice of their location every single day, in case a surprise test was to be given.[49] This led to considerable anger and even legal challenges by athletes. Tennis star Andy Murray said that the rules "are so draconian that it makes it almost impossible to live a normal life."[50] In another example, in June 2014, elite Dutch judo athlete Henk Grol described a degrading physical examination he was forced to undergo while providing a urine sample to drug testers at the Budapest Grand Prix. Another competitor simply refused the test, telling the testers: "I'm not going to bend over for you."[51]

Equity is also a concern.[52] Lance Armstrong was given a lifetime ban from sport and could lose much of his lifetime earnings, totaling more than a reported $100 million. Yet, witnesses who testified against him in antidoping proceedings, some of whom were guilty of the same violations, were given six-month bans and some have continued their careers in professional cycling, broadcasting, and sports management. When I spoke to officials at USADA, they told me that the rules for sanctioning athletes were followed in the Armstrong case—and I don't doubt this assertion. But it does leave open the question of whether the right rules are in place. Armstrong quipped to me, "What's next, the death penalty?"

Even the US district court judge who refused to halt the USADA investigation into Armstrong's doping activities expressed concerns about equity in antidoping sanctions. He wrote that if the agency "is promising lesser sanctions against other allegedly offending riders in exchange for their testimony against Armstrong, it is difficult to avoid the conclusion that [USADA] is motivated more by politics and a desire for media attention."[53] The judge's conclusion may or may not be unfair to USADA—impossible for independent observers to determine—because it is not clear to whom USADA is actually accountable. The agency receives most of its funding from US taxpayers, but it is not a federal agency.[54] Professor Paul Dimeo explains a resulting tradeoff: "It may sometimes be necessary to make a strong example—as USADA did with Armstrong—but the outcome is that some athletes suffer a great deal more than the others."[55]

Along with Verner Møller of Aarhus University in Denmark, Dimeo argues that antidoping may be harming the very essence of the sport of cycling.[56] They say it's a "farce" that the Tour de France titles stripped from Armstrong have not been re-awarded. But, they add, the fact that a winner cannot be found means that re-awarding the titles would also be a "farce." They argue that the combination of both athletes who doped and the antidoping policies that caught them has left the sport without a legitimate history.

Armstrong disagrees. He says common sense says that he won those races, tainted as they were: "We all know what we know and it was a dirty sport." Armstrong points to the fact that he was stripped of his Tour de France titles (the yellow jersey) and yet, the so-called secondary classifications in the Tour—the green jersey for points winners and the polka dotted jersey for overall winner of the mountain stages—have not been stripped from winners who admitted doping. He sends me to Wikipedia, where his name has been stripped, while others who doped remain. "Where is the uniformity of rules?" he asks.

Armstrong remains defiant: "Ask my peers who rode when I rode who won those years. They'll tell you. How can you not name a winner?" Armstrong says that cycling is treated differently than other sports. When an athlete loses a medal in the Olympics, it is awarded to someone else. Armstrong's bronze medal for the cycling time trials at the 2000 Sydney Games was stripped and not re-awarded. The winner of the gold medal that year, Viatcheslav Ekimov, was accused by another cyclist (Floyd Landis)[57] of doping, and the silver medalist, Jan Ullrich, admitted publicly to doping. Ullrich sounds like Armstrong when he explains his 1997 Tour de France victory:

> At that time, nearly everyone was using doping substances and I used nothing that the others were not using. In my view you can only call it cheating on my part when it is clear that I have gained an unfair advantage. That was not the case. All I wanted was everyone to have the same chances of winning.[58]

Ekimov and Ullrich still have their 2000 Olympic medals.[59]

Maybe cycling should follow the example of weight lifting, which changed weight classes in 1992 to try to move past its ugly history.[60] The point of changing the weight classes was an effort to "re-boot" the sport for a new era. In cycling the equivalent would be to move the Tour de France to Japan, and start fresh with a new Tour and, crucially, a new record book. The new record book would relegate doping-tainted performances to the history books, giving athletes a new set of goals to aim for. Of course, doping in weight lifting has not abated. But it has a new history.

The case of Lance Armstrong illustrates that many athletes within a sport can be guilty of violating the rules of that sport, but the punishments handed out by its governing body can vary widely, with just a few athletes or even a single one punished with exceptional severity. Debates will surely continue over whether Armstrong actually "won" the seven Tour de France titles—his peers may have their own answers to that question, which is what Armstrong says really counts the most. Regardless, Armstrong clearly received differential treatment from his peers during cycling's EPO era

The wicked problem of antidoping policies has other disturbing facets, too. The majority of athletes compete without doping, and without ever being accused of doing so, but they still can't entirely escape the shadow of doping. For instance, the end of a competition is no longer the final verdict on who wins and who loses: antidoping policies are such that we have to wait ten years for a result to stand, as that is the statute of limitations under which a doping violation can be sanctioned.[61] The provisional nature of sporting event results does not seem fair to athletes or to spectators. British marathoner Mara Yamauchi expresses the frustration: "If I get asked 'Did you come in sixth in Beijing?' What do I say? Yes, I think so, oh wait, no, maybe, it depends, ask me in two years, not sure . . ."[62]

The consequences to athletes who follow the rules can be significant. Adam Nelson, a US shot putter, won a silver medal in 2004 in Athens. In 2012, he learned that the first place finisher from Ukraine had been retroactively stripped of his gold medal based on

Jan Ullrich (left) in the 1997 Tour de France, which he won. Udo Bolts is leading the way.

new doping results.[63] Nelson later arranged to pick up the gold medal in a food court at the Atlanta airport. He lamented what was lost: "I feel like our country was robbed of a medal at the relevant time. One of the biggest parts of an Olympic career is when you hear your anthem and see your flag when you stand on that podium. That's something I can never replace." He also lost millions of dollars in potential sponsorship money. Yes, he ultimately received his medal, but he also lost a tremendous amount that can never be recovered.

The negative consequences experienced by athletes who follow the rules can be traced to a lack of basic information on the prevalence of doping in sport and on the effectiveness of antidoping policies. And that lack of information is puzzling, because, as an academic policy researcher, it seems to me that we already have the tools (notably, randomized control trials) with which we could discover how widespread doping is.[64] It would be straightforward to design a testing regime, complemented by surveys and interviews, focused on quantifying the prevalence of detectable doping among athletes, their trends over time, and the corresponding efficacy of different antidoping efforts. Testing serves many purposes, of course, but one purpose should be to help evaluate the value of testing regimes.

Officials at antidoping agencies tell me that they are constantly thinking about how better to assess effectiveness.[65] In the meantime, for athletes justice is meted out unevenly, affecting both those who break the rules and those who don't. Surely, antidoping agencies can do better.

A Way Forward on Antidoping in Sport

Travis Tygart and Lance Armstrong may have been on opposite sides of the issue of doping in cycling, but there is one thing they agree on: athletes will dope. In early 2016, Tygart told *Sports Illustrated*, referring to human growth hormone: "If it does all that good, and there's no way to get caught using it, call me crazy, but logic tells me that unless these athletes don't want to win, it's a hard sell not to do it."[66] Around the same time, Armstrong told me, speaking about doping in cycling, "Throw into the mix EPO, the most powerful performance enhancer known to man. And with it easy to not get caught, people say 'fuck it' and use it."[67]

A way forward on doping in elite sport starts with points that seem to be broadly agreed on within the sports community:*

- Athletes will take performance-enhancing substances if they actually or even allegedly can improve performance.
- Some substances will be banned from use.
- Science allows reliable detection of some but not all substances that might be banned.
- There are inevitable trade-offs between athletes' rights and certain rules that might make implementing antidoping regulations easier to implement.
- Due process for athletes matters.

With these points of agreement as a place to start, I propose that antidoping rules and regulations follow four principles as the rule-makers and regulators search for reforms.

Antidoping rules need to be simplified. The WADA prohibited list includes almost 300 individual substances plus three methods. This sets up a fantastically complicated set of tasks for antidoping agencies. And science will only continue to develop substances that may aid performance, meaning that the WADA list is bound to grow. Enforcing this complexity requires money, far more than is presently available or may ever be. Complexity also invites challenges over science, such as in the Tysse case, which leaves enforcement in the hands of a small number of experts. One way to simplify antidoping regulations would be to remove the spirit of sport criterion as the basis for a substance or method being included on the prohibited list. The reliance on objective criteria would have the benefit of removing ambiguity.

---

*   Antidoping efforts in amateur sport are an even more wicked problem; see Paul Dimeo, "Amateur Doping Shaping Up to Be Sport's Latest Test as Cycling Bans Rack Up," *The Conversation,* February 18, 2016, https://theconversation. com/amateur-doping-shaping-up-to-be-sports-latest-test-as-cycling-bans-rack-up-53543.

Antidoping rules need to be evidence based. Not only do antidoping agencies not know how many athletes dope, they do not have robust knowledge of the performance-enhancing benefits of the chemicals and substances on the prohibited list. Everyone would benefit from knowing the state of scientific knowledge on how certain substances either benefit performance or present health risks and for whom. For some substances—such as EPO and steroids—the effects will no doubt be large and detectable; for others, the effects may be much smaller or even undetectable. Are substances to be considered guilty until proven innocent? Or vice versa: are they to be considered innocent until proven guilty? Having better evidence on the exact performance-enhancing effects of substances and methods that are already banned or might be banned would facilitate simplification and athlete participation in the process.

Antidoping rules need to be athlete legitimized. Imagine if the banned list were to be drawn up by athletes, not by scientific experts. Armed with knowledge of performance-enhancing benefits of specific substances and the risks of their use, athletes (or their representatives) who are covered by the WADA code could vote on which substances should appear on the list. Presently, and as discussed in chapter 9, caffeine is not banned by WADA but offers demonstrable performance-enhancing benefits with little risk to the athlete. Perhaps athletes would judge other substances to be in the same category as caffeine, especially if the performance-enhancing effects are of the same magnitude of caffeine or less. More important, a prohibited list more transparently assembled and voted on by athletes would have far greater legitimacy than one put together and imposed by experts who don't have to compete under antidoping regulations.

Antidoping rules need to be rigorously evaluated. Whatever regime is put into place for antidoping, it should be evaluated rigorously and continuously to see if it actually works. Here, too, athletes deserve a greater role—in determining how far antidoping regulation should go with respect to individual rights and privacy, and with respect to the due process afforded to individuals who are accused of and sanctioned for breaking doping rules. For decades, antidoping regulations have been viewed as something that sports organizations force on athletes, with a low level of athlete representation or involvement. It is time for athletes to take a leading role in implementing antidoping regulations, aided by experts and sports organizations. Such implementation will be far more robust if everyone knows how well it is working.

These principles suggest an approach to antidoping that is more pragmatic, more transparent, and more accountable than the current system. Until a more simplified approach is put into place, we should expect little to change in the battle against doping.

Chapter 7

Hacking the Athlete and the Games

You are a miracle of modern technology.

And you are much better for it. I'll venture a guess that you were vaccinated at an early age against multiple diseases, a technology that has altered the biological fabric of your body in such a way as to enhance your performance against various debilitating, even fatal, diseases. There is a fair chance that you have had laser surgery on your eyes to improve your vision, and if not, you probably wear glasses, a technological prosthetic that enables you to enhance your visual acuity. You may have even undergone an enhancement procedure to boost your appearance—perhaps a boob job or liposuction or you've had the shape of your nose changed.

If you are like me, you've gone under the surgeon's knife to fix an injury or to restore capabilities that you might have lost. In my case, it was knee surgery after tearing cartilage in my left knee playing soccer. My wife has had more sports injuries than I can count. Her repaired anterior cruciate ligament in her knee was advertised as "better than the original." As a ten-month-old, my youngest child badly burned the skin on his palm, necessitating a skin graft from under his arm. He has a wicked scar, but today he is an exceptional athlete with full use of his hand.

Thanks, technology.

We are, all of us, better than we otherwise would have been thanks to technology. We perform better in daily life—and when we push our bodies to extremes—thanks to a large suite of technological augmentations. Some of us look better (or think we do) than we would otherwise, thanks to augmentation. If you were born with a birth defect or you are among those who lost limbs or body function due to war or disease, modern technology does much more than make you look better—it may also dramatically enhance your ability to function in the world.

In general, we tend to like the technological augmentation of the human form that enhances our abilities.* But augmentation can become problematic in the context of sport, where, in principle, fairness of competition is held up as a virtue. Technological augmentation forces us to turn abstract appeals to fairness into practical rules for what that might mean in actual competitions. Establishing such rules is not easy. And it is getting more difficult.

As if changing the human form isn't difficult enough, technology changes the nature of competition itself. For example, televised, high-definition instant replay allows fans to get a better view of the games than officials, threatening the legitimacy of referee judgments. Similarly, the equipment used in sport changes competition, whether it is ultrasleek swimsuits or grooved golf clubs that allow professionals to impart incredible spin on golf balls. Technology does not stand still, and that often means that the rules for the games we play are in a constant state of renegotiation.

Thanks a lot, technology.

This chapter considers two types of "hacks" in sport.† In many contexts, hacking the human is commonplace and accepted. In 2014, Americans underwent 15.6 million cosmetic plastic surgery

---

*   Yes, there are occasionally debates about innovations like vaccines.
†   I use the slangy term "hack" to refer to a "clever solution to a tricky problem"; see "Definition of Hack: A Clever Solution to a Tricky Problem," Urban Dictionary. com, http://www.urbandictionary.com/define.php?term=hack&defid=3916807. Improving (or even repairing) the human form after millions of years of evolution requires some cleverness. Further, as humans and technology become more symbiotic, the term "hack" seems appropriate.

procedures, from breast implants to butt lifts.* We look to technology to improve our performance. Athletes are no different than other people; they also look to technology to improve their performance. Such improvements are forcing sport to make some hard decisions.

The other type of hack that this chapter considers is the technological augmentation of the games themselves. People routinely hack computers and mobile phones by stripping them down to their component parts and then rebuilding them to work better. Sport is not much different. Most sports depend on technologies—a dependence that provides ample opportunity for would-be hackers: shoes, swimsuits, balls, sticks, bats, and so on. How we watch games also depends on technologies. In the past, technology was largely confined to radio, then TV, instant replay, slow motion, high definition, and even analytic measurements of the games themselves. Today, tennis has HawkEye technology to assist officials in making line calls, and baseball has Quest-Tec, which can objectively identify balls and strikes but is not (so far) used by officials. But some technologies—hidden motors in bikes, prosthetic legs that go too fast, high-tech brooms in the sport of curling—are judged to go over the edge of acceptability.

Hacking the human and hacking the game raise the same fundamental questions: How much is too much? How far is too far? When does cleverness go over the edge?

Two Boys, Worlds Apart

In the mid-1980s, about seven months apart, two bouncing baby boys came into the world on different continents of the southern hemisphere. One was born with a "birth defect," and the other developed a serious childhood disease. Both became elite athletes. Their respective stories force us to confront some difficult questions

---

* This statistic does not include reconstructive procedures. The most common surgical procedure for women was breast augmentation; nose reshaping was the most common procedure for men; see "American Society of Plastic Surgeons, 2014 Plastic Surgery Statistics Report," Plasticsurgery.org, http://www.plasticsurgery.org/Documents/news-resources/statistics/2014-statistics/plastic-surgery-statsitics-full-report.pdf.

Lionel Messi playing for FC Barcelona in 2011.

about where modern science and technology meet the biological human in the context of sport.

Baby Oscar was born November 22, 1986, in Johannesburg, South Africa. Oscar came into the world without fibula bones, the ones that go from the knees to the feet. His parents decided that the best course of action for their baby was to have him grow up walking on prosthetic legs.[1] One month before his first birthday, Oscar's legs were amputated below the knee.

Four months before that operation, on June 24, 1987, baby Lionel was born in Rosario, Argentina. When he was eleven years old, he was diagnosed with a condition called "growth hormone deficiency," which results from the pituitary gland failing to produce enough growth hormone.[2] The condition generally leads to a child being much smaller than peers of the same age.[3]

Both children were active in sports as they grew up. Oscar played rugby, water polo, and tennis, and he wrestled. He began a competitive sprinting career in January 2004 at age seventeen, following a rugby injury.[4] He soon became a top sprinter, running on prosthetic blades. In the 2004 Paralympics in Athens, just a few months after taking up competitive sprinting, Oscar won a gold medal in the 200 meters and a bronze medal in the 100 meters. Not long after, Oscar started racing against able-bodied athletes in IAAF competitions, and doing well. He soon shot to worldwide fame—Oscar Pistorius, the Blade Runner.

By the time little Leo's family discovered his medical condition, he had already distinguished himself as a soccer player. When he was only eight years old, he joined Newell's Old Boys, a club team in Rosario. When his medical condition emerged, the club agreed to help his parents pay for expensive treatments that involved regular injections of human growth hormone to compensate for the fact that his body did not produce enough. The talented boy caught the eye of coaches at River Plate, a top club team from Buenos Aires, but his medical condition put them off. However, FC Barcelona, the giant Spanish club, took a chance on Leo. He, too, shot to worldwide fame—Lionel Messi, arguably the greatest soccer player ever.

Pistorius and Messi have modern technology to thank for their ability to excel in competitive athletics. The use of human growth hormone to treat children with deficiencies had been performed for

Oscar Pistorius at the London Paralympics in 2012.

several decades prior to Messi's treatment.[5] The "blade" used by Pistorius was invented by Van Phillips, an amputee who lost his left leg below the knee in a water skiing accident in 1976, when he was twenty-one years old.[6] He turned the accident into motivation and spent years, first at Northwestern University, then at the University of Utah, working to create a new type of prosthetic leg. What he came up with was modeled on the legs of kangaroos and cheetahs.

Although the stories of Messi and Pistorius are uplifting, they force us to confront some difficult questions. Human growth hormone is considered a performance-enhancing substance and is banned by WADA and the NFL, among other sports organizations. Messi was administered the hormone by his soccer club as he was growing to enhance his ability to perform as a soccer player. On the one hand, many children have benefitted from such treatments; on the other hand, Lionel Messi the global superstar would not be where he is without the enhancement afforded by modern medical technologies. For a comparison, consider Diego Maradona, an Argentinean soccer star from an earlier generation who was allegedly given steroids while a youth to aid in his development.[7] Today, almost no questions are asked about the role of technological enhancement in the making of Lionel Messi.

Oscar Pistorius is not so fortunate. Lots of questions were asked about him as he emerged on the world athletic stage. After he began to experience success on the track running against able-bodied athletes, the IAAF introduced a rule in 2007, focused specifically on Pistorius, prohibiting the "use of any technical device that incorporates springs, wheels, or any other element that provides the user with an advantage over another athlete not using such a device."[8] Under this rule, Pistorius was determined by the IAAF to be ineligible to compete against able-bodied athletes.

Pistorius appealed the decision to CAS. The appeal hinged on answering a metaphysical question—how fast would Pistorius have run had he been born with functioning legs below the knee? In other words, did the blades give him an advantage over other athletes that the hypothetical able-bodied Oscar Pistorius would not have had? Because there never was an able-bodied Pistorius, CAS looked to scientists to answer the question.

In its judgment, CAS concluded that the IAAF was in fact fixing the rules to prevent Pistorius from competing and that "at least some IAAF officials had determined that they did not want Mr. Pistorius to be acknowledged as eligible to compete in international IAAF-sanctioned events, regardless of the results that properly conducted scientific studies might demonstrate."[9] The court did not find the IAAF arguments compelling. It upheld Pistorius's appeal and noted that their decision to allow him to run in London was for this one case and not a blanket judgment on blades or other technological aids. CAS concluded that resolving such disputes "must be viewed as just one of the challenges of 21st Century life." It was right.

A New Challenge for Sport in the Twenty-first Century

It's true. Technological augmentation of the human form is common in sport. Consider eye correction. Better eyesight is correlated with achievement in elite athletics. Michael Peter, an optometrist who works with the Carolina Panthers football team, took a survey in 2009–10 and found that the following proportions of professional athletes needed vision correction:

- 17.1 percent of the NFL
- 16 percent of the NBA
- 29.6 percent of the MLB
- 20.2 percent of the NHL

These numbers compare to 59 percent of eighteen- to thirty-four-year-olds among the general population who need vision correction. Peter concluded that having better vision is associated with athletic achievement: "You really do have to see to play."[10]

Various technologies are available to improve eyesight today, ranging from corrective eyewear to laser surgery. Some athletes even use tinted contact lenses in an effort to improve their sight—for example, amber lenses are supposed to help baseball players.

Writing in *Slate*, William Saletan observes that Tiger Woods and many other professional athletes have used laser eye surgery to improve their eyesight beyond 20/20:

> Golfers Scott Hoch, Hale Irwin, Tom Kite, and Mike Weir have hit the 20/15 mark. So have baseball players Jeff Bagwell, Jeff Cirillo, Jeff Conine, Jose Cruz Jr., Wally Joyner, Greg Maddux, Mark Redman, and Larry Walker. Amar'e Stoudemire and Rip Hamilton of the NBA have done it, along with NFL players Troy Aikman, Ray Buchanan, Tiki Barber, Wayne Chrebet, and Danny Kanell.[11]

Eyesight enhancement is not prohibited by any league or sports federation. Yet, it would clearly fail the test that was applied by the IAAF to Oscar Pistorius. It is a technology that gives the athlete with corrected vision an advantage over others that he or she would not naturally have.

Why are some technological augmentations allowed and others banned? Where should a line be drawn?

Oscar Pistorius participated in the London 2012 Olympics. He ran in the 400 meters, finishing eighth in one of the semifinals. He also participated in the 4x400-meter relay, anchoring the South African team that finished eighth. Imagine what might have happened had Pistorius finished first in his races or set a new world record. In the 2012 Paralympics, which followed the Olympics, Pistorius was bested in the 200 meters by Alan Oliveira of Brazil, who also ran on blades. After the race, Pistorius complained that Oliveira's blades were too long, giving him an unfair advantage.[12] If that seems ironic, given Pistorius's claims before CAS, it is.

Oscar Pistorius is far from the only athlete to take advantage of modern technology in order to enhance his athletic performance. In Tennessee in 2015, at Sweetwater High School, DJ Vanderwerf was the quarterback of the football team, a power forward on the basketball team, and a pitcher for the baseball team. Vanderwerf had had his lower left leg amputated when he was nine months old. He plays sports on a prosthetic leg.[13] In Germany, Markus Rehm is a long jumper who jumps off of his prosthetic leg. He is such a good jumper that he threatens to outjump all jumpers who jump off of their human leg, and even to break the world record. Rehm spent much of the first half of 2016 trying, but ultimately failing, to secure eligibility for participating in the 2016 Rio Olympics.[14]

Prosthetics are but one sort of technological augmentation of the human form for sport performance enhancement. Other modifications involve far more involved procedures. Consider the case of combat sports. In 2007, Nick Diaz and KJ Noons faced off in a mixed martial arts (MMA) cage match. MMA is a brutal sport in which two fighters brawl until one cannot continue any further. In this fight, Diaz was the favorite, but Noons had his own plans. Noons's background as a professional boxer gave him the skills to elude Diaz's attempts to grab him for a takedown while inflicting damage to Diaz's face with carefully placed punches.

An MMA website described the result:

> Noons delivered a knee that caught Diaz flush in the face, opening a deep gash above his right eye. Seconds after the cut was cleared by a doctor, Noons dropped Diaz with a right hook—and then opened a gash above the dazed fighter's other eye while throwing haymakers from above.[15]

Diaz was a bloody mess, prompting the fight's doctor to call the fight in Noons's favor.

Diaz's bleeding was not just the result of being hit, but "it was also the result of dozens of improperly sutured cuts Diaz had previously suffered in his fighting life. They had only healed superficially, leaving behind ground chuck underneath."[16] Soon after that fight, Diaz was approached by a plastic surgeon, Frank Stile, who suggested that Diaz's propensity to bleed when hit might be fixed by taking comparatively unused tissue from a cadaver and using it to replace Diaz's well-used facial tissue. Boxers had long used plastic surgery to try to limit facial bleeding, so why not do it in a more brutal combat sport?[17]

Diaz agreed to undergo the procedure, and in the process had several facial bones shaved down in order to reduce the chances of being cut upon being hit. Dr. Stile explains that, from his perspective, such surgery "is not enhancement." Rather, he says, "it levels the playing field. It gives [fighters] the ability to be like they were never cut before."[18] From this perspective, the face is like a worn-out knee ligament. When it no longer works, we can get a relatively unused one from a dead person and replace it. And for Diaz, the procedure worked. In the thirteen fights after facing Noons through 2015, Diaz hardly bled.[19] Today, the use of plastic surgery in MMA is becoming mainstream, even being called "the norm for cut-prone fighters who are trying to prolong their careers."[20]

Baseball also has a surgical procedure that has become mainstream. "Tommy John surgery" is named for the Los Angeles Dodgers pitcher who first underwent a surgery to replace a damaged ligament (the ulnar collateral ligament, or UCL) in his throwing arm with a tendon from his other forearm. John returned from the surgery to pitch fourteen more years in the major leagues. The UCL injury was first identified in 1946 among javelin throwers.[21] The surgery is today fairly common, with 235 pitchers undergoing the procedure from 1999 to 2014.[22] But the performance-enhancing benefits of Tommy John surgery have probably been oversold.

A 2014 study of 179 pitchers who underwent Tommy John surgery found that the surgery offered a reliable way for injured athletes to return to professional baseball, but that they did not necessarily have enhanced performance once they got back.[23] The study found that more than 97 percent of pitchers were able to return to professional baseball after the surgery, 83 percent to the major leagues. "In comparison with controls, pitchers who underwent UCL reconstruction had a lower ERA [earned run average, a measure of pitching effectiveness] and WHIP [walks plus hits per inning pitched, another metric of pitching effectiveness], had a lower losing percentage, and gave up fewer hits per inning." These positive outcomes have led to a perception among coaches (30 percent), parents (37 percent), high school athletes (51 percent), and college athletes (26 percent) that proactive Tommy John surgery (in the absence of injury) will offer performance-enhancing benefits.[24] Yet, "to date, there are no data to support or even consider prophylactic UCL reconstruction to improve throwing velocity or prevent injuries in the future." The myth of the performance-enhancing benefits of Tommy John surgery has outstripped the evidence.[25]

We have seen how twenty-first-century medical technologies can add body parts where none existed (Pistorius), can enhance development (Messi) and performance (many golfers, baseball players, and others), can replace and reshape body parts that don't work well (Diaz), and can repurpose body parts (Tommy John). Modern technologies can also remove body parts that inhibit performance.

Consider Simona Halep. At the start of the 2016 tennis season, she sat at number two in the world, trailing only Serena Williams in the World Tennis Association rankings. Halep's rise through the rankings was motivated by her intense desire to excel, which is characteristic of many elite athletes. In 2014, she looked back: "A few years ago I was looking up the rankings on the Internet and I saw I was on the fourth page. I said my dream was to be on the first page."[26] In 2009, Halep was ranked 210 in the world, and she faced a big obstacle to improving. Her breasts were too big.

Halep explained, "It's the weight that troubles me. My ability to react quickly, my breasts make me uncomfortable when I play."[27] Halep elected to have breast reduction surgery, and the results were immediate. In 2010, she jumped to number 81 in the world; by 2013, she sat just outside the top ten. Halep is not alone, as other elite athletes have elected to have breast reduction surgery, including Jana Rawlinson, an Australian runner, who had breast implants removed to facilitate her running.[28]

Most observers of sport focus little attention on technological augmentation, and when attention is focused on these issues, it typically emphasizes what some might regard as the lurid—breasts!—over the more fundamental issues related to the ethics of competition. Even academics have paid little attention to this issue. Ryan Rodenberg and Herlanda Hampton of Florida State University observe that "in researching the policy implications stemming from the surgical manipulation of athletes, the relevant literature is scant."[29]

We don't even have the language to talk about the issue. In this chapter, I use the phrase "technological augmentation." Rodenberg and Hampton coined the phrase "surgical doping." When an elite cyclist was found with a motor hidden in her bike's frame, many commentators called it "mechanical doping." More general discussions of the fusion of technology and the human use far-out terms like "transhumanism," the "techno-human condition," and even "human cyborgs."[30] None of the augmentations discussed in this chapter are covered by a regulatory regime, and those that do face regulation, such as Pistorious's blades, have been considered as one-off cases, meaning that rules have to be reconsidered for each case, such as when Markus Rehm petitioned to jump in the 2016 Olympics. He won't be the last athlete to try to crossover from the Paralympics to the Olympics.

Despite the increasing presence of technologically enhanced athletes looking to break down barriers, there is little consistency in rules across sport (and even within individual sports) as to what technological enhancements are allowed and what are not. Some observers have argued that technological enhancements are a form of doping that could be regulated under WADA, for example. Others see technological enhancements as a completely different category than doping, requiring new regulations and oversight. Some philosophize the issue and ask, What is the difference between a repair to an injury and a modification to make one perform better? Still others think, What's the big deal?

The need for a regulatory regime may grow, however—the enhancements discussed so far are just the tip of the iceberg, according to Mark Hamilton of Ashland University.[31] He says that the possibilities are "endless," and he mentions liposuction as a means of weight loss for wrestlers, elective ligament surgery for professional golfers wanting longer drives, and tendon surgery so sprinters can run faster. Power lifters could have metal knee joints implanted to aid strength and stability. As medical science progresses, the list of possible augmentations becomes longer and longer.

The issues raised by enhancement are long-standing in the Paralympics, where judgments must be made about how to group athletes with different types of disabilities. The Paralympics' classification methods illustrate the challenges of arriving at rules to govern fair competition more generally.

The Paralympics have identified ten different kinds of impairments that make an athlete eligible for entering competition.[32] These include physical impairments, such as the loss of a limb; visual impairments; and cognitive impairments. However, not all conditions are equally impairing across sports, requiring the Paralympics to make judgment calls that place athletes into different categories. And those judgments can sometimes be difficult and controversial.

In 2006, Victoria Arlen was eleven years old, a happy and healthy athletic child who dreamed of swimming in the Olympics. That April, she suddenly became sick, losing thirty pounds in two weeks. Her condition worsened, and she fell into a vegetative state. The news got even worse: "Her parents and family were told not to expect a recovery and to prepare for the possibility that Victoria would die."[33]

Arlen was brought home after doctors told her family not to expect her condition to improve. Several years later, she was diagnosed with a rare condition, transverse myelitis.[34] She was trapped in her body and communicated with her parents by blinking her eyes. This condition lasted into 2010, when she made a remarkable recovery. However, she remained paralyzed from the waist down.

In July 2010, Arlen returned to swimming with the encouragement of her fellow triplets, both brothers. She excelled. She did so well that she sought to qualify for the 2012 London Paralympic Games. She did qualify—but the Paralympics Classification Committee ruled her ineligible on the eve of the competition.

Under the Paralympic classification system in place for the London Olympics (and since), swimmers are grouped into forty-one categories. There are ten categories of physical impairment for all swimming events except the breaststroke, which has nine categories. There are also three categories of visual impairment and one for intellectual impairment. The Paralympics explain that "this, to a certain extent, is similar to grouping athletes by age, gender, or weight."[35] For instance, sprinters are classified into male and female categories, wrestlers and boxers are classified by weight, and senior competitions are organized by age.

Such a complex system of classification is bound to result in controversies over categorization. Arlen's case in 2012 was one such controversy. She was ruled ineligible to compete under any of the forty-one categories. The issue in her case was the fact that the nature of her medical condition is such that she could recover in the future. The Paralympic rules require that an athlete's disability be permanent. Because Arlen's paralysis is not necessarily permanent, and because on the eve of the 2012 Olympics there was a possibility that she might yet walk again and even fully recover, she was ruled ineligible.

After an outcry, Arlen was granted a temporary reprieve for the Paralympics and was able to compete, but under the condition that her eligibility would be reviewed within a year.[36] In London, she won a gold medal and three silvers in freestyle events. Upon returning home to New Hampshire, she was greeted with a celebratory parade. She threw out the first pitch at a Boston Red Sox game.[37] She was a hero.

But just one year later, her Paralympic career ended when the International Paralympic Committee (IPC) ruled again that she was ineligible to participate, and this time the ruling stuck. Peter Van de Vliet, the medical and scientific director of the IPC classification committee, explained the uniqueness of Arlen's case: "If you're classifying an amputee, either they've got a leg or they haven't, and in 12 months, they still won't have a leg." In this case, "According to the rules, athletes have to provide evidence of permanent impairment to compete in the Paralympics, and we do not have satisfactory confirmation of that."[38]

The ruling proved controversial. The New Hampshire governor and two US senators expressed their displeasure to the IPC. One of Arlen's parents called the decision "cruel and heartbreaking." But the Paralympics stood firm in enforcing its rules. Van de Vliet explained: "There's no question that she's a great athlete, and no question that she's not faking. But not every illness constitutes an entry into the Paralympics. And every sport has its rules, and we were provided with medical evidence that does not conform to the diagnosis of a permanent impairment."[39] In late 2015, Arlen joined ESPN as a reporter, her career as a professional athlete apparently over.[40]

The vexing, and some would say impossibly difficult, decisions made in the Paralympics are bound to become more common outside the Paralympics as well: technology is blurring the distinction between abled and disabled. The issue of "permanent disability" is sure to become problematic. What happens, for instance, if technology allows the visually impaired to regain or improve their sight? What happens if science results in the paralyzed regaining lost capabilities? The line between repair and improvement is sure to become more blurred, as will the difference between the prosthetic and the human. The challenges presented by enhanced athletes will pose further challenges for athletics organizations of the twenty-first century.

How Technology Makes Enforcing the Rules Easier and Harder

Not just athletes are changed by technology; the games are too. For years, the international soccer community has debated the introduction of "goal line technology" to help officials determine if a ball crosses the goal line. In soccer, such decisions can determine the outcome of a match.

Similar technologies are common in tennis and cricket (the Hawk-Eye system), and the use of video replay has expanded to many college and professional sports. Part of the application of technology to refereeing games is about reducing the uncertainty in judgments, but another part is about legitimacy; that is, the general acceptance of referee judgments and the overall integrity of competition. Technology, it turns out, presents challenges to legitimacy and the key to preserving legitimacy. Let me explain.

In general, people—especially the sports-viewing public—understand uncertainties just fine. Studies of public understanding of probabilities related to weather forecasts indicate that, when it comes to the weather, the public actually has an appreciation for probabilistic information, even when the information is provided with no mention of the possibility that the forecast might be wrong. It turns out that we each have enough experience with weather forecasts to be able to develop a sense of their accuracy.

Such research on the public understanding of science suggests that we should be cautious about assuming how the public might react to information in other contexts as well.[41] Now let's apply this thinking to sports. Consider that most sports broadcasts are accompanied by a wealth of statistical information, some of which is very sophisticated. The role of technology-assisted refereeing in sports is primarily about legitimacy—the better that referees understand what just happened on the field of play, the more likely they are to make the right calls, which in turn means that the players and the fans are more likely to regard the outcome of a competition as fair, and a system that delivers fair outcomes is more likely to be regarded by athletes and fans as legitimate.[42]

Consider two shots on goal in the World Cup that occurred forty-four years apart. In the 1966 World Cup final, England was awarded a goal in extra time against West Germany when the ball may or may not have crossed the goal line after ricocheting straight down off the crossbar.[43] Video evidence remains inconclusive (though one analysis conducted thirty years later by engineers at Oxford University found that the ball was six centimeters short of fully crossing the line).[44] Nonetheless, the goal was given and became part of football lore. Uncertainty still lingers over whether the ball actually crossed the goal line, and a half century later, some Germany supporters still feel wronged.

In contrast, the persistence of uncertainty today is often not possible. In the 2010 World Cup, England's Frank Lampard had an obvious goal disallowed, also against Germany, this time in the quarterfinals. Like its doppelganger generations before, Lampard's shot ricocheted downward off the cross bar. In this case, however, the ball undoubtedly crossed the goal line, according to the video replays. Although Germans with long memories called it payback for 1966, the English felt aggrieved, and most neutral observers found the incident problematic: one of the most important events to occur on the pitch was missed by the officials but seen clearly by millions around the world. There was no hiding behind fuzzy black-and-white television imagery. The wrong decision was there for everyone to see.

It is this difference between what the referee can detect on the pitch and what television viewers can see at home—with ultra-slow-motion replays in high definition—that has led to the introduction of technological aids to assist referees. Equipped with this high-tech assistance, human referees are now faced with about the same level of uncertainty that remote spectators (the fans watching their TVs) must deal with. Referees' uncertainty has been realigned with spectators' uncertainty.

But sports have stopped short of trying to reduce uncertainty in every decision that referees make. It's just not practical or affordable—or perhaps even necessary from a legitimacy standpoint—to do so. In soccer, goal-line technologies are used to detect whether balls cross the goal line, not to detect whether balls go out of bounds or who should have subsequent possession. In tennis, the Hawk-Eye system is used sparingly, with players granted a limited number of challenges to deploy it in a match. In professional cricket and basketball, video replay as an officiating aid is also limited to certain situations.

With the introduction of technology, uncertainty does not go away. During the 2013 French Open, Ukrainian tennis player Sergiy Stakhovsky received much attention (and a fine from officials) for taking a picture of a ball mark on the clay with his iPhone and then tweeting it to document a dispute over a ball that was ruled out.[45] When Stakhovsky had done the same thing in Munich a few weeks earlier, several of his colleagues on the professional tennis tour tweeted back to dispute his complaint. The introduction of technology has not eliminated line call disputes, and social media has created new challenges for officials. One can only guess what John McEnroe, the famously controversial and colorful tennis star of the 1970s and 1980s, might have done with an iPhone and a Twitter account.

However, technology can create incentives that help human referees perform better. A 2011 study by David Hamermesh and colleagues in the *American Economic Review* looked at more than 3.5 million pitches in Major League Baseball games from 2004 to 2008 to assess whether umpires displayed biases in how they ruled balls and strikes.[46] The study found a small but significant bias in how umpires ruled depending on whether the umpire's "race" was the same or different than the pitcher or batter. When the umpire was being evaluated by a computerized system (or performed before an exceptionally large crowd or in an important game), however, the bias went away. The presence of the technology helped umpires overcome potential biases when they knew that they would be evaluated objectively.

Technology also creates new problems. In February 2016, Colorado State University was hosting Boise State in basketball. The teams had played a close game that went to overtime. With 0.8 seconds left, Boise State had the ball in its half with the score tied at 84. Boise State inbounded the ball to James Webb III, who took two quick steps and, before the buzzer, launched a one-handed shot as he was falling out of bounds. Miraculously, the ball went in. Boise State won, right?

Nope. The referees believed that the game clock had not started on time, so they went to the video replay. The video replay technology allowed the referees to compare when the clock started, when it should have started, and how long it took for Webb to get the shot off. The referees determined, based on the video replay, that Webb took about 1.2 seconds to get his shot off, more than the 0.8 seconds remaining. The shot was waved off, and the game went into a second overtime, from which CSU emerged victorious.

It did not take long for TV viewers and reporters to perform their own timing of the final play to discover that Webb's shot was launched in only 0.6 seconds, not the 1.2 seconds claimed by the referees. What had happened? The software used by the replay technology had a bug—it counted the elapsed time twice as fast as what really occurred. The Mountain West Conference, in which both teams played, issued a statement explaining that Boise State should have won the game. Under NCAA rules, protests of such mistakes are not allowed, so Colorado State kept the victory. The conference announced that changes would be made to the rules governing the use of video replays and the episode would be used as a future teaching tool.[47] Technology doesn't necessarily get rid of uncertainty—it may just move it from one setting to another.

The improved alignment of refereeing decisions and what the public observes on television through the introduction of technology is to be applauded. When such decisions fall out of alignment— whether less or more precise than what the public demands—sport faces a legitimacy crisis that then necessitates innovation.

For instance, sometimes we look to technology to do the impossible. The struggles that the NFL has faced in defining a "catch" illustrate this point. Here is an experiment that you can try right now. Pick up a ball (or any tossable object). Throw the ball to your nearest companion and ask him or her to catch it. Now answer this: Did he or she catch your throw? I bet that neither one of you will have any difficulty answering either yes or no. Understanding the catching of a ball doesn't require nuance, subtlety, or litigious interpretation. That used to be the case in the NFL. But not anymore.

As recently as 1996, the NFL needed only 109 words to define what it meant to "catch" a football.* This is the number of words that appear in the prior paragraph. By 2015, the NFL definition of a "catch" had swollen to almost 600 words,† and the definition of a catch had become an endless point of controversy among fans, players, officials, and the media.

Defining a catch became difficult after the introduction of high-definition slow-motion instant replay. Today's television technology allows viewers to have a far better look at the act of catching a ball than referees could ever hope for on the field. Using instant replay can help referees have the same view as everyone else, but it also forces the NFL to define more precisely what a catch actually is. It was clever when the folksy TV commentator and former coach John Madden used to explain that a player getting one knee down in-bounds while making a catch was equivalent to having two feet come down in bounds. Madden wasn't invoking any real rule, just helping the viewer to make sense of referee judgments. High-definition TV and instant replay has consigned folksy interpretations of the rules to the era of vacuum tubes and low-definition broadcasts.

Today, referees need to be able to address what happens when the player bobbles the ball, or the ball touches the ground while it is being firmly held, or when the ball is jarred loose and hits the ground just after a player crosses the goal line for a touchdown. Ev-

---

* Specifically, rules 7 and 8 under "Passing Guidelines" in the 1996 NFL Rulebook, accessed here: https://web.archive.org/web/19961223132153/http://www.nfl. com/fans/rules/pass.html.

† Specifically, rule 8, sections 2 and 3, in the 2015 NFL Rulebook, accessed here: http://operations.nfl.com/the-rules/2015-nfl-rulebook/#rule8.

eryone watching can see when these things occur, often in excruciating detail. Then the definition of a "catch" gets tough. The act of catching a ball is not, it turns out, a discrete event like a ball crossing a goal line. Whatever a catch is, it is ultimately a judgment made by a referee. Judging if a ball was caught or not is more like judging if pass interference occurred ("pass interference" is called when the defender makes prohibited contact with a would-be receiver while a pass is in the air) than it is like determining if a ball crossed a goal line. The closer we look at the making of a catch, the more contingencies we see, which has led to more considerations being identified that referees must be aware of. Hence, the word count in NFL rules for what it means to catch a ball has increased by 600 percent.

The best way for the NFL to deal with challenges over the definition of catching the ball is to accept that it can't be precisely defined. The NFL should simply go back to letting referees decide if a ball was caught or not, based on the sort of general guidance provided in the old 109-word definition. Such an approach is not all that radical, as the NFL routinely determines that some decisions are not reviewable, such as whether a field goal that passes over the upright is good or not.[48] In that case, technology could certainly be used, but a decision has been made not to go there. And football has survived. Using technology in sport in a smart way means giving up the idea that its use can eliminate uncertainty—and that means that sometimes it is better to figure out how to live with uncertainties rather than try to completely eliminate them.

Let's consider one more example that illustrates this last point. In baseball, pitches are judged to be strikes or balls by a human umpire. In 2015, FiveThirtyEight, a website owned by ESPN, published an evaluation of umpire accuracy in MLB. It found that the average MLB umpire is 86 percent accurate in judging balls and strikes.[49] In a game that involves 280 pitches (for both teams), the umpire might make 40 mistakes. That is a lot of mistakes.

The technology exists to standardize the calling of balls and strikes in baseball,[50] and the technology has been tested in the minor leagues. There are arguments for and against adopting the technology. An argument for adopting it is that it would standardize the definition and the strike zone and apply the standard impartially to each player.[51] However, some observers argue that umpires and their judgment are a key part of the game.[52] Wherever you come out on this issue, at its core is the notion of uncertainty and judgment. Is umpire error (14 percent on average) part of the game of baseball? Or is umpire error something to be reduced and, ideally, eliminated? In 2003, Arizona Diamondbacks pitcher Curt Schilling answered this question by taking a baseball bat to one of the cameras of an early computerized pitch-calling system.[53] Your answer to this question gets to the core of what you think baseball is as a sport and the role that technology has in it.

Put me down on the side of keeping the imperfect umpires in place. Why? I can think of at least three reasons. First, for better or worse, human umpires are part of the tradition of baseball. Even if computers are more accurate, deploying them completely changes that tradition, which is an important norm of the sport. Second, umpire uncertainty is also essential to the game of baseball. Remove the umps and you have a different game. Finally, if baseball is, as Pittsburgh Pirate first baseman Willie Stargell once said, "a reflection of life," then uncertainty in the application of the rules deserves a prominent place in the game.

Technology and the "Purity" of Sport

Technology has long been a source of angst because it forces us to contemplate change. Change can be good and change can be not-so-good. For those who view sport in terms of an ideal of purity, change resulting from technology is a threat. The director of development for the IAAF, Elio Locatelli, said of Oscar Pistorious: "With all due respect, we cannot accept something that provides advantages. It affects the purity of sport."[54] However, the definition of "something that provides advantages" is not clear. Matt Albuquerque, the founder of a prosthetics company, says that concern over purity masks a fear of losing a competitive advantage: "I've seen it. Able-bodied people do fear this advantage on the part of the amputee. They fear that you aren't just 'normal' again, you're better than human."[55]

In 2008, Silvia Camporesi, an ethicist at King's College London, observed: "It is plausible to think that in 50 years, or maybe less, the 'natural' able-bodied athletes will just appear anachronistic." She continued: "As our concept of what is 'natural' depends on what we are used to, and evolves with our society and culture, so does our concept of 'purity' of sport."[56] Chris Cooper, an expert in the science of athletic performance at the University of Essex in the United Kingdom, suggests that genetic profiling may soon allow us to identify "specific genetic adaptations that improve sporting performance." If so, Cooper asks, as do Paralympics officials, "Will there be different classes [of competition] dependent on different sequences of key molecules in the body?" Cooper says that he once would have considered this "a fantasy" but "now I am not so sure."[57]

Both athletes and sport will continue to be transformed by technology. Such transformations will create both opportunity and demand for change. Thanks technology. Thanks a lot. Sport will have to confront change, whether participants like it or not. What sort of medical enhancements should be allowed? Where is the boundary between the Olympics and the Paralympics? Is there even a boundary? What does it mean to catch a football? Should umpires be replaced by robots?

The bodies that oversee sport don't yet have answers to these questions, as they are just starting to be asked. But they had better start addressing them soon. Like other difficult questions that we have encountered thus far, the best answers—better thought of as temporary resolutions—will come from a commitment to transparency, openness, discussion, and debate. What is sport? It's what we make it. And technology guarantees that we will be constantly remaking sport as innovation proceeds.

Chapter 8

When Mother Nature Cheats

"Can someone be a girl for 17 years and 11 months and suddenly become a boy in the 18th year?" This question was asked by Saraswati Chand, older sister of Dutee Chand, an incredibly talented young Indian sprinter.[1] In June 2014, Chand helped India achieve its only two gold medals at the Sixteenth Asian Junior Athletics Championships. She won the 100-meter sprint and anchored the 4x400-meter relay.[2] It was a proud moment for Chand and for India.

But that moment did not last very long. One month later, Chand was contacted by the Sports Authority of India (SAI), a governmental body, and told that she would not be selected to represent the nation at the upcoming Commonwealth Games in Glasgow, Scotland.[3] The authorities told Chand that she had failed a medical test; specifically, the test indicated that she had a testosterone level in excess of that allowed by the international federation that oversees track and field, the IAAF. According to the *Indian Express*, "After her Taipei gold, whispers of her 'masculine build' had grown stronger and the Athletics Federation of India (AFI) had asked the SAI to test her for excess androgen."[4] Chand failed the test and was suspended from international competition.

This chapter is about the long history of sex testing in sport. Dutee Chand is one of many athletes to have questions raised about their eligibility to participate in women's sporting events. This chapter focuses on track and field, but similar issues arise across sports. The IAAF created separate competitions for men and women in 1928.[5] Almost a century later, the IAAF and the International Olympic Committee continue to struggle with determining which individuals are eligible to participate in women's events.

After being suspended, Chand took her case to the Court of Arbitration for Sport, the Swiss-based organization that settles disputes within international sport. CAS ruled in her favor in July 2015 and suspended the IAAF testosterone policy for two years. That ruling was just the latest development in efforts by sports officials to figure out a scientifically valid and procedurally fair way to determine an athlete's eligibility to compete as a man or a woman in elite sports. After more than fifty years of IAAF missteps in trying to implement policies that were variously deeply flawed and well meaning, Chand's appeal provided a chance to get the male/female eligibility question right.

We often look to science to provide clear-cut answers to difficult questions. In this case, the question was, who is a female for purposes of elite athletic competition? Unfortunately, however, science is pluralistic and the world is complicated. CAS discovered this quickly, explaining in its expert judgment that, "The expert witnesses each relied on different published papers to support his or her view" and "no single study has established, to an appropriate level of certainty, a scientific basis to come to a definitive conclusion one way or the other."[6]

Yet, the court agreed that testosterone could, potentially, be used for purposes of eligibility. The problem is that many other physical characteristics could also be used, as we will see, such as chromosomal makeup, the presence of reproductive organs, and even height; each of these markers is problematic, because it does not always succeed as an indicator of who is a woman. Testosterone, it turns out, is similarly problematic. In addition, the court found that high testosterone in a female does not necessarily offer performance benefits so large as to justify creating "a new category of ineligible female athletes within the female category" and that the use of this benchmark is thus "discriminatory."

Thus, as the court put it, the IAAF found itself "in the invidious position of having to reconcile the existence of a binary male/female system of athletics categorization with the biological reality that sex in humans is a continuum with no clear or singular boundary between men and women." The court will reinstate the testosterone rule only if the IAAF can prove that women with high testosterone benefit from a performance advantage so significant that they should be excluded from competing against other women.

With the testosterone rule on the ropes, a new eligibility policy is needed. What should it be? To answer this question, we'll look at the history of sex testing in sport, tackling the question of whether Mother Nature can break the rules by producing biological females unfit to compete in sports. The debate has relevance beyond sport and touches on how we think about sex, gender, and equality in broader global society, where there is anything but agreement on these sensitive issues.

Inequality on the Track and in the Board Room

The birth of the modern Olympic movement in the 1890s led by Pierre de Coubertin was accompanied by open opposition to female participation in the games. Coubertin explained that in the Olympics, "women have but one task, that of crowning the winner with garlands."[7] Such views have changed over time, with hard fought battles for greater equality gradually winning ground despite the sometimes fierce opposition of administrators, fans, and even athletes. However, in the context of setting policies to determine eligibility for participation in women's sporting events, such perspectives still exert considerable influence in the twenty-first century.

As one might expect, given the views expressed during the early modern Olympic era by Olympics officials, women's participation in the Summer Olympics early in the last century was quite low, at about 2 percent of all participants through 1924, the last games under Coubertin's leadership of the IOC. Women first participated in the Winter Games in 1924. In 2007, the Olympic charter recognized the goal "to encourage and support the promotion of women in sport at all levels and in all structures, with a view to implementing the principle of equality of men and women."[8] By the London Games of 2012, women made up about 44 percent of participants in 46 percent of all events. In the Sochi Winter Games of 2014, women were 40 percent of total athletes, and women's events represented 50 percent of the total competitions.[9]

Participation rates in athletic events do not tell the whole story of gender equality, however. The IOC notes that beyond the statistics of participation, "gender equality is a critical component of effective sports administration."[10] The Olympic movement comprises the IOC as well as hundreds of international and national sports federations covering forty-one summer and fifteen winter sports. A 2013 survey of 1,550 people in leadership positions in international sports bodies found that only 13 percent were women; fourteen of the fifty-six executive committees included no women at all.[11] As participation in the games has become more equal, the governance of those games has remained decidedly unequal.

Sports organizations have so far fallen well short of achieving the goal of gender equality expressed in the Olympic charter and the policies put into place to determine eligibility for participation in women's athletic events.

Science has taught us that biological sex does not divide into two neat categories, but instead is highly complex and is not determined by any single characteristic or even a single combination of characteristics. This fact presents problems for sex testing in sport. According to the World Health Organization, "gender" is "typically described in terms of masculinity and femininity, [and] is a social construction that varies across different cultures and over time."[12] The IAAF and IOC have looked to science to settle disputes over sex and gender, both of which are complex and imprecise categories that do not always correlate with one another in a neat manner.

I use the phrase "sex testing" here to refer to the current IAAF and IOC policies for determining eligibility to participate in women's athletic events. I recognize that other phrases are sometimes preferred (such as "gender verification," "gender testing," "femininity testing," "hyperandrogenism policy," and "testosterone policy").[13] The phrase "sex testing" should perhaps *always* appear in scare quotes, so as to draw attention to a wicked problem: sports organizations seek to apply scientific criteria based on biology to determine eligibility to participate in women's athletic events (hence, sex testing), but this approach is doomed to fail because sex is not binary, nor is sex the same thing as gender (hence the scare quotes, "sex testing").

Sex Testing Policies and Recent Controversies

The IAAF policy that Dutee Chand was suspended under is titled "Eligibility of Females with Hyperandrogenism to Compete in Women's Competition"; it is not formally a gender test, because it makes no determination of gender.[14] What it does determine is whether a female has a level of naturally occurring testosterone in her system that, under the terms of the policy, would prohibit her participation in women's events. As a practical matter, the policy determines who is and who is not a "woman" as defined in the context of athletic competition. Athletics are divided into women's and men's categories, not "low T" and "high T" categories.* From the perspective of sport, those who are eligible to participate in women's events are identified as women, and all others are men. There is no other category of competition, and it does not appear that there will be anytime soon.

The IAAF testosterone policy, and the IOC policy that followed in its footsteps, was the result of a prolonged dispute over the eligibility of another sprinter to compete in women's events. In 2009, South African sprinter Caster Semenya burst on the international scene at the World Track and Field Championships in Berlin. The eighteen-year-old was participating in her first major international race, and she dominated the field in the 800 meters, taking the gold medal by beating the second place finisher by 2.45 seconds.†

Immediately, questions about gender verification based on Semenya's appearance were raised by competitors in the race. Elisa Cusma of Italy, who finished sixth in the race, complained to the Italian me-

---

* But as the previous chapter suggests, we could, if we so desire, create competitions of Low T vs. High T individuals. Sport is, after all, what we make it.

† See IAAF, "Regulations Governing Eligibility of Females with Hyperandrogenism." Semenya's winning time in Berlin was 2 seconds off of a world record time. See Cheryl Cooky, Ranissa Dycuss, and Shari L. Dworkin, "'What Makes a Woman a Woman' versus 'Our First Lady of Sport': A Comparative Analysis of the United States and the South African Media Coverage of Caster Semenya," *Journal of Sport and Social Issues* 37 (2013): 31–56.

dia: "These kind of people should not run with us. For me, she's not a woman. She's a man."[15] The fifth-place finisher, Russia's Mariya Savinova, said: "Just look at her."* Later, in an article about Semenya in the *New Yorker*, Ariel Levy explained what people saw when they looked at her: "Semenya is breathtakingly butch. Her torso is like the chest plate on a suit of armor. She has a strong jawline, and a build that slides straight from her ribs to her hips."[16]

The response by the IAAF to the challenges to Semenya's eligibility caused the organization embarrassment. Such challenges to eligibility were supposed to be handled confidentially, but the IAAF confirmed the investigation into Semenya's eligibility immedi-

Caster Semenya at the 2011 Bislett Games.

ately after the race.[17] A few months later, the results of the IAAF investigation were leaked to the press. The *Daily Telegraph* (Australia) reported that Semenya had been raised as a girl and that she had external female genitalia and internal male testes.[18] The leaked report prompted reactions across the world, with Semenya becoming an international media sensation.

----

*   In late 2014, Savinova was accused of participating in systematic doping in a German television series, prompting a major investigation. See Uwe-Jens Lindner, "ARD Documentation Covers Doping and Cover-Up Apparatus in Russia to Grab Active Athletes, Coaches and Insiders," Pressportal.de, March 12, 2014, http://www.presseportal.de/meldung/2896900/t. The *New York Times* called her the "face of Russia's doping scandal." See Colleen Curry, "The Face of Russia's Doping Scandal: Mariya Savinova," *New York Times*, November 10, 2015, http://nytlive.nytimes.com/womenintheworld/2015/11/10/the-face-of-russias-doping-scandal-mariya-savinova/.

Almost a year later, in June, 2010, the IAAF announced publicly the results of its investigation and concluded that Semenya was eligible to "compete with immediate effect."[19] But the damage had been done. Semenya, who had undergone a year of public scrutiny and uncertainty, said, "I have been subjected to unwarranted and invasive scrutiny of the most intimate and private details of my being."[20] The IAAF did not fare well either, as the organization appeared inept at handling the controversy.

Immediately after the Semenya controversy broke, in December 2009, an IAAF committee started meeting to develop a new policy for determining eligibility for participating in women's athletic events.[21] The new policy was released in May 2011. The focus of the policy was hyperandrogenism, which, according to the IAAF, is "a term used to describe the excessive production of androgenic hormones in females. The androgenic hormone of specific interest for the purposes of the new Regulations is the performance enhancing hormone, testosterone." Hyperandrogenism (HA) deserves regulation, according to the IAAF, because the condition "proved to be controversial since the individuals concerned often display masculine traits and have an uncommon athletic capacity in relation to their fellow female competitors."[22]

Under the new policy, a female would be eligible to participate in IAAF women's events if she were recognized in law as a female and compliant with the new IAAF regulations. Specifically, the IAAF regulations state that "no female with HA shall be eligible to compete in a women's competition if she has functional androgen levels (testosterone) that are in the male range." The IAAF abandoned all mention of "gender verification" or "gender policy." The new policy established a new class of individuals in the sporting world: women who are prohibited from competing in athletic competition. From the standpoint of women's events, these individuals would not qualify as women.

In regard to being judged to be in violation of the IAAF hyperandrogenism policy, the IAAF explains that "these conditions may necessitate the athlete undergoing treatment by her personal physician to normalize her androgen levels."[23] Caster Semenya reportedly underwent treatment of some sort, during her year of uncertain standing in 2009 to 2010.[24] According to the *Toronto Star*, to secure continuing eligibility, Semenya "must have surgery or receive hormone therapy prescribed by an expert IAAF medical panel and submit to regular monitoring."[25] When asked about the treatment, Semenya replied, "I can't really say anything." At the 2012 London Games, Semenya carried the flag for South Africa in the opening ceremonies, and she went home with a silver medal in the 800 meters, 1.8 seconds slower than she had run in Berlin.[26] In 2016, Semenya qualified for the Rio Olympics, running some of the fastest times of the year.[27]

Like Semenya, India's Dutee Chand was found to be in violation of the IAAF's hyperandrogenism policy. She was told that to regain eligibility she could have surgery or start a hormone regime to "normalize" her testosterone levels.[28] Chand chose a different path. She filed an appeal against the IAAF policy with CAS, seeking to have the AFI "decision [to ban her] overturned and the hyperandrogenism regulations declared invalid and void." Chand's subsequent victory in that arbitration is what has left the IAAF in need of a new approach.

Fraud and Fairness:
Failed Efforts to Tame the Wicked Problem

The need for a policy to determine eligibility for participation in women's sporting events results from two frequently expressed concerns. One is about fraud, specifically the fear that men will seek to impersonate women athletes in pursuit of athletic successes. From this perspective, regulation is needed to keep men out of women's athletics. The second is concern about fairness among female competitors, based on a belief that certain naturally occurring physical characteristics offer an unfair advantage to certain women. From this perspective, regulation is needed to keep superwomen out of women's athletics.

A close look at both these concerns finds them to be unfounded: neither men nor superwomen pose a threat to women's athletics. To the contrary, sex testing regulations violate human dignity and are contrary to the expressed values of the IOC and IAAF. But I'm getting ahead of myself. Let's take a closer look at the notions of fraud and fairness as the basis for sex testing in sport.

Fraud

There are no examples of a man posing as a woman in elite athletics in at least the past fifty years and probably longer.[*] Yet, urban myths have developed surrounding the role of sex testing in preventing such fraud from occurring.[29] Gender fraud in sport is a very good example of what Ole Bjorn Rekdal calls an "academic urban legend"—a falsehood repeated so often by academics (and others) that it comes to be accepted as true.[30] Vanessa Heggie, a historian, argues that a "mythology of gender fraud" was created coincident with the Cold War and the success of Eastern Bloc female athletes in international competitions. In 1952, the *Washington Post* noted that some of these athletes had distinctively masculine characteristics, at least by contemporary Western standards, and that save for these women, the medal tally "wouldn't even have been close between Russia and the USA save for the almost complete dominance of the Russian women in the heftier field events and the gymnastics. . . . In the non-bicep division, though, in the more graceful swimming and diving events where feminine form counts more than feminine muscle, the American girls were all-conquering. Each to her liking, perhaps."[31]

Forms of gender verification existed before the Cold War, but as a consequence of concerns about masculine-looking women from the Eastern Bloc, formal sex testing was introduced in the 1960s by sporting organizations; nations no longer trusted each other to regulate their own athletes.[32] According to Heggie, female athletes had to undergo nude visual inspections in 1966 at the European Athletics Championships and the following year at the Pan-American

---

[*]   There are, however, examples of women posing as men in order to participate in sport. For instance, Kathrine Switzer entered the 1967 Boston Marathon (then closed to women) by using her initials on the application form. She ran the race and was physically attacked on the course by one of the race organizers; see Kathrine Switzer, "The Girl Who Started It All," *Runner's World*, May 2007, http://kathrineswitzer.com/site/wp-content/uploads/SwitzerStory_RunnersWorld.pdf.

Games in Winnipeg. Such inspections came to be known as "naked parades."

In 1967, the IOC tried to be more scientific with the use of a "buccal smear" consisting of a swab taken from inside the cheek.[33] The swab allowed medical experts to perform a Barr body test intended to identify the presence of multiple X chromosomes and thus, in theory, provide an objective basis for distinguishing women and men. Most women have an XX chromosome pair, and most men have an XY pair.[34] The test was applied through the 1970s and 1980s. But scientists discovered that biological sex is more complicated than can be indicated by the Barr body test. Writing in the British medical journal *The Lancet*, two doctors explained that the test was abandoned as unreliable because it falsely identified as men certain women with various genetic make-ups and falsely identified as women certain men with a different set of genetic combinations.[35]

In 1990, the IAAF convened a set of experts to develop new and improved procedures for distinguishing female from male. The result was a more sophisticated and comprehensive set of tests. The new tests were used in the 1996 Summer Olympics in Atlanta, where 8 of 3,387 female athletes failed them, although all were allowed to compete as women.[36] The IOC abandoned the use of genetic tests in 1999, before the 2000 Sydney Summer Games, in favor of a "suspicion-based" approach, which set the stage for the controversy over Caster Semenya at the end of the decade.[37]

Although the history of sex testing in athletics includes concern about fraud, the evidence shows little basis for such concerns. Today, concern over fraud as a problem that needs to be addressed has taken a backseat to concerns over fairness.

Fairness

The notion of sex testing as a means to ensure fairness among women in competition also has a long history. Writing in 1974, Eduardo Hay of the IOC Medical Commission provided a window into the thinking behind the policies of that era: "Today the purpose of the femininity tests carried out on women athletes taking part in the Olympic Games is to make sure that all female athletes compete under identical anatomical conditions."[38] In 2011, the IOC announced the purpose of its new policy in substantially similar language, explaining that the purpose was to "guarantee the fairness and integrity of female competitions for all female athletes."[39]

But are genetic differences an issue of fairness in athletics? There are certain genetic or, more generally, biological traits that give some individuals an advantage over others in the games that we play. For example, tall individuals have some advantages in basketball. In general, such biological differences and anomalies are celebrated when they result in competitive advantages. Consider the following three examples.

- *Marfan syndrome.* Flo Hyman was a US volleyball star who stood 6 feet 5 inches (196 cm tall). On her death in 1986, it was discovered that she had a genetic condition called Marfan syndrome, which is characterized by tallness and by heart problems. Hyman's sporting career was celebrated, despite the advantages that she gained from her unique genetic condition.[40] Athletes are warned about the health effects of Marfan syndrome, but no sporting body has regulations against participants with the condition.* As a genetic condition, Marfan syndrome has not been deemed by sporting bodies to offer an unfair advantage and is not regulated as a matter of fairness.

- *Acromegaly, or gigantism.* Gheorghe Mureşan, who played basketball for Romania and in the NBA, stands 7 feet 7 inches (231 cm) tall. He, as well as a number of basketball players in the United States and internationally, has a condition that leads to growing to an unusual size. Called "gigantism" in youths and "acromegaly" in adults, it results from the overproduction of growth hormone in the pituitary gland, typically as a result of a tumor. The condition can cause severe health problems. Human growth hormone is considered a

---

* In 2014, University of Baylor basketball star player Isiah Austin withdrew from the NBA draft and retired from basketball upon learning that he had Marfan syndrome; see "Isaiah Austin Has Marfan Syndrome," ESPN.go.com, June 23, 2014, http://espn. go.com/nba/draft2014/story/_/id/11119553/former-baylor-star-isaiah-austin-career-ending-medical-condition.

form of doping when introduced into the body by other than natural means. But when found in excess as a natural condition, it is not regulated as providing an unfair advantage to athletes.

- *Hereditary polycythemia.* Eero Antero Mäntyranta was a Finnish cross-country skier who had hereditary polycythemia, a condition that enabled his body to produce more red blood cells than is typical.[41] As a consequence, he derived endurance benefits because his body produced extra erythropoietin (EPO). As discussed in chapter 5, synthetic EPO is the substance that cyclists, in particular, have used for doping purposes to gain an unfair competitive advantage. Even though Mäntyranta had a rare genetic condition that gave him benefits over others, his athletic career was celebrated. Hereditary polycythemia is not regulated by any sporting body as a matter of fairness, despite the advantages that it may convey.

Unique genetic or biological conditions are not, in themselves, problematic in sport competition as a matter of fairness even when they give one athlete an advantage over others. Further, athletes with natural conditions that provide benefits are not barred or penalized, even if those same conditions are impermissible if attained through doping. The same goes for testosterone, the subject of the IOC and IAAF sex testing policies.

Consequently, rather than remedying an unfairness, the IAAF and IOC policies are manifestly unfair, according to Shawn Crincoli, a law professor at Touro College in New York, because the policies regulate testosterone levels in women but not in men. Crincoli argues that "the new rules treat men and women differently from one another without demonstrating an acceptable rationale supporting the regulation of androgens in women, but not men. This unequal treatment is the hallmark of discrimination based on sex."[42] Men who produce higher levels of testosterone than other men are not judged to have an unfair advantage requiring regulation.[43] Cases of biological or genetic differentiation among athletes and the differential treatment of men and women with rare levels of testosterone suggest that the issue of fairness is not the whole story behind these regulations.

Embracing the Wicked Problem: Science, Sex, and Gender

In difficult social or political contexts, we often hope that science will forge a path to decision making that sidesteps the messiness of culture, values, and politics.[44] If only scientists could identify the specific biological factors or the factors that clearly distinguish male from female, then the issue of sex testing in athletics would be easy to resolve in an objective manner via the application of objective criteria. These delineating factors have been the Holy Grail of sex testing since the 1960s. Like the Holy Grail, they have not yet been found.

Looking ahead, we should not expect science to identify unique biological factors that cleanly distinguish male from female. The World Health Organization explains some of the complexities:

> Humans are born with 46 chromosomes in 23 pairs. The X and Y chromosomes determine a person's sex. Most women are 46XX and most men are 46XY. Research suggests, however, that in a few births per thousand, some individuals will be born with a single sex chromosome (45X or 45Y) (sex monosomies) and some will be born with three or more sex chromosomes (47XXX, 47XYY or 47XXY, etc.—sex polysomies). In addition, some males are born 46XX due to the translocation of a tiny section of the sex-determining region of the Y chromosome. Similarly, some females are also born 46XY due to mutations in the Y chromosome. Clearly, there are not only females who are XX and males who are XY, but there is a range of chromosome complements, hormone balances, and phenotypic variations that determine sex.[45]

A vocabulary has developed to describe different variations in biological sex: "disorders of sexual development," "differences of sexual development," "intersex," and so on.[46] Whatever term one prefers, the key point to comprehend is that scientific understandings of biological sex do not support a binary view of male and female, but a far more nuanced perspective.

This complexity seems to have been accepted by the IAAF committee, which developed a hyperandrogenism policy in 2011, declaring that "we must find ways to take into account that sex is not neatly divided into only two categories in the real world."[47] However, the policy recommended by the IAAF and IOC seeks to use a scientific threshold of testosterone concentrations as the basis for creating exactly such a neat divide between male and female insofar as sporting competition is concerned.

When justifying the focus on testosterone, both the IOC and the IAAF present the science of sex in binary fashion. According to the IOC: "The androgenic effects on the human body explain why men perform better than women in most sports and are, in fact, the very reason for the distinction between male and female competition in most sports."[48] The IAAF voices a similar view: "Men typically achieve better performances in sport because they benefit from higher levels of androgens than women and this is predominantly why, for reasons of fairness, competition in Athletics is divided into separate men's and women's classifications."[49] Both the science and the history presented by the IOC and IAAF are highly questionable.

Let's start with the science. First, testosterone is not a control knob for athletic performance: the "benefit" of testosterone level to any individual athlete is unclear. Katrina Karkazis and Rebecca Jordan-Young, two influential scholars who have studied controversies over sex testing in sport, observe that although testosterone "matters" in athletic performance, "you can't use testosterone to predict who is going to do better on any physical feat. You also can't infer that people who do better have more testosterone."[50] The CAS judgment on Dutee Chand expressed a similar view, citing evidence that testosterone has some impact on performance, but pointing out that testosterone has not been shown to be more significant than "nutrition, access to specialist training facilities and coaching, and other genetic and biological variations." Setting aside fairness, scientific research does not support claims to a significant advantage at the individual level. After all, the IAAF and IOC recognize that many women who are androgen insensitive (meaning their bodies do not acknowledge testosterone) excel in women's athletics.

Although there is ongoing debate and research over the effects of testosterone on athletic performance, here I depart from Karkazis and Jordan-Young, who helped Dutee Chand in her case before CAS, and who argue that testosterone has no effect on performance. I will readily grant that it may indeed, as CAS concluded. But whether it does or does not, my view is that testosterone simply does not matter—as a practical matter. Let us suppose for the sake of argument that some women have testosterone levels that are similar to those levels observed in most men. Let us further suppose that this amount of testosterone can be associated with some greater athletic achievement, say speed or strength. The appropriate response is, "So what?"

Imagine the previous paragraph rewritten with "height" substituted for "testosterone." There are notable examples of female athletes with exceptional height, generally attained only by men, who have achieved sporting successes.

Further, challenging the exact role of testosterone in athletic performance gives more legitimacy to the IAAF and IOC policies than they deserve. The practical importance of naturally occurring testosterone in a woman should be no more significant than that of hereditary polycythemia. The role of hormones in athletic performance is a really interesting scientific topic, but it is inherently no more relevant to athletics policy than any other naturally occurring characteristic of the human athlete, man or woman.

Second, testosterone is not a "male hormone," nor is there a natural "male level" exclusive of females, using the phrases of the IAAF. As Karkazis and Jordan-Young explain, "All people produce testosterone, and it is important for body functions and organs well beyond those we think of as masculine, like the heart and liver." Men are typically taller than women, but height is not considered a uniquely male characteristic, nor is tallness in a woman viewed to be an excursion into "maleness." Yet, the IAAF frames as unfair the participation of women who "benefit" from "male levels of testosterone."[51] Characterizing certain levels of testosterone as a "male level" and then applying that criterion is to engage in spectacularly circular reasoning. Imagine if, instead of using testosterone as a yardstick, we defined a "male level of height" and judged all women who exceed that height as benefiting from male levels of height. It sounds ridiculous because it is.

More precisely, to assign a biological measure to a male or female category is to confuse biology with how we think about biology. As Crincoli, the Touro College law professor, observes:

> There is no such thing as a correct biological amount of androgens for a female to be a woman; there is only data that show the statistical distribution of androgens that can be produced by the female body. . . . [A female] athlete cannot produce "excessive" androgens. She can only produce an amount that is a statistical outlier.[52]

We characterize a biological characteristic to be male or female based on what we think it means to be masculine and feminine. Sugar, spice, and everything nice? Feminine. Snips and snails and puppy-dogs' tails? Masculine.

Underlying the entire notion of sex testing in sport is a profound irony. Sex tests do not reveal gender; rather, our perceptions of gender determine how we have tested for biological sex. Such perceptions were clearly in play in 1974, when Eduardo Hay of the IOC Medical Commission justified sex testing of that era in terms of preserving what he saw to be the essence of being female: "Women are fighting against all discrimination, but fortunately still cling to their gifts of beauty, grace and maternity as endowments exclusive to them." His view of women was not in terms of strength, power, and speed, all of which define elite athletics.

Although the science of the role of androgens, testosterone in particular, on athletic performance in males and females remains complex and disputed (as one would expect in cutting-edge science), the argument of the IAAF and IOC is also scientifically suspect.

Testosterone was not isolated until 1927 and was not synthesized until 1935.[53] Androgens were thus largely unknown when international sport was divided into men's and women's categories. Clearly, androgens had nothing to do with the division of sporting events into men's and women's categories. There are multiple reasons why this categorization was made, not least because the early

twentieth century was a period of public advocacy of women's suf-
frage and rights.[54]

The inclusion of women in the Olympics had very little to do
with fairness. The early Olympic movement was openly hostile to
the inclusion of women in elite sport competitions. In 1912, Pierre
de Coubertin—he who thought a woman's place was behind a gar-
land— gravely declared: "The Olympic Games . . . [are] the solemn
and periodic exaltation of male athleticism with internationalism as
a base, loyalty as a means, art for its setting and female applause as
reward."[55] As recently as the 1992 Summer Olympics in Barcelona,
women made up less than 30 percent of the competing athletes.[56] It
wasn't until 2007 that the IOC added text to its charter recognizing
"the principle of equality of men and women."[57]

What about individuals who do not have the typical biological
traits of women? Tough luck, according to the IOC's Hay, who in
1974 explained, "If the Medical Commission of the International
Olympic Committee had wanted to satisfy everybody, we would
undoubtedly, at the present moment, have Olympic Games divided
into chromosomic groups. For it is easily forgotten, at this stage,
that the sole purpose of the Medical Commission in this investigation of femininity, is to ensure the physical equality of the women
athletes competing against each other."[58]

What would happen when a woman was found to have atypi-
cal biological characteristics? She would go away, as Hay explained:
"Once the anomaly is detected, the athlete concerned must with-
draw, but nobody, not even the members of her team, may know
the reason."

Women who were deemed to be feminine enough received an
official document certifying that fact: "Each athlete who has passed
the tests receives a certificate of femininity signed by the President
of the Medical Commission of the International Olympic Committee." Hay's view of "femininity" in Olympic sports was not grounded
in any objective scientific standard. He explained: "The instructions
issued by the IOC to its Medical Commission are exclusively sporting in their aim and in no way seek to open up a scientific discussion
of the matter."[59] In the 1970s, femininity was the sort of thing that

you recognized when you saw it. And in some respects, under the IAAF's 2011 hyperandrogenism policy, it still was.

The 2011 policy was focused on androgens rather than chromosomes, but was otherwise substantially similar to the approach advocated by the IOC forty years ago.[60] Although the IAAF no longer uses the term "femininity" in its regulations, it nonetheless displays a marked focus on what are broadly considered "feminine" physical characteristics, such as (lack of) body hair and the size and shape of breasts.[61] The IAAF explains that "XY women with complete androgen insensitivity" are acceptable because "their tissues don't respond to the masculinizing call of testosterone."[62] This raises a question: Is the issue the presence of biological testosterone or, instead, the "masculinizing" effects that the testosterone has had on appearance?

Evidence suggests the latter. An examination of the language used by the IAAF and IOC suggests that social stereotypes of masculine and feminine characteristics are a key factor in the perceived need for the regulations.[63] For example, the IAAF enumerates as one of the underlying principles of the hyperandrogenism policy "a respect for the very essence of the male and female classifications in Athletics."[64] The IOC offered a similar rationale when announcing its acceptance of the new policy: "These rules should respect the essence of the male/female classification."[65]

What is the "essence" of the male/female classification? Neither organization formally defines this concept, but both suggest what is meant.* The IOC provides a hint: "Some women develop male-like body characteristics due to an overproduction of male sex hormones, so-called 'androgens.'"[66] In the IAAF regulations, seven of the nine "clinical signs" of potential hyperandrogenism focus on the athlete's physical characteristics, with two of these focusing on her breast size and shape, reinforcing a stereotype of what the male ath-

---

*   I Googled the "essence" of male and female. The only things that turned up were aftershaves and perfumes. Despite being a central concept of the IAAF and IOC regulations, the meaning of the "essence" of the male/female classification remains elusive.

letics administrator might emphasize to be important about being a woman (see figure 8.1).

The IAAF policy encourages a focus on physical appearance as the basis for a complaint and investigation. Katrina Karkazis and her colleagues write, "It is troubling that more than half of the indicators of hyperandrogenism identified by the IAAF policy to determine which female athletes should undergo sex testing are entangled with deeply subjective and stereotypical Western definitions of femininity."[68] These stereotypes are reflected in the opposite of the IAAF criteria for identifying possible cases of hyperandrogenism: full breasts, little or no facial or body hair, high voice, small muscles, wide hips. In other words, not Caster Semenya.

One key difference between the IOC policy of the 1970s and the IAAF's stand in 2011 is that female athletes today are offered a remedy for their "condition." Whereas in the 1970s athletes who did not conform were expected to silently disappear, athletes today are offered the opportunity to undergo chemical treatment or surgery to meet IAAF criteria for eligibility to participate in women's events. It is difficult to view this option as anything other than a chance to get the twenty-first century equivalent of a "certificate of femininity" through the gender-normalizing magic of science.

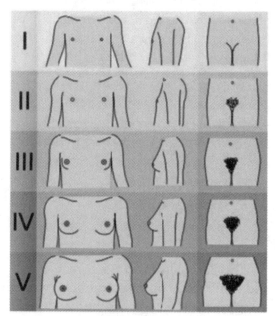

Figure 8.1. The Tanner-Whitehouse Scale, used by the IAAF as one of nine "clinical signs" used to identify possible hyperandrogenism in female athletes. (*Source:* IAAF Hyperandrogenism Regulations, Appendices.)

Sporting Ideals in Theory and Practice

To be scientifically sound and practically possible, policies for determining eligibility for participating in women's athletics should acknowledge the complexities of science and society. Historian Vanessa Heggie observes that "the changing nature of these judgments [about eligibility for participation in women's sports events] reflects a great deal about our cultural, social and national prejudices."[67] Given the realities of human biology, any policy that asks science to distinguish between two ambiguous sex categories opens the door to couching cultural, social, and national prejudices in scientific claims.

Alice Dreger of Northwestern University, a leading scholar of sex testing in athletics, sums up the overall challenge facing sport decision makers: "Humans like their sex categories neat, but nature doesn't care. Nature doesn't actually have a line between the sexes. If we want a line, we have to draw it on nature."[69] There are countless "objective" biological criteria that could be used as a litmus test of "woman-ness":

- A height of less than two meters
- An XY chromosome combination
- Testosterone less than a threshold amount
- Breasts scored at level III or greater on the Tanner-Whitehouse Scale
- Having a uterus
- Having menstruated
- Having given birth

This list could go on. Some may seem sensible—at first glance—and some may appear ridiculous. All can be objectively measured using scientific techniques. But all are problematic in the exact same way: they may differentiate between men and women in many cases, but not all.

As Dreger notes: "Can you decide what ultimately makes someone male, female, or other? Practically speaking, sure. That is to say, you can go ahead and make a decision. You won't be the first."[70] Such demarcations inevitably harm some women, like Caster Semenya and Dutee Chand.

What about Treating Gender Like Sports Organizations Treat Nationality?

So how should sports organizations use what we know about science to draw a line between men and women for purposes of competition? The answer seems obvious: they shouldn't. Science has been having the hardest time trying to figure out what makes a man a man and a woman a woman. And society keeps changing its mind about that question (not to mention that different societies in different parts of the world have different opinions). We should stop searching for the Holy Grail of the biological "essence" of male and female and instead take a more pragmatic approach.

Some observers have come to a similar conclusion and have recommended a policy of "anything goes," in which an athlete simply determines his or her gender, and that is that.[71] This approach has the feature of respecting the dignity of the athlete, but presents some practical obstacles. For instance, even though fraud has not been a significant problem in the past, opening up participation to anyone on their say-so would increase the chances of fraud. Perhaps more problematic, those opposed to this approach to classification in sporting events could cause much mischief by entering men into women's competitions to make a mockery of an "anything goes" policy.

Sporting organizations have dealt with a similar challenge in another context, and the resolution offers some guidance on how to deal with segregating women and men in competition. Nationality refers to the country (or political body, as not all sporting nations are independent, sovereign countries—Scotland, for instance, is not [as of this writing] a sovereign state) that the athlete represents in competition.[72] Sporting bodies have learned that nationality is not the same thing as legal citizenship. In the pursuit of sporting success, some nations have shown a willingness to give out passports to elite athletes who have very few ties to the country whose name is on their new passport.[73] That practice has forced sports organizations to come up with new rules governing nationality.

Just as with some opponents of sex-testing, some critics of nationality guidelines see the fundamental ambiguity in such rules and call for them to be abolished.[74] Others see in the rules the "very essence" of nationality. For instance, when it was revealed that the teenage Manchester United star Adnan Januzaj, a Belgian citizen of Albanian descent, would be eligible to play for the England national team, Arsenal's Jack Wilshere prompted a row by tweeting: "The only people who should play for England are English people."[*] Kevin Pietersen, a cricket player who was born in South Africa but, after moving to England, played for the England national team, took exception to the comment and replied with a list of English sports stars of various national lineages: "Interested to know how you define foreigner . . . ? Would that include me, Strauss, Trott, Prior, Justin Rose, Froome, Mo Farah?"

Sporting bodies, wisely, have never waded into the thicket of defining the "very essence" of nationality, lest it open up issues of ethnicity, historical conquest and subjugation, race, and politics. But these bodies also reject a policy of "anything goes" that would risk turning national sport competition into a club-like competition where athletes are traded, bought, and sold. Nor do these bodies generally rely on legal citizenship. For instance, according to FIFA's rules, citizenship is not a sufficient basis for eligibility to play on national soccer teams.[75]

Sporting bodies recognize, in practice if not in words, that nations are social constructs and as such are real and important elements of our contemporary world. Those bodies have adopted procedural guidelines to reflect the reality of nationalism while avoiding making a mockery of the categorization. Consequently, there are strict criteria for changing nationalities.[†] As with the issue of sex testing, the procedural guidelines for determining national-

---

[*]   Under FIFA's rules, Januzaj could have chosen among England, Belgium, Albania, Kosovo, Serbia, and Turkey. He ultimately chose to play for Belgium. See Owen Gibson, "Kevin Pietersen Argues with Jack Wilshere on Twitter over Englishness," *Guardian*, October 9, 2013, http://www.theguardian.com/sport/2013/oct/09/ kevin-pietersen-jack-wilshere-twitter-englishness.

[†]   Similarly, policies for changing gender categories are different than those used in the first instance. A full treatment of that topic goes beyond the scope of this chapter.

ity are openly debated and challenged and found by some to be un-satisfactory. But unlike the sex testing guidelines, sporting bodies do not appeal to scientific criteria to determine nationality (though one could easily imagine the use of genetic tests to determine ancestry for purposes of nationality). The key issue is that despite scientific evidence to the contrary, those who govern sporting bodies (like many people) appear to still believe in binary differentiation between men and women. In other words, they reject the idea that science can determine "English-ness" but accept the idea that science can identify "female-ness." This belief becomes problematic when sports administrators seek to turn it into a regulation based on science.

What would a procedural approach to determining eligibility for participation in women's events look like if it were modeled on nationality guidelines? Here are some thoughts:

- Legal status alone would be insufficient, and it may or may not be necessary (currently some countries recognize men and women, others recognize a greater number of genders, and still others have no formal policy regarding gender status).*

- Participation in the men's or women's competitions would be determined initially by the athlete in the first instance of participating in organized national or international elite competition segregated into men's and women's categories. This would in almost all cases take place at the youth or junior level.†

- On reaching senior competition and legal adulthood, the

---

* For comparison, see Russell Goldman, "Here's a List of 58 Gender Options for Facebook Users," February 13, 2014, ANC News, http://abcnews.go.com/blogs/headlines/2014/02/heres-a-list-of-58-gender-options-for-facebook-users/ Germany has created a legal "third gender." See Bill Chappell, "Germany Offers Third Gender Option on Birth Certificates," NPR, November 1, 2013, http://www.npr.org/sections/thetwo-way/2013/11/01/242366812/germany-offers-third-gender-option-on-birth-certificates.

† A key term here is "elite." A girl who plays recreational soccer on a boys team at age ten could hardly be said to be making a decision about gender. Thus, delineating when such a decision is made is key to this approach. If we depart from "anything goes," then a line must be drawn somewhere.

athlete would sign an affidavit testifying to his or her gender.

- Consistency in participation in men's or women's competitions would be required from the first instance through senior (i.e., adult competitions).

- In those cases where an athlete wishes to change gender categories, policies and procedures would cover this contingency.*

Challenges under this approach would focus on whether procedures were followed for determining eligibility, and not on medical tests or examinations, and certainly not on the "essence" of femininity.

Becoming an elite athlete is a monumental achievement, requiring years of commitment and effort. It also requires some luck in having the physical capabilities necessary to achieve at the highest levels of competition. Many exceptional athletes have exceptional, even freakish, physical characteristics. Some athletes have an appearance that may challenge or be at odds with conventional social gender norms. Sporting bodies should embrace this diversity, rather than trying to "normalize" it.

The policy recommended here has three distinct advantages over other proposals that have been advanced.

First, this policy is consistent with the current state of scientific understanding of biological sex and gender. Any effort to implement a biological test to distinguish men from women is bound to fail in the sense of producing false positives and false negatives. Such failures have been shown repeatedly to violate human dignity. A policy consistent with scientific understandings and evidence would eschew any such test.

Second, it places the onus of responsibility for determining gender on the athlete rather than on an international sports organization.

---

*   Many sports organizations already have such policies and procedures in place. See IAAF, "Regulations Governing Eligibility of Athletes Who Have Undergone Sex Reassignment to Compete in Women's Competition," http://www.iaaf.org/download/download?filename=e08ef22e-09ff-43eb-a338-fe127e99fc28.pdf&urlslug=IAAF%20Regulations%20Governing%20Eligibility%20of%20Athletes%20Who%20Have%20Undergone%20Sex%20Reassignment%20to%20Compete%20in%20Women%27s%20Competitions%20.

Third, despite recognizing that gender is a social construction, it acknowledges and reinforces the fact that gender is very real in terms of its social functions. Considerations of gender have changed over time and will continue to change in the future. As society changes, how individuals see themselves will also change. The policy recommended here rejects the idea of the "very essence" of men and women and is capable of evolving as social norms change. How those norms change involves complex sociological, cultural, and political factors. Sporting bodies should not be in the business of trying to supersede these factors, much less codify them via regulation.

So under the approach recommended here, what would the response be when a woman who looks "butch," with bulging muscles and a deep voice, wins an athletic competition? It would be to give her a medal and our applause, and to be thankful that after more than a half century, sport was finally able to leave "sex testing" behind.

PART III

WINNING THE WAR FOR SPORT

Chapter 9

Can Science Save Sport?

As a professor, I sometimes play tricks on students in my graduate seminars on policy and decision making. One of these is
to present them with a wicked problem and then ask them to solve
it. The trick, as you now know, is that wicked problems cannot be
solved—they can only be managed. After students inevitably struggle with "solving" the wicked problem, they often admit defeat and
then recommend that a committee of super smart experts be put
together to solve the problem. I return all such recommendations,
with a note that says "Incomplete, please try again."

Like my students, sports officials tend to outsource difficult
problems to experts, especially scientific experts. We see this in
doping and sex testing, where medical science is invoked as an answer; in match fixing, where aggregated data on betting patterns is
supposed to identify suspicious competitions; and in technological
augmentation, where academics are supposed to be able to discover
how fast Oscar Pistorius would have run in an alternate universe
where he was born with fibula bones in his legs. Science—the systematic pursuit of knowledge—offers the tantalizing prospect of
taming wicked problems without all of the messiness that politics
and values tend to bring to such issues.

For instance, just before the 2015 IAAF Track and Field World
Championships in Beijing, controversy erupted when a German TV
series revealed leaked data on pervasive, unpunished doping in elite
sports. The IAAF and WADA, the World Anti-Doping Agency, were

put on the defensive. The best response that Craig Reedie, the president of WADA, could muster was to put his faith in science: "At the end of the day," said Reedie, "I'm quite certain science will prevail and we'll come through this."[1]

Although Reedie's response was hardly inspiring, he did have a point. In some of the battlegrounds we've just visited, such as doping, well-used science can indeed contribute to more effective decision making, because many of the issues surrounding antidoping are amenable to research and empirical analyses. But science has its limits. Indeed, all the science in the world cannot resolve the question of how to define a woman. Sometimes, the most important contribution that science can make to decision making is to tell us what we can and cannot know. Knowing when and how to use expertise is essential to managing wicked problems.

This chapter comes back to the issue of doping in sport to consider how science might be more effectively marshaled as a tool in antidoping regulations. More science—greater expertise—is often held up as the solution to doping in sport. In this chapter, I take a different position: if we really want to reduce the amount of doping in sport, let's rely *less* on experts, but let's also use science better and more legitimately.

Science is one of the keys to more effective governance of sport, whether the issue is doping, match fixing, sex testing, or other controversies at the edge. However, those who govern sport must use science wisely. Here, too, we find a fine edge. Evidence suggests that some of the most important sports governance institutions are not up to this challenge. This chapter concludes with some straightforward advice to sports organizations and academics on how science might be better used in sports governance.

Living with Uncomfortable Knowledge

One of the problems with experts is that they don't always tell you what you want to hear. Sometimes they deliver "uncomfortable knowledge."* What decision makers do with uncomfortable knowl-

---

* I borrow this phrase from Steve Rayner at Oxford, who joined it with the notions

edge says a lot about their commitment to grappling with difficult challenges.

At the 2011 Play the Game conference in Cologne, Germany, I heard Dick Pound, a member of the International Olympic Committee since 1978 and the founding president of WADA, make some very strong claims about the unwillingness of sports officials to police doping.[2] It doesn't get more uncomfortable than a leading voice in international sport claiming that his peers aren't willing to do their jobs. At the 2013 Play the Game conference in Aarhus, Denmark, Pound was back with even stronger statements, including an admission that antidoping agencies don't really know how many athletes dope and don't really want to know.[3] Pound had chaired an internal WADA committee that concluded: "There is no general appetite to undertake the effort and expense of a successful effort to deliver doping-free sport."[4] The report laid blame on athletes, national and international sports organizations, and governments.

As we have since learned through the IAAF scandal and allegations of systematic doping among athletes in Russia, Kenya, Ethiopia, and elsewhere, the situation appears even worse than Pound suggested. Throughout 2015 and 2016, Russia was rocked by one revelation after another of systematic, even state-sponsored, doping among its athletes. For instance, a whistle-blower to the *New York Times* reported that during the 2014 Sochi Winter Olympics, "in a dark-of-night operation, Russian antidoping experts and members of the intelligence service surreptitiously replaced urine samples tainted by performance-enhancing drugs with clean urine collected months earlier, somehow breaking into the supposedly tamper-proof bottles that are the standard at international competitions."[5] Such accusations led to a debate over whether Russian athletes should be allowed to participate in the Rio Summer Games. A couple of months before the Rio games began, the IAAF decided to ban Russian track and field athletes, and the IOC and CAS backed that ban. However, Russian athletes who could prove that they had not gone along with the Russian doping regime, and who were clean,

---

of "wicked problems" and "clumsy solutions" to offer a pithy description of what it means to tackle the most vexing policy challenges.

would be allowed to compete in Brazil as "neutral athletes." A similar ban was imposed for similar reasons on Kenyan athletes—and similar individual exemptions were permitted.

One of the sometimes-frustrating things about science is that it can define the scale of some problems but not solve them. The most authoritative study on the prevalence of doping among elite athletes suggests that between 14 percent and 39 percent of elite track and field athletes take prohibited performance-enhancing drugs.[6] That study used questionnaires as well as biological parameters to come up with estimates. These numbers are consistent with an internal IAAF survey taken at the 2011 World Championships that indicated that 29 percent of athletes were doping. The results of that survey were suppressed by the IAAF and WADA until 2015, when the UK parliament released them to the public.[7] Through much of 2016, however, the IAAF and WADA continued to refuse to allow the study to be published in the scientific literature.[8] The scale of doping is a perfect example of "uncomfortable knowledge."

With the evidence that we do have, we can do some simple math. There were 1,933 athletes at the 2015 IAAF World Championships in Beijing: 1,043 men and 890 women. If 14 percent doped—the low end of recent research findings—then we can infer that 271 athletes were doping. If we use the top of the range, 39 percent, then we're looking at 754 dopers. That year, the IAAF announced that two athletes had been caught doping. Although that

Svetlana Podobedova of Kazakhstan won a gold medal at the London 2012 Olympics but was provisionally stripped of the medal in June 2016, in the wake of the Russian doping scandal.

number may increase if urine and blood tests are reexamined, there is clearly a huge gap between the estimated prevalence of doping and the number of athletes who are caught and sanctioned. Either hundreds of dopers are beating the system or very few athletes dope and the research on doping prevalence is badly flawed. The former seems much more likely.

I decided to take a look at this issue myself in an attempt to understand what antidoping agencies know about doping prevalence and the role that their programs play in reducing it. What I discovered reinforced Dick Pound's impressions: sometimes sports organizations don't want to discuss uncomfortable knowledge.

I approached WADA with some simple questions. How many athletes fall under testing regimes globally? How many athletes were tested in 2013? How many associated sanctions resulted?

WADA responded that it does not know the answers to these questions, explaining that the tests are administered by 655 different agencies that have signed on to the WADA code and that not all agencies share their results. Fair enough. In WADA's defense, this is an overwhelming landscape and WADA's resources, less than $30 million per year, limit what sort of work it can do.

But this means that important questions—questions at the core of any evidence-based antidoping policy—cannot be answered. How many athletes dope? We don't know. Is that number increasing or decreasing? We don't know. How well does testing serve as a deterrent? We don't know. And most important: Are antidoping policies working? You guessed it. We don't know.

Antidoping officials tell me that these are the wrong questions to ask, because the true purpose of drug testing in sport is deterrence, not detection. However, it is hard to know how well an emphasis on deterrence is working without solid data on the prevalence of doping among elite athletes. Current testing around the world, both by organizations that adhere to the WADA code and the US professional leagues, detects evidence of doping in 1 percent or less of samples, a number that hasn't changed since 1985.[9]

I then asked the same questions of officials at the US Anti-Doping Agency, USADA. Like WADA, USADA does not collect or report data suitable for researchers to assess the prevalence of doping or the effectiveness of antidoping programs. In other words, there are essentially no studies that use drug-testing data to estimate doping prevalence because that data is not collected for that purpose. Travis Tygart, the head of USADA, did tell me that USADA would be open to new research ideas focused on better understanding prevalence and program effectiveness.

Drug testing in sport, as currently implemented, appears to catch the occasional cheater and may deter many others, but we don't know much more than that about if and how drug testing works; we certainly don't know enough to design, implement, and evaluate an effective antidoping strategy. For that, we need to know whether the number of athletes doping is trending up or down based on a reliable measure of what proportion of athletes dope. The problem, and its inherent wickedness, is very different if 1 percent of athletes dope than if 50 percent of them do.

Estimating the number of elite athletes who dope is actually straightforward and perfectly suited to the tools of science. Determining this number is no more difficult than other efforts by scientists to quantify unknowns, such as estimates of the number of planets in the galaxy or the incidence of rare diseases. To assess the prevalence of sports doping requires two things: one, a reliable estimate of the total population of elite athletes; and two, methods to estimate how many in that population use banned performance-enhancing substances. Such methods could include a randomized testing protocol and parallel independent methods such as surveys that do not rely on testing data.

Data on the population of elite athletes are readily available. For instance, at the Rio 2016 Summer Olympics, about 11,000 athletes participated, representing more than 200 countries. Each country conducted Olympic trials with its own pool of registered, domestic competitors seeking to qualify for the games. So counting athletes is pretty easy, especially in professional leagues with team rosters. For the methodologies to estimate prevalence, because screening every athlete every year is impractical, antidoping agencies could carry out randomized tests and surveys focused not on catching cheaters, but on quantifying how many cheaters there are. Studies of prevalence could be carried out at a small additional cost to the agencies' regulatory programs. A range of approaches could also be employed by independent academics; to approach the issue from different directions usually helps produce a more accurate picture of that problem.

Coming up with more robust knowledge of doping prevalence and antidoping policy effectiveness is certainly possible. But sports agencies have deliberately avoided the uncomfortable question of how many athletes are doping and how that has changed over time. Recent history helps us to understand why.

On Seeing and Not Seeing

A lot of countries—183 in total—have signed on to the United Nations' International Convention against Doping in Sport.[10] The treaty legitimizes national bodies to oversee antidoping regulations put in place by WADA. For instance, USADA is recognized by the US Congress as the nongovernmental body responsible for fulfilling the US obligations under the treaty.[11] USADA receives close to $10 million per year from the US government to play this role.[12] Although this may sound like a lot of money, it is not very much in the context of thousands of elite athletes competing in dozens of sports. With limited resources, antidoping agencies face difficult choices in how they prioritize their activities.

Sometimes athletic performance suggests that something funny is going on. Consider the L'Alpe d'Huez climbs of the Tour de France: data suggest that something was going on in the Tour de France starting in the early 1990s, when times improved by about 10 percent almost instantaneously. Some observers have concluded that similar demonstrations of biking prowess, still on the record books, were the result of doping. For instance, the French newspaper *Le Monde* raised questions about the "mutant" performances of Miguel Indurain in the 1990s.[13] The only riders in the Tour who ascended L'Alpe d'Huez faster than Indurain were Lance Armstrong, Jan Ullrich, and Marco Pantani, each of whom doped. But "mutant" times, by themselves, are not sufficient to prove a doping violation such that an athlete can be sanctioned.

Furthermore, looking at performances by athletes and then making accusations of possible doping is certainly not fair to athletes. But it is a perfectly understandable thing to do given the poor performance by antidoping agencies. After all, if as many as 40 out of every 100 athletes are dopers, but only 1 of them is actually caught, then there is good reason to suspect that at least some of the best performers are doping. As we will see below, such suspicions are backed up by research that looks at performances across a set of elite athletes, and not individual performances. Still, detecting doping, whether in performance data or through drug testing, is tricky for several reasons.

First, performance data alone cannot offer definitive proof of violations of the WADA code. Athletic records are broken all the time. It would be a shame if every record-breaking performance was clouded by speculation and allegation of doping violations. But this is exactly what happened when Ye Shiwen, a Chinese swimmer, won the gold medal in the 400-meter individual medley at London 2012, shaving five seconds off of her personal best time. Ross Tucker, a sports scientist with expertise in human performance, wrote: "Don't shy away from the question [of doping] just because it's politically incorrect—look where that got sport before."[14] China's athletics programs have long been accused of systematic doping, so no one would be surprised to learn that Ye Shiwen doped. Yet, if she did not, then the accusations were deeply unfair to her. That cloud of uncertainty harms the athlete and sport.

Simon Ernst and Perikles Simon of Johannes-Gutenberg University in Germany are among the researchers who think that they can detect evidence of doping in performance data for a large set of elite athletes.[15] They claim that the signature of EPO can be seen in the annual top twenty times in the men's 5,000-meter race. Figure 9.1 shows a dramatic improvement in times from 1991 to 1996, what these authors call "the EPO effect," similar to the climb times of L'Alpe d'Huez in the Tour de France. Ernst and Simon also claim that drug testing leaves an imprint on performances, at least for a while. They assert that "the introduction of EPO testing in 2000 led to significant increases in running times." The release of a new EPO test in 2008 was accompanied by a short-lived decrease in race times. Both "bumps" can be seen in figure 9.1. Ernst and Simon caution, however, that "the concrete connection with doping can only be made by assumption or in retrospect."

A second reason why doping is so hard to detect and reduce is that dopers are often one step ahead of their pursuers. Simon argues

Figure 9.1. Men's Times for the 5000 Meters, 1986–2010

that the drug-testing protocols used to identify doping are fraught with loopholes that athletes can easily take advantage of.[16] For instance, whereas anabolic steroids are readily detectable, substances like EPO, human growth hormone, and testosterone can be administered at levels ("microdoses") that enhance performance but are not detectable by current methods. Such techniques raise some difficult questions; for instance, if a violation of the WADA regulations occurs but cannot be detected by contemporary scientific methods, should the substance even be on the WADA list? Simon explains that the large disparity between anonymous admission to doping and formal detection by oversight agencies is partly due to the fact that only about $6 million per year is spent on developing new tests to identify the presence of prohibited drugs in an athlete's system, in contrast to $350 million spent on giving existing drug tests.

In their study, Ernst and Simon also looked at men's 100-meter times and identified a large reduction in times from 2006 to 2011 (shown in figure 9.2; they also found a similar improvement at the 200 meters, not shown here). They speculate that the improvement was due to the introduction of a newly developed and banned substance, Insulin-like Growth Factor-1 (IGF-1), into the medicine cabinet of sprinters: "In our opinion, IGF-1 is the source for the most recent improvements in male short-distance running."[17] Over this time period, the use of IGF-1 was not detectable by drug testers. Ernst and Simon note that there are other possible explanations, such as the use of other drugs or different populations and training of athletes. Drugs that improve performance and are banned but cannot be reliably detected are one of the thorniest challenges facing antidoping efforts.

A third reason for difficulty in detecting doping is that sports governance bodies may not want to hear the results of drug tests, and thus they have an incentive to downplay or cover up doping violations. The leadership of the Union Cycliste Internationale (UCI), which oversees cycling, was accused of covering up a drug test that Lance Armstrong failed, of taking a bribe, and of being financially involved with Armstrong's team. Similarly, the IAAF in 2015 and

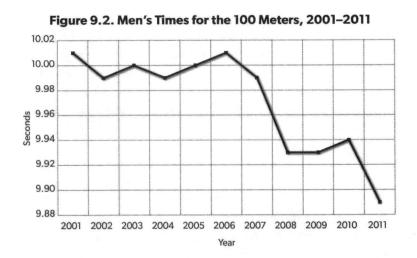

Figure 9.2. Men's Times for the 100 Meters, 2001–2011

2016 faced accusations that it covered up failed doping tests. The case of Erik Tysse, discussed in chapter 5, shows that antidoping science can be wielded sloppily. USADA's Tygart explained the general problem in the context of WADA's slow response to the allegations surrounding Russia: "Since it was founded in 2000, the United States Anti-Doping Agency has advocated separation between those who promote sport and those who police it. To do otherwise is to have the fox guarding the henhouse. WADA's governing rules allow its board members also to serve in an executive capacity for sports organizations. This inevitably gives rise to conflicts of interest."[18] An organization that fails to catch and punish cheaters might simply be poor at the job of catching cheaters. But, equally, it might be good at catching cheaters but bad at sharing the news and punishing the offenders.

In the 1980s and 1990s, the US Olympic Committee was accused of covering up failed doping tests of some of its most prominent athletes.[19] Carl Lewis, America's fastest sprinter in the late 1980s, admitted in 2003 that he had failed three drug tests before the 1988 Olympics but was allowed to compete, which he says was typical for US athletes of that era: "There were hundreds of people getting off."[20] Lewis was awarded the gold in Seoul after Ben Johnson was disqualified for steroid use. Dick Pound, former WADA chairman, explained: "There's this psychological aspect about it: nobody wants to catch anybody. There's no incentive. Countries are embarrassed if their nationals are caught. And sports are embarrassed if someone from their sport is caught."[21]

One Way to Simplify Antidoping Regulations: Apply the Caffeine Test

Let's say that athletes and administrators decide that they truly do wish to improve antidoping policies. How might science be used better? In addition to collecting robust evidence on prevalence and policy effectiveness, there is a need to simplify antidoping regimes. The number of substances on the WADA prohibited list has steadily increased over recent years. A swelling list requires more resources for enforcement and asks science to provide more evidence—evidence that in some cases can be uncertain and contestable (think Erik Tysse), which requires even more resources to defend if challenged. A key aspect of coping with a wicked problem is to determine what matters and what does not. In antidoping efforts, as in every area of regulation, difficult choices must be made about what to prioritize.

For improving antidoping policies, coffee can help us think more clearly. I don't mean just having a cup to enhance our thinking performance. Every day, people around the world drink more than 2 billion cups of coffee and more than 5 billion cups of tea.[22] If you are like me, and like billions of other people around the world, then you drink coffee or tea for its performance-enhancing qualities. These qualities have been known for millennia. One myth holds that Muhammed, overcome by sleepiness, was served coffee by the archangel Gabriel that gave him the energy to "unhorse forty men and make forty women happy."[23] While the enhanced strength and virility attributed to coffee in this myth may be a bit overstated, there is little doubt that caffeine, the stimulant in coffee and tea, does enhance physical performance.

A 2008 scientific review of the effects of caffeine in performance enhancement found "reasonable but not unanimous support that caffeine can be beneficial for" the endurance sports of running, cycling, and cross-country skiing.[24] The review also found benefits for high-intensity events lasting less than twenty minutes, including running, cycling, swimming, and rowing. The benefits for team and racquet sports were less clear, perhaps due to lesser effects, but also possibly due to the inability of researchers to detect those effects.

The magnitude of caffeine's performance-enhancing effect varied across the more than two dozen studies surveyed, ranging from no observed effect to an improvement of as much as 7 percent. One study looked at the benefits of caffeine in a simulation of the 1-kilometer cycling time trial and found a performance benefit of 2.4 seconds, a 3.1 percent improvement.[25] To put this amount of performance improvement into context, consider Ed Clancy of Great Britain, who won the 1-kilometer sprint in the London Olympic 2012 Games with a time just over 1 minute.[26] Second place was 3.3 percent slower, and tenth place was 6.7 percent slower. The performance benefit, at least according to this study, was just about the same as the difference between first and second places, or between second and tenth. Studies aside, many professional cyclists report consuming caffeine before races.* Given both common sense and the state of scientific understanding, downing a few espressos before a race is not at all surprising.

Knowing that caffeine is a documented performance-enhancing substance and that its effects in some sports and for some people is of a magnitude similar to observed differences between athletes, you might think that caffeine would be prohibited in competition. It once was, but now it's not.

In 1984, the IOC included caffeine (above a certain threshold) as a banned substance. In 1988, an Australian pentathlete, Alex Watson, was tossed out of the games after failing a urine test, which showed evidence of caffeine above the allowed threshold. He had, by his own admission, consumed more than a dozen cups of coffee and several caffeinated sodas on the day of his competition.[27] Watson initially received a lifetime ban, which was later reduced to two years, and he competed for Australia in the 1992 Olympics in Barcelona.

Despite its infrequent application, the prohibition against caffeine lasted until 2004, when WADA issued its first "prohibited list." Caffeine was not included. WADA has explained that the drug's ubiquity in society and its differential effects on people as reasons for leaving it off the list.[28] In contrast, the NCAA prohibits caffeine over a certain threshold for college athletes in the United States. That threshold can be reached by drinking two 12-ounce Starbucks coffees in the hours before a drug test.[29] However, no college athlete has ever been sanctioned under the NCAA prohibition.

As a performance-enhancing drug that is allowed under WADA and (de facto) by the NCAA, caffeine offers a useful metric for thinking about how antidoping policies might be improved. The 2016 WADA prohibited list identified almost 300 drugs and methods, as well as "other substances with similar chemical structure or similar

---

* A fun video of cyclists explaining the coffee habits in the Vuelta a España 2015 is at http://leastthing.blogspot.com/2015/08/caffeine-and-cycling.html.

biological effect(s)" to those that appear on the list.[30] This lengthy roster places an enormous burden on antidoping regulators because tests are needed to detect the presence of the prohibited substances. Tests cost money and take time. The first WADA prohibited list in 2004 identified more than 120 drugs and methods; over the course of a decade, the list grew by 150 percent.[31]

Advances in modern medicine and chemistry ensure that the potential for continued growth in the WADA list is unlimited. Although an ever-expanding list provides a rationale for expanding budgets and activities of antidoping agencies, simple mathematics tells us that an ever-expanding list means a losing battle for sport. The science of antidoping simply cannot keep up, nor can the policing of athletes. Simplification is called for.

That's where caffeine comes in. Because caffeine is both allowed and has a significant performance-enhancing effect, it offers a convenient threshold for deciding whether a substance belongs on the WADA list. If a substance cannot be shown to have a performance-enhancing effect that is larger than caffeine, then why is it included in the list? Employing such a threshold necessarily implies that we have solid scientific evidence of the performance-enhancing qualities of all substances that are candidates for inclusion on the list.

It turns out, however, that a lack of evidence does not prevent WADA from including a substance on its list. The WADA director of science, Oliver Rabin, explains: "Now the real challenge is when we are asked to take decisions on substances for which there is almost no scientific literature available. Thus, you have to extrapolate either from similar compounds or classes of similar substances."[32] In 2012, at a meeting of the WADA Foundation Board, Arne Ljungqvist, then chair of the IOC Medical Commission, explained that substances were added to the list based on a "gut feeling," not robust evidence. Gut feelings are not the stuff of successful regulations.[33] But obtaining robust evidence is difficult, not least because it requires studies of elite athletes, many of whom are far more likely to be interested in competing than in being lab rats. There are no easy answers to what role evidence should play in creating the WADA banned list, but the answers have profound implications for the scope of the WADA list.

A more radical proposal would be to empower elite athletes who are regulated by WADA to help determine which substances appear on the prohibited list. Currently, the list is overseen by a panel of scientific and technical experts who share their recommendations with signatories to the WADA code. Athletes have little representation or voice. Under the alternative model, experts would make a case for why they recommend that a substance be included on (or removed from) the list, and athletes governed by the regulations would have the final say in which substances are added to (or deleted from) the list. I'll return to the subject of empowered athletes in chapter 11.

The caffeine test leads to some difficult questions. Should a substance be viewed as guilty (of performance-enhancing effects greater than caffeine) until proven innocent, or innocent until proven guilty? If the substance has performance-enhancing effects, is it safe? Is it even detectable? In making such judgments, who gets to decide what is safe? Scientists and other experts? Administrators? Athletes?

Through an open discussion and debate of such questions, antidoping regulators would be empowered to implement a simpler, more robust, transparent, and arguably more effective approach to the oversight of performance-enhancing substances and methods in sport. If athletes play a more direct role in determining what is on the banned list, the list may be viewed as being more legitimate by athletes and the public alike.

Organizing to Secure Independent Advice

Even if athletes were to take on a more prominent role in antidoping or other areas of sports governance, the need to consult experts for their judgment and advice will remain. Sports has a long history of relying on a narrow set of experts over and over again. For instance, Dick Pound was the first president of WADA and has been a long-serving member of the IOC. He was also the chairman of the WADA commission that was asked to look into the IAAF scandal that emerged in 2015. He also chaired the WADA committee that looked at the effectiveness of doping tests in 2012. And the 2004

Olympic Games Study Commission. And the investigation into the Salt Lake City scandal in the late 1990s. His is a distinguished résumé to be sure, but why ask so much of just one man?

Consider also Richard McLaren, a Canadian lawyer who is a CAS arbitrator who might be selected to render judgments on cases brought before that body. He was one of the arbitrators who decided the Dutee Chand case in 2015. And the Tysse case in 2011. And he sat on the 2015 WADA committee that looked into the allegations against the IAAF that was chaired by Dick Pound. He was also appointed by WADA as the sole "independent person" to investigate the allegations raised against Russia at Sochi 2014. McLaren has been very gracious in responding to various questions I've asked him over the years and has undoubtedly helped to make sport better. But, again, why ask one man to render so many crucial judgments? And it is typically *men* who make such decisions. Only one woman was involved in the Chand and Tysse CAS arbitrations; no woman was on the IAAF investigative committee chaired by Dick Pound. Of the 365 CAS arbitrators from almost 80 countries listed by CAS in 2016, fewer than 30 (or less than 8 percent) were women.[34]

In addition to consulting only a narrow set of experts, sports organizations have demonstrated an inability to understand what "independent" advice actually means. For example, in 2011, FIFA appointed an "independent" body to provide advice on governance reforms. The body was quickly shown to be far from what most people would consider independent. Its chair, Mark Pieth, a Swiss professor, was paid $128,000 plus $5,000 per day to produce a white paper on FIFA reform, payments that were undisclosed until a Swiss newspaper revealed them.[35] The FIFA governance committee comprised twelve people, six of whom had financial or employment connections with FIFA.[36] After the committee disbanded, Pieth revealed that members had collectively been paid more than $800,000 for their work, plus an additional $300,000 in travel expenses.[37] Only one member of the committee, anticorruption expert Alexandra Wrage, refused to take FIFA's money. She ultimately resigned from the committee in protest over its conflicts of interest and weak performance.

A recounting of conflicts of interest, nepotism, and the lack of independence in sports advisory bodies could fill a thick (and boring) encyclopedia. I'll add just one more example. In 2015, Sebastian Coe was elected to the presidency of the IAAF, an organization that was quickly enveloped in scandal due to the various allegations against Russia. One of the issues that Coe was asked about upon assuming the presidency was his role as a "Nike ambassador," which paid him a healthy salary every year, and how that role jibed with the IAAF Code of Ethics, which prohibits such cozy relationships with IAAF corporate partners.[38] Coe initially refused to acknowledge that his role with Nike represented any sort of conflict, despite IAAF guidelines saying otherwise. The IAAF ethics committee agreed with Coe, and issued a statement saying that he could keep his Nike appointment and salary if he wished to.[39] One of the members of that ethics committee was the head of the Brazilian Olympic Committee, which had a reported $25 million to $40 million partnership with Nike.[40] Coe eventually relented and resigned the Nike position, but the IAAF's readiness to turn a blind eye to conflicts of interest was obvious.

In February 2016, FIFA adopted a number of reforms in response to its governance crisis (explored in the next chapter). Among them was the adoption of the definition of what it means to be an "independent" advisor to FIFA. The criteria allow an individual to be paid $125,000 by FIFA and still be considered independent of FIFA.[41] For most people, $125,000 is not pocket change; the average income in developed countries is about one-third that amount, or $45,000.[42] FIFA's definition of independence ensures that the experts and advisers that it relies on will be beholden to the organization. What's the point of getting independent advice if it's not independent?

Governments, universities, nonprofit organizations, and businesses have long grappled with issues of conflict of interest.[43] After all, when securing advice, the best advice is based on evidence and professional judgment unclouded by the prospect of a paycheck. That is why independence is so valued. Conflicts of interest are about more than just appearances. The NFL's role in concussion research provides an example of what can go awry when conflicts of interest arise in sports settings. It matters most to those closest to sport, the athletes.

Consequences of Conflicts of Interest

Football has never been more popular. The 2016 Super Bowl between the Denver Broncos and Carolina Panthers was the second-most-watched TV program ever in the United States, trailing only the 2015 Super Bowl. In fact, the twenty-one most-watched programs ever are all Super Bowls. In 2015, almost 50 million people attended college football games. More than 1 million boys played high school football, making it the most played high school sport, a status it has held since data were first collected in 1969.

Despite football's immense popularity among spectators and players, the sport is facing an existential threat due to the long-term health risks presented by repetitive injuries to the head. A new disease has even been associated with these injuries—chronic traumatic encephalopathy, or CTE, the subject of the movie *Concussion,* starring Will Smith as Bennet Omalu, the Nigerian doctor who discovered the disease.

If the NFL, the NCAA, high schools, players, and parents are to make informed decisions about football, robust evidence about the health risks of playing football is needed. However, just like other areas where science runs into politics, money, and culture, securing a solid foundation of science in the context of football has proven problematic. In early 2016, ESPN reported that the NFL had become the nation's largest and most powerful funder of brain research, exceeding money spent by the National Institutes of Health (NIH). On the one hand, such investments are to be commended. Federal research dollars are limited, and despite the popularity and visibility of football, the sport's risks directly affect far fewer people than other health concerns.

On the other hand, the role that the NFL has played in research has undercut its credibility and the ability to secure solid science in support of understanding the risks of football, and thus our ability to take steps to make the game safer for children, college students, and professionals alike. ESPN reported that the NFL has favored some league-friendly scientists over others by directing where funding is awarded and where it is not. There is a troubling association between views on the science of concussions and the relationship of some scientists with the NFL. One researcher quipped, "It felt like we were going back to the stage where the people who were funded by Big Tobacco were saying smoking is not harmful."[44] Based on ESPN's allegations, the US Congress investigated and concluded that "the NFL improperly attempted to influence the grant selection process at NIH."[45]

This, happily, is not a wicked problem. There's a fairly straightforward solution. The NFL should indeed fund research—a lot of it! But it should do so in a completely hands-off manner. That could mean donating money to authoritative research bodies, like those associated with the NIH, to run a competitive research program without interference. Once the scientific agenda is set, the NFL must step back and allow the research process to take place. Science agencies have strict conflict-of-interest guidelines, and these guidelines should be employed rigorously to ensure that funding decisions are made by individuals who are open and transparent.

For independent advice, the NFL needs to outsource its expert advisory process. The league's Head, Neck, and Spine Committee is an internal body that may serve important roles, but an independent adviser is not one of them.

Independent advice could be secured by asking the US National Research Council (NRC) to establish an advisory body. The NFL and the NRC could negotiate the scientific questions to be addressed by the body, and the NFL could pay for the committee's work, but its work would be overseen by the NRC completely independently of the NFL. More broadly, if the NFL doesn't act to secure independent advice, Congress or the president could create a national commission on the "future of football" designed as an honest broker to evaluate current science, to suggest future research directions, and to generate alternative paths forward for the nation's most popular sport.

What we learn about the risks of football may not always be welcome or pleasant, but preserving what is loved about the sport depends on being honest with the players and fans. That means establishing a robust system for securing expert advice. If the NFL can do that, it will teach a lesson with relevance much broader than just to sport.

How to Better Use Science to Support Sport

The role of science in decision making has been the subject of much attention in recent years, mainly because science matters today so much more in policy and politics than it did in past generations. Sport is no different, as we've seen. Science shows up as a critical factor in decision making related to doping, sex testing, and technological enhancement (both of athletes and of sport). Science also plays an important role in detecting evidence of match fixing and in debates over the economics of amateurism. Sport faces the same challenges as found in other areas of decision making in the effective use of science and in avoiding its abuse.

Here, I suggest a few simple guidelines for how sport can better use science to support effective decision making. I focus on three issues:

- When to rely on science
- How to use science
- Who to tap for their expertise

When Should Science Play a Role in Decision Making?

There are some questions for which science doesn't much matter to the answer. For instance, consider this easy question: What is your favorite sports team? Surely, you did not need to consult data, theory, or the academic peer-reviewed literature to answer this question. The reply came from somewhere in your gut, based on your experiences and emotions. But ask a different question, such as, How many people identify Arsenal as their favorite team?* Answering such a question requires collecting data, perhaps by a social scientist employing robust research methods.

---

*   The answer, of course, is "All right-thinking people," but I digress.

The key distinction here is that there are some questions that are best answered with evidence, and there are other questions for which evidence doesn't much matter to the answer. The former are questions of policy and the latter are questions of politics. In the abstract, making such a distinction is easy; in the real world, policy and politics are all mixed up.

Consider again the issue of sex testing. For many decades, sports administrators, probably like most people in society, believed that identifying a woman was a simple matter of biology. Even as it became apparent that the biology of sex was anything but simple, many held out hope for an unambiguous, scientific delineation between males and females, even if that line was somewhat complex. But as we saw in chapter 8, although many biological variables might be used to classify someone as a woman for sporting purposes, all are problematic in some way. Any demarcation chosen for purposes of regulation will therefore reflect not just science but also gut feelings and emotions.

The fact that we classify a "woman" based on a complex brew of science *and* values does not mean that we can't use a biological characteristic as a regulatory device, but it does mean that in implementing such a regulation we should be aware that we are not just depending on science. That is how characteristics such as breast size and shape came to be a part of the recent IAAF regulations focused on testosterone. In difficult issues, both in and out of sport, there is a tendency to hide or ignore matters related to values behind technical discussions. When we do that, it doesn't make the values go away; they are still there, stealthily nestled smack dab in the middle of the putatively technical discussions.

Values aren't the only challenge to effectively identifying when to rely on science. Uncertainty and ignorance matter, too. Uncertainty refers to situations where more than one outcome is consistent with what we know. For instance, chapter 5 explored the case of Erik Tysse, the Norwegian race walker sanctioned for doping. Did he in fact dope? Based on the evidence, I am uncertain, meaning maybe he did, and maybe he didn't. Ignorance refers to situations where we don't even know enough to hazard a reasonable guess. For instance, how many soccer matches were fixed in the lower divisions

of Italy and Turkey in 2015? We don't even know enough to be uncertain about an answer; we are simply ignorant.

One goal of science in decision making is to turn ignorance into
uncertainty, and uncertainty into knowledge appropriate for decision making. Wisdom lies in knowing which issues are amenable to
such transformations. In principle, antidoping agencies should have
been able to determine to anyone's satisfaction whether Tysse doped
or not. Instead, sloppiness and missteps created a permanent state
of uncertainty, and perhaps even an injustice. By contrast, quantifying the scope of match fixing in lower tiers of professional soccer (or
probably any sport) may be prohibitive as a matter of cost and other
practicalities. Consequently, decision making may have to proceed
in the face of fundamental ignorance. The point here is that sports
governance should proceed with a clear-eyed sense of what science
can and can't do in the context of uncertainties and ignorance.

How Do We Use Science?

The troubled relationship between the NFL and science can be used
to illustrate some of the different ways that sport can use experts to
help inform decision making. There are at least four roles that sport
needs experts to perform, and all are important depending on the
context. Clearly identifying what is expected from experts is one of
the most important factors in using science (and other expertise) in
decision making. Here are those roles:[46]

- *The pure scientist* seeks to focus only on facts and has no
  interaction with a decision maker. For instance, a medical
  researcher might conduct studies of the long-term health
  consequences of repetitive head injuries. That study would
  be available to the NFL in the scientific literature. The "pure
  scientist" has no direct connection with a decision maker.

- *The science arbiter* answers specific factual questions posed by
  the decision maker. The NFL might ask a group of experts to
  summarize the scientific literature on health risks associated
  with playing football. To take another example, FIFA could

ask a group of governance experts to summarize best practices for organizational reform. Collectively, society has a lot of experience soliciting advice from experts in a way that is transparent and deals effectively with actual or perceived conflicts of interest.

- *The issue advocate* seeks to argue for a particular course of action. For instance, Dr. Bennet Omalu has argued that children should be prohibited from playing tackle football. Former NFL quarterback Danny Kanell takes the opposite position. Both are advocates for a course of action. Sometimes, advocacy is based on financial incentives, but not always. When experts are enlisted to offer advice, it is important to know where they stand on issues as well as what they are expert in so that advice can be appropriately balanced among competing interests.

- *The honest broker of options* seeks to expand, or at least clarify, the scope of choice available to the decision maker. The honest broker doesn't try to tell you what to do, but rather what the options are and the possible costs and benefits associated with each course of action. Typically, an honest broker is a committee rather than an individual. Omalu and Kanell might make good members of an honest broker committee on the future of football, but neither would be expected to be able to play the role of an honest broker by himself, because each man has a particular view and interests.

Whatever role an expert plays, if he or she claims to be independent, then he or she needs to be seen to be independent, by disclosing actual or potential conflicts of interest. Sports organizations have, for the most part, yet to adopt the sort of conflict-of-interest policies that governments, businesses, and other organizations routinely use when relying on experts. Whether the issue is concussions in the NFL, governance of FIFA, or consideration of drugs for inclusion on the WADA prohibited list, decision making in sport will make better use of expertise with more attention to independence and transparency in the selection of experts and in the specific roles that they are asked to play.

Who Should Sports Organizations Tap as Experts?

If the questions to be addressed with science are clearly identified and the roles of experts are well understood, then the choice of which experts to tap becomes much easier. Nowadays, it is of course common for a decision maker to decide what answer they want and to carefully cherry pick the science or expertise to rationalize that decision. Such tactics are standard practice in adversarial settings such as in courts and in arbitration. They are less useful when expert advice is actually desired to inform decision making.

The experiences of Professor Paul Dimeo and USA Cycling (USAC) provide a case study in what can go wrong when an organization sets up a process for soliciting expert advice but really isn't interested in the advice it gets. In early 2016, Dimeo was asked by USAC to serve as the chair of a new antidoping committee. He explained how he saw his role as chair on the committee: "To take a balanced account of the members' views, to help organize the meetings, assure everyone has a voice and to assist (not overly influence) decision-making."[47] Dimeo, who is cited in several places in this book, is well known for raising questions about how well antidoping efforts are working and whether a new approach might be needed. For USAC it was an inspired choice. Or so it seemed.

Just two months after Dimeo was chosen to chair the USAC antidoping committee, the organization asked him to step down from the committee. The reason was an interview that Dimeo gave with the *Sunday Times* in which he suggested, as he had many times before, that substances on the WADA prohibited list, including EPO and blood transfusions, might have appropriate medical uses for athletes. Such substances are, after all, from the world of medicine in the first place. Dimeo explained:

> Clean sport is a construction that has developed over time without pause for reflection on how the wider world has changed. People can access drugs more easily, can learn about them in an instant on the Internet, and sport has become much more scientific. The ideal of the natural athlete is an anachronism. Meanwhile, testing has not stopped athletes from doping. Given these circumstances, alongside the cases of relatively innocent

athletes being sanctioned, maybe there is a better way of approaching all this.[49]

Dimeo's comments were judged to be unacceptable. Derek Bouchard-Hall, the CEO of USAC explained: "While we welcome dissenting opinion within our committee, the conversation must focus on the problem at hand: how to eliminate doping from American cycling."[48] Apparently, raising questions about the present doping regime was not welcomed by USAC. The episode proved embarrassing for USAC and difficult for Dimeo, who explained, "I have been cast in the role of villain and my reputation damaged. I would be careful to work with any anti-doping organization now; I would certainly be much more cautious about the terms of engagement."

Michael Ask, CEO of Anti-doping Denmark, offers some good advice for both academics and sports organizations. He says that antidoping agencies need to understand the constructive role that critique can sometimes play:

> Anti-doping organizations are bound by legislation and regulations from governments and WADA, whereas academics traditionally, and rightly so, refer to the right to research freely and independently. For anti-doping organizations, it means that we sometimes have to enforce rules and regulations that might not necessarily agree with our personal views. However, I think that we could be more courageous in public and outline some of the unsuitability's [sic] of the system. That is the only way we can influence the decision makers and make the system better.

For academics, he says that critique has to be grounded and constructive:

> Researchers can of course freely criticize all aspects of the doping system, but I think they often score some cheap points by just criticizing without pointing to solutions at the same time. The WADA Code and the anti-doping regulations are results of international compromises, and I find that researchers have a tendency to forget the complexity of that fact.[50]

The USAC fiasco could have been avoided with a clearer up-front statement of what the organization expected from its expert advisers. Did it want a set of science arbitrators to render a group judgment on a specific question (or questions) that could be addressed with evidence? Or did it want the committee to perform an honest broker function by exploring—and even critiquing—alternative approaches to antidoping regulation and implementation? Dimeo would have been a perfect chair for the latter, but perhaps not the former. Absent such clarification, it looks like USAC simply wanted the benefits of having an expert committee without thinking through what that actually implied. Of course, such clarity of purpose makes it more difficult for organizations to use experts as props to rationalize decisions already made. For many observers of sports organizations, that is precisely the point.

Focusing on the who, what, and how of expert advice can provide a solid foundation for sports organizations to better use science in how they make decisions. Of course, a prior step is the need for a sincere commitment to using science even when the advice from experts is uncomfortable or unwelcome. Ultimately, sports organizations have no obligation to take the advice they are given; advice is just that—to be considered, not to be obeyed. By being more transparent and open about expertise, including issues such as conflict of interests, sports organizations can become more accountable to their stakeholders, and bring their practices more in line with expectations of organizations in the twenty-first century. Using science wisely is a matter of good governance, and as we will see next, many sports organizations have work to do in that area, too.

Chapter 10

Against Autonomy

It was like a scene out of a Jason Bourne movie. At 6:00 on the morning of May 27, 2015, plain-clothed Swiss police entered the posh Baur au Lac Hotel in Zurich, Switzerland, to arrest members of an alleged international criminal syndicate. The surprise raid at the early hour meant that seven suspects were taken into custody without incident, although one was able to escape the hotel without being caught because he saw the arrests being made as he was eating his breakfast. The suspects were ushered out of the hotel behind white sheets to save them embarrassment.

The suspects' identities were not kept quiet for long, thanks to Twitter and a hard-working press corps. They included top officials from FIFA, the Swiss-based international organization that oversees soccer competitions around the world, and several of its business partners. The police action was the result of an unprecedented coordinated effort between the US and Swiss governments. It also marked the onset of a global crisis for FIFA. Less than a week later, FIFA President Sepp Blatter announced his intention to step down, leading to the election of Gianni Infantino in February 2016.

The crisis garnered an incredible amount of global media attention. *USA Today* observed that the snowballing FIFA scandal was "an above-the-fold story in almost every major newspaper worldwide" and, in the traditionally soccer-disinterested United States, it was "a national news story that has reached people who couldn't tell Ronaldo from Waldo."[1] In February 2016, when FIFA elected its new

Figure 10.1. The Front Pages of Major Papers around the World the Day after the FIFA Scandal Broke in May 2015

president, major US cable networks ESPN and Fox Sports provided hours of live coverage and analysis.

The attention paid to the FIFA scandal since 2015 reflected a change in how the media and the public viewed sports governance. The topic was once niche and esoteric, but by 2016, it had gone viral. It wasn't just FIFA either; the alphabet soup of sports governing bodies—IAAF, WADA, ITF, CAS, and others—were increasingly newsworthy, and not because of what was happening in competitions. Several factors help to explain why governance has become a more important focus since the FIFA scandal broke.

First off, sport has become big-time. Big money, big politics, big media. The cost to put on the 2014 Sochi Winter Olympic Games was a reported $50 billion; Qatar is investing more than $200 billion in preparations for the 2022 FIFA World Cup. In the United States, major college coaches routinely are awarded contracts in the tens of millions of dollars, and TV networks pay billions of dollars for the rights to air college football and basketball tournaments. And wherever there is big money to be found, governments, businesses, and the media are not far away. As we saw in chapter 2, although sport is not big business in a relative sense, the amount of money in sport has grown to the point where corruption is a significant risk, especially in the absence of oversight.

Another reason why the governance of sport matters more today is that the boundaries between the politics of sport, once an esoteric niche, and the broader politics of governing society have become blurred. As one expert in international politics explains in the context of the FIFA controversy, "The debate over FIFA suggests that sport today has come not to reflect politics, as in the past, but also, in some sense, to substitute for it."[2] The FIFA scandal surfaced remarkable allegations of government collusion to secure the hosting rights for the World Cup. Did the French president dictate how a French member of FIFA's Executive Committee would vote? Did Qatar and Thailand strike a deal over natural gas to secure the Thai vote for the 2022 World Cup? Did Germany lift an arms embargo on Saudi Arabia to secure its vote for the 2006 World Cup? Did the Russian government give a Picasso painting from the archives of the State Hermitage Museum in St. Petersburg to a FIFA official to gain his support? With the potent combination of sport, politics, and money coming together in an increasingly globalized world, it's no wonder people are ever more captivated by issues of sports governance

Behind every major sport and sporting event is a typically hidden superstructure of organizations, people, money, politics, and power. For most of us, this superstructure seldom comes into view, and when it does, we get to see only a fleeting glimpse.

Sport governance has been out of sight for so long because of the long-standing view that sport should be free to govern itself; in the jargon of the sports world, sport should be *autonomous*. That is a principle endorsed by no less an institution than the United Nations, which in October 2014 passed a resolution supporting the independence of sport. Thomas Bach, the former Olympic fencer who heads up the IOC, goes so far as to call athletic competition "the only area of human existence which has achieved universal law," arguing that it is incumbent on politicians to respect the autonomy of sport.

No institution better illustrates the perils associated with leaving sport to govern itself than FIFA. On May 31, 2011 (which was also the 100th anniversary of the launch of the *Titanic*), Sepp Blatter told the world, "I am the captain, we will weather the storm together," meaning that he would see FIFA through its crisis.[3] The controversies surrounding FIFA have included allegations of corruption such as bribery in the process of selecting the 2018 and 2022 World Cup venues (Russia and Qatar)and payoffs (delivered in brown envelopes) for votes in advance of the 2011 FIFA presidential election.[4] In 2011, those at the helm of the good ship FIFA believed it was unsinkable, but almost exactly four years later, FIFA hit the iceberg that is the US Department of Justice. Sepp Blatter was forced to step down in 2015, as FIFA administrators, one after another, were relieved of their duties. In 2016, FIFA revealed that several top FIFA officials, including Blatter, had arranged for secret bonus payments totaling some $80 million to be paid to each other. Some of these bonuses were put into place in the days after the raid on the Baur au Lac Hotel, guaranteeing payment even if the official were to lose his job.[5]

This chapter is about the governance of international sport, and by "governance" I mean "the making and implementation of rules, and the exercise of power, within a given domain of activi-

ty."[6] I've obviously already discussed many issues of governance in the other chapters of this book, but here we dive more deeply into the subject, looking to explain why the governance of sport is such a troubled area these days and what might be done about it.

Sepp Blatter in 2007, announcing the selection of Rio as the venue for the 2014 World Cup.

FIFA has been doing its best to steal the sordid spotlight in recent years, but it has been facing some stiff competition. A wide variety of sports have been experiencing breakdowns in governance:

- The International Weightlifting Federation (IWF), located in Budapest, Hungary, has faced accusations of financial mismanagement, with millions of dollars provided by the IOC unaccounted for.[7]

- The Fédération Internationale de Volleyball (FIVB), located in Switzerland, has faced accusations of illegitimate political actions to keep a leadership regime in power, as well as accusations of financial mismanagement of its funding.[8]

- The Union Cycliste Internationale, or the UCI (discussed in chapter 6), also located in Switzerland, in association with the doping scandal involving Lance Armstrong and his teammates, has faced accusations of bribery and financial conflicts of interest.[9]

- The IAAF, as discussed in previous chapters, stands accused of covering up institutionalized doping by Russian athletes and also extorting athletes who tested positive for banned substances. In addition, the IAAF, along with WADA, stood in the way of the publication of research on doping prevalence that WADA had commissioned.[10]

Many more examples could be cited—a fact that suggests that what we're looking at here isn't an unsightly but limited case of governance acne, but an outbreak of governance plague. In other words, the rash of failures in sports governance is epidemic—there are some shared, fundamental weaknesses in the governance of international sporting bodies. This chapter seeks to characterize this epidemic by looking at a few cases. It begins by taking a close look at a tragic example of the human consequences of poor governance through the story of Mario Goijman, a former Argentinean volleyball official. It then explores institutions of sports governance through a closer look at WADA and its subsidiary organizations that oversee antidoping. The chapter then returns to FIFA and asks why, with such outrage focused on the organization, FIFA has done what it wants for many years with impunity and only recently has been brought to account. Goijman's story puts a human face on the consequences of governance failures while FIFA's troubles illustrate what can happen when sports bodies lack basic mechanisms of accountability characteristic of governments and businesses in the twenty-first century. Sports bodies have a lot of catching up to do.

The Tragedy of Mario Goijman

Late on a Friday evening in March 2012, outside of Buenos Aires, Argentinean police and government officials arrived at the home of Mario Goijman with orders to evict him and confiscate his belongings. From 1996 to 2002, Goijman was the president of the Argentinean Volleyball Federation, which hosted the 2002 Men's World Championships. Once a successful businessman, he was a broken and ill man when he was evicted from his home, a victim of the inability of international sporting associations to deal with corruption within their ranks.[11]

The officials had shown up on Goijman's doorstep that evening because of a dispute that had left Goijman responsible for bank loans that he had personally taken on as part of hosting the 2002 championships. The story of that dispute and its tragic consequences for one man provides a window into what is often a dark and corrupt world of international sports governance, far from the headlines.

Goijman's battle against the international body that oversees volleyball competitions, the FIVB, began in 2002, shortly before the Men's World Championships in Argentina. Based on information that he had gleaned as an insider, Goijman decided to blow the whistle on the FIVB and went public with allegations that the books of the federation contained financial irregularities. Goijman alleged that corruption stemmed from the top of the federation and its president, Rubén Acosta.

For his part, Acosta, who had headed the FIVB since 1984 and who was also a member of the prestigious IOC, denied the allegations and in turn accused Goijman of committing his own financial irregularities. Acosta immediately suspended Goijman from the FIVB; he later suspended the entire Argentinean Volleyball Federation after it came to the support of Goijman. Supporters of Acosta subsequently established a new volleyball federation in Argentina. In this battle of Argentinean sports officials, Goijman lost big-time.

For anyone paying attention, which was very few outside of the small volleyball community, it was a situation of dueling accusations with little basis for judging what may have been true and what may have been false. The dispute could have disappeared as a historical footnote.

However, it turned out that some of the people who were paying attention to the dispute had the power to turn footnotes into headlines. In 2003, Swiss authorities raided the headquarters of the FIVB in Lausanne and turned up documents that supported Goijman's allegations. Around the same time, the ethics committee of the IOC began an investigation of Acosta that resulted in a recommendation of sanctions, prompting his subsequent resignation from the IOC, at which point the investigation was discontinued, because he was no longer under the IOC's jurisdiction.

A Swiss court later judged that FIVB accounts had in fact been falsified, but did not determine that the falsification had resulted from criminal intent. Jens Sejer Andersen, who heads Play the Game, a Danish nonprofit organization focused on sports governance, took up Goijman's cause. Andersen came into possession of leaked internal FIVB documents that led him to conclude that Acosta had skimmed more than US $33 million from the organization's accounts. Yet none of these revelations led to the resolution of Goijman's predicament. More than a decade later, Goijman continued to suffer the consequences of the retribution from Acosta and the FIVB for speaking out.

I first encountered Goijman in October 2011 in Germany at the biennial Play the Game conference. Goijman, a grandfatherly figure, spoke passionately and emotionally at that conference about his experiences and troubles, and it was clear that the events had taken an enormous toll on him emotionally, if not physically. I was at the conference to present a paper on the governance of FIFA. Having never heard of Goijman or Acosta, I decided to dig a little deeper.

As the head of the Argentinean Volleyball Federation, Goijman was the lead individual responsible for organizing the 2002 Men's

World Championships. Part of this responsibility involved contributing his own savings and taking out substantial bank loans to finance the games, a reported US $800,000—his entire life savings. Goijman told me that he was expected to contribute his personal funds because of the sorry state of the Argentinean economy at the time. Besides, he told me, he was not worried about the loans, as the games were expected to generate a 30 percent return. He proceeded under the expectation that the borrowed money would be repaid by the contracted partnership he had with the FIVB.

Under such circumstances, one might question the wisdom of blowing the whistle on an organization immediately after loaning it a substantial sum of money, because the results were probably predictable. The FIVB refused to reimburse the Argentinean Volleyball Federation (and thus Goijman) for the loans that it had taken, leaving Goijman personally responsible for the debt. The FIVB also focused its sights on the Argentinean Volleyball Federation and anyone who offered Goijman support. Goijman's inability to repay the loans is what ultimately led to the police arriving on his doorstep to repossess his home and the last of his belongings.

My repeated inquiries to the FIVB press office in Switzerland and FeVA (the current Argentinean Volleyball Federation, and the one that replaced the one headed by Goijman) received no response. But I was able to speak to Doug Beal, the CEO of USA Volleyball and the head coach of the US volleyball team at the 2002 Men's World Championships in Argentina. Beal also serves on the Board of Administration of the FIVB.

Beal told me that during the time that the FIVB was run by Acosta, the organization was essentially a "one-person dictatorship." Beal explained: "Nobody asked too many questions, because he was bringing in a lot of money and significantly raising the profile of the sport, particularly in the Olympics and particularly with the addition of the beach discipline in '96. Acosta was certainly receiving significant commissions for some time before it was an approved or well-known practice, and the total amount may likely never be known." Such payments to sport administrators are the sort of practice revealed to the world in the FIFA scandal. Unfortunately, they are not limited to FIFA.

Of the dispute between Goijman and Acosta, Beal said, "Goijman didn't react as most people did [to Acosta] by bending to his every whim and will. Acosta decided to dismiss him from the volleyball world." Beal told me that the practice of having individuals take personal responsibility for loans to finance a championship is not something that USA Volleyball would ever allow to happen or agree to do. Beal's recounting of the events and disputes matches up well with the evidence collected by Andersen at Play the Game and that is publicly available. By essentially all accounts, Goijman got screwed —and that is putting it mildly—and the organizations that oversee his sport, from the Argentine federation to the FIVB all the way up to the IOC, failed comprehensively to right this wrong.

Goijman's personal experiences illustrate what can be the seamy underside of the governance of international sports organizations. Corruption in sports governance is bad enough in the context of sport but has potentially far greater consequences than simply on the games themselves. Allegations of the consequences of poor sports governance are not just about money; they can take heavy a human toll.

For instance, human rights attorney and former Olympic swimmer for Canada Nikki Dryden has complained that following the 2010 drowning death of Fran Crippen, an American open-water swimmer, at the UAE World Cup, 300 meters from the finish line of the 10-kilometer race. Dryden says that FINA, the international swimming federation, "refused to participate with the USA Swimming Task Force to help with a thorough, transparent investigation," despite claims that the event should not have been held given what may have been excessively warm water and a shortage of lifeguards.[12] When the actions of sports organizations provoke concern, one question almost always gets asked, sooner or later: "Who is accountable?" For many years, the answer to this question has been, "No one, really."

In another case with even broader consequences, Jack Warner, the Trinidad and Tobago government official who was suspended in 2011 from the FIFA Executive Committee for ethical violations, was accused of mismanaging funds that had been raised to aid those suffering in the aftermath of the 2010 Haiti earthquake. According to the London *Sunday Times*, Warner collected $750,000 from FIFA and its vice president, Moon Jung-Chung (who is also part of the South Korean family that owns Hyundai). The president of the Haitian soccer association, Yves Jean-Bart, says that only $60,000 reached Haiti. Warner reportedly did not account for the remaining funds and in 2015 was indicted by the US Department of Justice on corruption charges.[13]

The United States and Europe, in particular, are familiar with using governmental and nongovernmental bodies to help root out and clean up corruption. Yet, such practices are far from universal. Jean Loup-Chappelet, a professor of public management at the Swiss Graduate School of Public Administration and a leading expert on sports governance, notes that only ten countries around the world have laws against bribery in sports, likely a consequence of the relative immaturity of these bodies as well as the long-standing notion that they should operate autonomously. Even within Europe (including Switzerland), where most international sports bodies reside, a complex tapestry of laws and enforcement makes dealing with corruption a challenge.[14]

For Mario Goijman, the sorry state of accountability among sports bodies was consequential. When the police showed up at his house in October 2012, Goijman put a gun to his head to attempt suicide and had to be hospitalized. Andersen at Play the Game has asked the FIVB to enter into a process of arbitration to resolve the outstanding dispute over the 2002 loans still held in Goijman's name. "By showing generosity and willingness to open a dialogue with the [Argentinean Volleyball Federation] and Goijman," Andersen argued, "the FIVB will send an important welcoming signal to those future leaders inside and outside volleyball who wish to preserve the integrity of sport and its institutions." Andersen told me that in 2016, Goijman lived in a small rented house and continued to suffer the consequences of the loss of his life savings.

Beal at USA Volleyball made his position clear. He told me that the $800,000 owed by Goijman "may sound like a lot" but is "not too much to the FIVB." Andersen agrees: The "FIVB does not publish its annual accounts but is widely believed to be among the most wealthy sports federations." Beal cited the well-run and quite successful 2002 Men's World Championships that Goijman pulled off in a difficult financial period for Argentina and its federation when he concluded, "My very strong opinion is that the FIVB should just pay this disputed amount, or some negotiated amount. It would clearly get rid of this stigma on our sport and send a positive message about supporting our world events and our long-time partners and do the right thing." But the FIVB has chosen not to engage with Goijman, much less help him to recover any of his savings.

The tragedy of Mario Goijman is an example of how international sporting organizations have been controlled by small groups of unaccountable men (and it is mostly men) who operate from secretive organizations, most of them headquartered in Switzerland, where oversight has been lax and autonomy has triumphed. Understanding why change is difficult requires knowing a bit about accountability and international organizations.

The People and Institutions That Caught Lance Armstrong

WADA is at the center of the modern antidoping regime. Headquartered in Montreal, Canada, and established in 1998, WADA is a remarkable organization in many respects, perhaps most importantly because it represents the first global governance regime for sport, one recognized in an international treaty that has been signed by more than 190 countries. The treaty is called the International Convention against Doping in Sport.[15] WADA was established as a Swiss foundation and the international treaty recognized WADA to oversee doping in the Olympic sports. WADA is governed and funded by governments and the IOC.[16] The fact that WADA is incorporated in Switzerland but headquartered in Canada illustrates some of the complexities of such organizations.

Even amid all the complexity, arguably, WADA is maybe the world's best example of coordinated global governance in any area, including nuclear weapons, the environment, and human rights. This speaks to the broad appeal and significance of sport among nations and people.

According to WADA, "doping is defined as the occurrence of one or more of the anti-doping rule violations."[17] Doping rules are part of the rules of the games, like the fact that the 100-meter dash is 100 meters and athletes cannot start before the gun or leave their lane. "Anti-doping rules," WADA explains, "like Competition rules, are sport rules governing the conditions under which sport is played. Athletes or other Persons accept these rules as a condition of participation and shall be bound by these rules." WADA is more than just a sports organization, though, because of the international treaty—it is a unique hybrid of sports organization and governmental body under international law.

We can look at the role played by WADA in antidoping efforts by returning to the case of Lance Armstrong and doping in professional cycling. One of the provisions of the international treaty on doping is that each nation is encouraged to have a national antidoping program to implement the WADA code at the domestic level. In the United States, this responsibility falls to an organization called the US Anti-Doping Agency, or USADA, headquartered in Colorado Springs, at the foot of the Rocky Mountains in Colorado.

The US Congress gave USADA special authority to oversee antidoping efforts under the international treaty.[18] US taxpayers provide almost $10 million per year, more than half, of USADA's total support.[19] USADA has responsibility for overseeing the antidoping regulations for those US athletes who compete under an organization called USA Cycling, as well as other US athletes who fall under the jurisdiction of the WADA code.[20] A nonprofit incorporated in Colorado, USA Cycling is the US member of the UCI, the international body that oversees cycling competitions worldwide, including the Tour de France (which is privately owned). The UCI is a member of the IOC, and thus falls under the jurisdiction of WADA.

The institutional context is important in the Armstrong case, but institutions are of course populated by real people. The head of USADA during the Lance Armstrong saga was a man named Travis Tygart, a lawyer who rose through the organization to become its CEO in 2007.[21] Tygart played sports in high school, playing on Florida state championship teams in basketball and baseball. One of his teammates was Chipper Jones, who would go on to a professional baseball career with the Atlanta Braves.[22] Tygart's focus on Armstrong resulted from a chance meeting with Jonathan Vaughters, a former member of Armstrong's cycling team, on a Colorado ski lift. According to Reed Abbergotti and Vanessa O'Connell of the *Wall Street Journal*, that chairlift "conversation made Tygart think about his mission."[23] Vaughters told Tygart that he had recommended that Floyd Landis, one of Armstrong's former teammates, come and talk to him about his experiences.

Landis was relatively unknown outside cycling circles, but that changed when he won the 2006 Tour de France. For a brief instant, he appeared to be the successor to Lance Armstrong. That dream did not last long, however, because only a few days after Landis's victory, he was notified that he had failed a drug test that showed unusually high levels of testosterone. Landis was subsequently stripped of his Tour de France victory and banned from cycling by USADA.[24]

Landis chose to appeal the ban. Under USADA, appeals to its judgments are considered as arbitration proceedings; USADA judgments do not carry the force of law because USADA is a nonprofit organization. The US Congress had decided in 1978 to place responsibility for settling disputes involving the Olympic sports outside the court system,[25] and the US Olympic Committee identified the American Arbitration Association (AAA) as the body that would resolve controversies under its constitution and bylaws. This was recognized officially in law in 1998,[26] and appeals of USADA judgments are heard under this system.

The appeal made by Landis was heard by a panel of three arbitrators in May 2007 at Pepperdine University in Malibu; the ruling was announced soon thereafter. In a strange twist, Greg LeMond, three-time winner of the Tour de France, testified that he had received a threatening call the night before. LeMond was able to trace the call to Landis's business manager. When this came out, the business manager was fired, but as Albergotti and O'Connell explain, "the damage had been done—Landis had been made to look terrible by the actions of a friend, and the hearings became a huge media spectacle." Not surprisingly, the arbitration panel's judgment went against Landis.[27] This left him with only one more appeal, to the

Court of Arbitration for Sport—the Swiss-based body that arbitrates disputes in international sport.

CAS is like a supreme court for sports arbitration. The organization is headquartered in Switzerland, where it is accountable to Swiss law. CAS was established in 1984 to settle disputes in international sports under the IOC. We've already talked about CAS in previous chapters, in the cases of Erik Tysse, Oscar Pistorius, and Dutee Chand. In principle, CAS helps to prevent disputes becoming messy jurisdictional issues. In this situation, Floyd Landis was an American cyclist competing in a private French race under the auspices of an organization (the UCI) headquartered in Switzerland, which operates under antidoping provisions overseen by WADA in Canada. Which laws apply to a doping violation that runs afoul of the rules of various nonprofits? Doping in sport is not illegal in the United States or in many other countries. CAS was created to cut through just this sort of potential messiness arising from the complexity of international sports.[28]

Landis lost his appeal to CAS.[29] He hit rock bottom a few years later, prompting him to contact Tygart and express his desire to tell him what he knew about doping in cycling, and about Lance Armstrong in particular. After hearing from Landis, Tygart contacted Jeff Novitsky, with the criminal investigation unit in the US Food and Drug Administration, to pass along what he had learned. In the early 2000s, Novitsky had been with the Internal Revenue Service on an investigation that uncovered the "massive steroid ring that supplied athletes in Major League Baseball, the National Football League, and Olympic track and field."[30] (As a result of that investigation, baseball player Barry Bonds and Olympic sprinter Marion Jones were both convicted of the criminal offenses of obstruction of justice and perjury.) Novitsky opened a criminal investigation of professional cycling focused on Lance Armstrong.

That investigation did not last long. The federal government decided not to pursue a case against Armstrong. Even so, the effort was significant because it compelled numerous professional cyclists and members of their entourages to testify on the record about doping in the sport. The role of the federal government in the Armstrong case is important and typically underappreciated. There is a convincing counterfactual argument to be made that if the case had been left just to sports bodies, Armstrong might never have been caught and punished.

Cyclists who testified against Armstrong under the short-lived US government investigation were subsequently more favorably inclined to testifying on the record to USADA when Travis Tygart approached them. And talk they did. On October 10, 2012, USADA released its "reasoned decision" on doping in professional cycling—a massive compilation of testimony, evidence, and analysis.[31] Armstrong was stripped of his seven Tour de France titles, admitted to doping on an Oprah Winfrey special, lost his sponsors, and continues to fight legal battles today.

But before all that, Armstrong tried to stop the investigation in its tracks. Unlike Landis, who appealed his decision under the rules of arbitration of the alphabet soup of USAC, USADA, AAA, UCI, IOC, and WADA, Armstrong decided to take his appeal outside the system of sports governance and into the US legal system. Months before the reasoned decision was released, Armstrong sued USADA in federal court in an effort to halt the investigation, arguing that USADA did not have the authority to sanction him. USADA asked for the suit to be dismissed.

Judge Sam Sparks sided with USADA. He wrote in his decision that courts are not generally the right place for such controversies: "Federal courts should not interfere with an amateur sports organization's disciplinary procedures. . . . To hold otherwise would be to turn federal judges into referees for a game in which they have no place, and about which they know little."[32] Sparks cited an earlier precedent to emphasize this conclusion: "It is hard to imagine a situation more illustrative of Judge Posner's famous words, that 'there can be few less suitable bodies than the federal courts for determining the eligibility, or the procedures for determining the eligibility, of athletes to participate in the Olympic Games.'" Instead, he pointed Armstrong toward the same arbitration processes that had heard Landis's appeals and, if necessary, the Swiss court system if Armstrong felt that CAS had violated Swiss law. Armstrong decided not to appeal the USADA sanction under the arbitration bodies, and his ban stuck.

The Armstrong case helps to illustrate the mushrooming of what has been called *lex sportiva,* or sports law. Recent decades have seen a growing body of policies, rules, jurisprudence, and institutions related to sport. Lorenzo Casini of the University of Rome describes this as "transnational law produced by sporting institutions"; others call it "international sports law."[33] International sports law has developed a great deal over the years. The Armstrong case helped to reinforce its legitimacy.

However, international sports law does face challenges. German speed skater Claudia Pechstein was suspended by the International Skating Union (ISU) in 2009 for two years for blood doping.[34] She never failed a drug test, but the ISU determined that there was circumstantial evidence of doping in her blood profiles. Pechstein appealed the case to CAS, claiming that her blood results indicated a hereditary condition. She lost the appeal. She returned to skating after serving her ban, but she did not end her fight to clear her name.

Pechstein sued the ISU in German court, which agreed to hear her case, which in effect meant that the CAS decision was not considered the last word on the matter.[35] One issue raised by the German court was the independence of CAS arbitrators, who are selected by a committee comprising members of the IOC, national Olympic committees, and international sports federations.[36] Because many CAS cases involve athletes against sports bodies, the fact that CAS arbitrators are selected by representatives of these bodies suggests a bias against athletes. The German court ruled that Pechstein

Speed skater Claudia Pechstein, photographed in Berlin in 2008, the year before she was suspended for blood doping. She has always protested her innocence.

deserved to have her case heard in a civil trial. A British lawyer who has represented athletes before CAS says that the Pechstein case might lead to the falling of "the wall of science" that often character-izes CAS cases on doping.[37] Pechstein's case has had its victories and losses in the German court system and is likely to unfold over the coming years before reaching its conclusion.[38]

However the Pechstein case is ultimately resolved, it seems clear that the CAS system of arbitration and the development of a *lex sportiva* are here to stay. But once we look under the hood of the system, we can see parts of the system that need tinkering. One fix that's needed is to create greater independence among CAS arbitra-tors, something that could be achieved, at least in part, by including more athletes and athlete representatives on CAS's arbitration com-mittees. A streamlined approach to antidoping that relies less on sci-ence, as suggested in the previous chapter, could also help to make arbitration more transparent and less of a dogfight between experts.

The development of a *lex sportiva* has come a long way. But it still has a long way to go.

The Uniqueness of Sports Organizations

Jens Sejer Andersen of Play the Game believes that 2015 was the year that "killed the autonomy of sport."[39] Scandal after scandal fo-cused attention on sports organizations and led to questions about their ability to self-govern. Andersen explains the challenge that these organizations face: "This notion of autonomy is not invented so corrupt people can hide behind it." Others agree. Gordon Smith, chief executive of the US Tennis Association, acknowledged the need for a more open flow of information in his sport when it faced accusations of widespread match fixing in 2016: "Look, I think the new watchword for tennis is transparency."[40] But calling for less au-tonomy and more transparency is one thing. Delivering it is anoth-er. Sport governance has developed over more than a century; fixing shortfalls won't be easy. National sports bodies, such as the NFL or the Premier League, are easier to keep in check because they are ultimately accountable to national laws, providing a sort of governance backstop. International bodies play by entirely different sets of rules, and they fly without a net.

Autonomy in sports has become increasingly problematic because sport is increasingly big business and, crucially, is increasingly associated with big business, thus providing opportunities and motivation for poor governance. For instance, the IOC reported revenue of about $8 billion for the four-year period ending with the London 2012 games.[41] To place this number into context: it is about the same as the 2013 revenue of all US Major League Baseball teams.[42] It is also about $1 billion more than the collective total revenue of the top twenty European soccer clubs in 2013.[43] Following the 2010 World Cup, FIFA boasted financial reserves of more than $1.2 billion.[44]

A billion dollars is a lot, but in the broader context of business, sport does not turn over particularly large amounts of money. For instance, Tesco, the British supermarket chain, had revenue of about $100 billion in 2014,[45] and the Shell oil company had revenue of about $450 billion.[46] Stefan Szymanski has shown that as part of the overall economy, sport and sport-related economic activity is fairly small.[47] Even so, the turnover of billions of dollars within the largest sporting organizations represents a significant increase from past years and provides considerable opportunities and incentives for corrupt behavior. The growth in the financial stakes associated with sport shows no sign of slowing down.[48]

Even though international sport and its finances have grown in size and significance, the organizations that govern the games are typically not businesses, but rather nonprofit associations. Mark Pieth of the Basel Institute of Governance and from 2011 to 2013 chair of FIFA's internal governance reform effort, writes that despite its nonprofit status, FIFA is "a potent corporate entity. This calls for a sequence of particular governance measures developed in the corporate world."[49] This view holds for other sports organizations as well. However, because of their unique governance structures, such bodies are not easily held accountable to standards of good governance because they are not considered to be businesses.

To understand international sports requires understanding the peculiar history and organization of the institutions that oversee international sports.[50] The most significant governance body is the International Olympic Committee, created in 1894. The IOC oversees what it calls the "Olympic Movement" defined as "the concerted, organized, universal and permanent action, carried out under the supreme authority of the IOC, of all individuals and entities who are inspired by the values of Olympism."[51] By "Olympism" the IOC is referring to its guiding philosophy—which we know from chapter 2 is sometimes equated with the spirit of sport—"based on the joy found in effort, the educational value of good example and respect for universal fundamental ethical principles."[52] In 2016, more than fifty sports were part of the Olympic movement, being played at either the Olympic Summer or Winter Games.[53]

The IOC coordinates the activities of national Olympic bodies and collaborates with international sports federations, such as FIFA, the FIVB, and the IWF, among many others. The international federations have many other responsibilities that go far beyond their collaboration with the IOC. For instance, FIFA oversees the quadrennial World Cup. FIFA also oversees and coordinates national soccer federations that, in turn, oversee the most popular professional leagues in the world, including the English Premier League and the German Bundesliga. Of course there are also many significant sports leagues, such as the NFL in the United States, that sit apart from the Olympic movement.

About sixty international sports organizations are headquartered in Switzerland, including the IOC and FIFA.[54] The IOC may seem like an international body, and it does have a close relationship with the United Nations, including special UN recognition and shared programs.[55] However, the IOC is not a part of the United Nations or any other multilateral institution—it is a nonprofit organization incorporated under the provisions of Swiss law. The IOC and several other global sports bodies receive special treatment under Swiss law, including tax and property privileges.[56]

For the IOC and other sports organizations, arrangements with the Swiss government date to more than a century ago, when the Swiss sought to encourage international governmental and nongovernmental organizations to set up shop in the country. The historical interest of the Swiss in hosting international organizations is not particular to sport; almost three hundred international bodies are headquartered in the small country.[57]

Because most international sports bodies are incorporated as associations—that is, as voluntary membership organizations—and are legally characterized as nonprofits, in general they are not subject to national or international laws or norms that govern business practices. To paraphrase sports governance doyen Dick Pound, this makes sports organizations nineteenth-century institutions operating in a twenty-first-century world.[58]

The difference in governance practices between public corporations such as the Swiss food giant Nestlé, multilateral institutions such as the United Nations, and sports organizations is striking. For example, if one wants to know the compensation of Ban Ki-Moon (about $240,000), the secretary-general of the United Nations, one can find that information on the UN website.[59] The same transparency applies to the CEO of Nestlé ($10.6 million).[60] However, if one had wished to know the salary of Sepp Blatter, the former president of FIFA, that information was simply not made available by FIFA during his seventeen-year reign.[61] Only after he was deposed did we learn that it was in the tens of millions of dollars.[62]

Leadership compensation disclosure is just one of many issues where private, nonprofit sports organizations differ from governmental, corporate, or nongovernmental multilateral organizations. In 2011, Pieth, the Swiss professor who was working for FIFA on governance reform, argued that the divergence in practices was increasingly problematic. He argued that the practices widely used in both corporations and in international bodies should be followed by sports organizations: "They are close to international organizations, but they are also businesses. There is a certain logic in applying the standards of both worlds."[63] In general, however, adopting such standards has proven difficult in practice, leaving corrupt officials in sports organizations better able to conceal their wrongdoing and escape any punishment.

Corruption in sports organizations located in Switzerland has been especially hard to prosecute. These bodies are subject to the provisions of Swiss law, and the Swiss government has historically been lax in its oversight. For example, as recently as 2006, bribery was not illegal under Swiss law. The Swiss government has taken steps in the past few years to tighten its oversight of sport bodies. In December 2014, it passed a law that would classify the leaders of sports organizations as "politically exposed persons," thus allowing investigators to examine their financial holdings and transactions.[64] The legislation is part of a broader set of reforms, tellingly called *lex Fifa*.[65]

All international sports organizations have corporate sponsors, and some have very large television contracts. However, sponsors have generally shown little interest in holding these bodies accountable when allegations of corruption have surfaced. Occasionally, a sponsor will issue a statement of concern,[66] but because sport is popular and makes them money, sponsors have shown little interest in much else. In general, sponsors have been quick to drop individual athletes when controversies arise—think Tiger Woods or Lance Armstrong—but have not shown the same resolve when it comes to organizations. But this may be changing. In 2016, several of Maria Sharapova's sponsors, including Nike and HEAD Tennis, stuck by her when she was suspended for doping. Sponsors have a crucially important role to play in sports governance, but what exactly that role consists of is still being worked out.

Learning from Governance Successes

Back in 2013, before the arrests and revelations of 2015 and 2016, I explored why FIFA, the subject of frequent allegations of corruption and poor governance practices, is so difficult to hold accountable.[67] The answer that I found is broadly applicable to international sports organizations that share similar characteristics.

Researchers looking at international organizations have identified six different mechanisms of accountability:[68]

- *Hierarchical accountability*: the power that superiors have over subordinates within an organization
- *Supervisory accountability*: relationships between organizations
- *Fiscal accountability*: controls over funding

- *Legal accountability*: the requirement that international bodies and their employees must abide by the laws of relevant jurisdictions in which those laws are applicable
- *Market accountability*: influence that is exercised by investors or consumers through market mechanisms
- *Public reputational accountability*: the reputation of an organization

The Olympic bribery scandal that emerged in the fall of 1998 led to comprehensive reforms of the IOC and provides an important precedent for how change can occur in international sport governance. The IOC scandal involved university scholarships provided by the Salt Lake Organizing Committee, or SLOC, which was seeking to bring the 2002 winter games to Salt Lake City.[69] The university scholarships were but the first domino to fall in a series of revelations involving not only the SLOC but also other bidders, including Nagano and Sydney, that included favors granted to sway votes, ranging from medical care to cosmetic surgery, jobs, and bribes. A Swiss member of the IOC suggested that as many as 7 percent of IOC members had taken bribes from potential host cities.[70]

The IOC and the SLOC created a number of investigative committees that by early 1999 had documented extensive instances of corrupt practices in the form of efforts by bidding cities to influence the IOC. The most significant investigative effort was put together by the US Olympic Committee and headed by former US senator George Mitchell, while the FBI opened an investigation to ascertain if relevant US corruption laws had been violated. The IOC set up its own commission to recommend reforms, and enlisted a number of prominent outsiders to serve on the commission, including former US diplomat Henry Kissinger.

An important motivator for change occurred in April 1999, when Congressman Henry Waxman introduced legislation under the US Foreign Corrupt Practices Act that would make it illegal for US corporations to contribute to the IOC unless it adopted the reforms recommended by the Mitchell Commission. Olympic sponsors were engaged in the issue and were a significant motivating force behind the creation of the IOC 2000 reform commission. Congressman Waxman explained his strategy in a press release:[71]

> I regret that this legislation has to be introduced. I had hoped that the IOC would adopt the necessary reforms on its own accord. It is apparent, however, that the IOC is reluctant to take strong and immediate action. Perhaps, the only thing that will get the IOC's attention is if American corporate money is cut off.

The US Congress followed up with a number of hearings on the IOC and opened an investigation into the practices employed to win the 1996 Atlanta Games, uncovering numerous instances of corrupt practices. The congressional threats and scrutiny had their desired effects. By December 2000, the IOC had adopted all the reforms that had been recommended by the IOC 2000 commission. Here again we see the importance of the US government stepping in when sports organizations fall short.

How was it that the IOC was held accountable and significant reforms were introduced? Of the seven mechanisms of accountability listed above, the interaction of legal and fiscal accountability were arguably the most important in this case. The fact that the scandal erupted in the United States meant that the US Congress had the authority to sanction the sponsors of the IOC under US anticorruption legislation. For members of the US Congress, the issue was a political winner because the victim of the scandal was the notion of fairness that is emblematic of the Olympics, and the bad guys were (often) bribe-seeking foreigners. The spectacle of members of the US Congress dressing down foreign IOC members made for excellent political theater.

Political theater sometimes coincides with policy reform. The threat posed by Congressman Waxman to Olympic sponsors was real and potentially enormously costly to their business interests. Thus, the legal authority exercised by the US Congress over the IOC was indirect but real. This authority facilitated the exercise of other forms of accountability, in particular fiscal accountability and public reputational accountability. Fiscal accountability was exercised through the various investigative committees that were established, particularly the Mitchell Commission and the IOC's parallel effort.

The investigations provided a steady stream of juicy revelations that kept the story fresh in the media and reinforced the efforts by members of the US Congress to secure political gain from the issue. Supervisory and peer accountability played considerably lesser roles. Ultimately, these various factors led to the exercise of hierarchical accountability, as the IOC had little choice but to accept the reforms brought to it by its committee.

The IOC experience can help us to understand the process of reform that FIFA has been going through since about 2010. I say "going through" because FIFA has not embraced or willingly taken on most of the reforms that have been recommended to it by governance experts such as Transparency International. FIFA thumbed its nose at those calling for reform for years. It was only after several individuals and organizations exposed themselves to the US legal system by using US banks in their corrupt activities that change was forced on FIFA. The legal accountability, as in the case of the IOC, snowballed, with FIFA's reputation and sponsors eventually becoming compromised. The reform of FIFA is a work in progress and is a process that will continue for years.*

Sports Governance for the Twenty-first Century: Less Autonomy, More Accountability

Good governance is like oxygen: when there's lot of it, it's rarely noted; when there's not enough or none at all, everyone pays attention. The sports world has seen crisis after crisis emerge in recent years revealing governance shortfalls. From FIFA to the UCI, the IAAF to WADA, the NFL to the IOC, the FIVB to the Confederation of North, Central American and Caribbean Association Football, a host of sports organizations have somehow fallen short of expectations for good governance.

---

*   I created a scorecard for evaluating how well FIFA is doing; see "An Evaluation of the FIFA Governance Reform Process of 2011–2013," in Stephen Frawley and Daryl Adair, eds., *Managing the Football World Cup* (London: Palgrave Macmillan UK, 2014), 197–221.

One reason for these shortfalls has been the demand by sports bodies for autonomy over their affairs. For the most part, the rest of society has agreed to this arrangement. In the United States, sports bodies run their affairs until they run into trouble, at which point the backstop, which is more than two hundred years of US jurisprudence and policy, comes into play. Sometimes, that backstop is helpful in addressing issues that sports bodies cannot resolve on their own, such as the dispute between the NFL and Tom Brady over deflated footballs. Other times, sports bodies would just as soon that government stay out of their affairs, as in the case of the NCAA pushing back against legal and legislative interventions into college sports.

In the international arena, autonomous sports organizations, for the most part, have no such backstop, for the simple reason that there is typically no international law or jurisprudence at the global level. There are a few exceptions. In the area of doping, nations around the world have signed on to an international treaty, but the shortfalls in that regime seen in recent years indicate that it is best viewed as a glass that has only started to be filled, and is far from a completed project. The sports world has embarked on creating its own jurisprudence—a *lex sportiva* developed under the judgments of CAS. Here, too, we see more work to be done. The independence of CAS has been challenged by athletes who demand greater representation, and its relative small size and limited number of cases decided means that a *lex sportiva* remains more of an aspiration than a reality.

The good news for sports organizations is that principles of good governance are well established in many settings, from government to business to civil society. These principles are not rocket science, and include basic notions of transparency and accountability. Even so, the struggle for many sports organizations has not been not knowing what good governance is, but actually putting it into place. When Sebastian Coe defied the conflict-of-interest guidelines of the IAAF on being elected to its presidency, and when Gianni Infantino rolled back one of the few governance reforms in FIFA on his assuming its presidency, it reflected a culture in which autonomy is used for private gain and personal power, rather than for promoting the broader interests of athletes, sponsors, and fans.

Despite such episodes, the outlook for better governance in sport is bright. Scandals draw attention, and with attention comes demands to do better. How we can provide the oxygen needed to sustain and respond to such demands is the subject of the next, and final, chapter.

Chapter 11

Governing Sport in the Twenty-first Century

Sport brings people together. In a world where we spend so much time focusing on our differences, sports reminds us of what we have in common. It is something everyone can share. So let's make sure it thrives.

Even if we set the high-minded stuff aside—like the spirit of sport—the fact remains that as a practical matter, sport brings many people pure joy. So let's get it right.

At present, however, sport is running into trouble. Billions of us still participate in sport, watch it, and love it, of course. But our shared enjoyment keeps running into the same obstacle: Can we admire what we don't trust? We see elite athletes achieving remarkable things—running faster than ever before, lifting more than ever before, jumping farther than ever before—but sometimes they, along with enablers and exploiters, do so by breaking the very rules that make sport possible. Put simply, they cheat.

The overarching theme of this book is that sport resolves the eternal conflict between the performance edge and the ethical edge through the creation and application of *rules*. The rules of sport take our highest-order values and turn them into on-the-ground practicalities. The rules take an abstract notion like fairness and turn it into something concrete, such as a rule that says everyone who runs a marathon has to run the same distance—they can't take shortcuts or hop on a bus.

But a lot of elite athletes and sport administrators seem to be jumping on metaphorical buses these days. Take, for instance, the scandals that have enveloped international track and field since 2013, centered on Russia, with many allegations of widespread, state-sponsored doping among Russia's elite athletes, encouraged by coaches, sports officials, and even politicians. The scandal claimed the leadership of the IAAF, the body that athletes trust to oversee their sport. Much discussion in the media in the lead-up to the 2016 Rio Olympics was not about the spectacle of athletic performance, but about the highly politicized battle over whether or not Russian track and field athletes would be allowed to compete in Rio at all.

Why are so many people breaking so many rules these days across sport?

We can point to several different reasons, but the most important of them is that the rules that sport is currently trying to implement reflect values that many of us don't relate to so much anymore. Sport is suffering from a stubborn adherence to aspirations that are outdated or simply not fit for the twenty-first century. Trying to implement rules that are built on a foundation of sand is a recipe for collapse. Across the battlefields surveyed in part II of this book, the values of amateurism, purity, uncertainty, and autonomy no longer serve the functions that they once did in creating a consensus as to what sport should be about. Trying to hang on to ideals that are no longer widely shared inevitably creates conflict and, eventually, institutional collapse. Some people argue that we need tougher and tougher measures to enforce the old values. For instance, clean sport, they argue, is nonnegotiable. Others say that it is impossible to enforce the old rules all—or even most—of the time, and that, consequently, sport should just let anything go.

In this concluding chapter, I complete our look at the edge by underscoring that sport in the twenty-first century needs to be reimagined in terms of a new quartet of values: professionalism, pragmatism, accountability, and transparency. I revisit a few of the battlegrounds discussed earlier and offer a perspective on how these battles might be reconsidered of in light of contemporary values. In some instances, sport is already being reconsidered in these terms—it is our language, institutions, and practices that need to catch up.

For example, in the debate over amateurism in college sports, a pragmatic middle ground for the enhanced compensation of athletes is already taking shape. But regardless of what shape college athletics professionalism ultimately takes, evolution in the values that underlie college sports is already occurring. The NCAA hasn't yet changed its rhetoric to reflect the new reality, suggesting that it may still be in denial about its own transformation of amateurism into a form of professionalism. Refusal by those who oversee college sports to accept that change is under way may lead to more profound sorts of change foisted on them, such as by Congress or the courts. In the face of such risks of political intervention into college sports, for those who would like to see college sports continue as a distinct category of competition, accepting that values have changed may be the wiser course of action.

Values are changing as well in the other battlefields, in most cases far less obviously than in college sports. Again, there are struggles to keep modern issues—like athletes with prosthetic limbs or intersex women—outside of the debate, lest bringing them into the debate will call into question old values. I argue that change is hard to hold back, so we might as well have the discussion anyway.

The chapter concludes by recommending that we keep in mind three principles to guide that discussion:

- Values underlie rules and rules underlie sport.
- Athlete participation in sport governance is essential.
- Governance at the edge is always a work in progress.

These principles are not about solutions, but about organizing a discussion. I am wary of falling into the trap that I set for my students—looking for solutions to wicked problems. Instead, sport needs to open itself up to a broader set of stakeholders, to more debate, to more ideas (even ones that will eventually be tossed aside) to be reimagined in a modern context. Let's return to the issue of college sports to illustrate such a reimagining, not as a solution, but as a way to engage a debate and discussion that might lead to a new consensus on what college sports are to be about.

When Values Are Changing: Emerging Pragmatism in College Sports

Chapter 4 ended by suggesting that big-time college athletics could move in one of two directions: toward a professional model or in the direction of legitimizing athletics as a vocation. Let's probe the professional model a little more, because it seems to me that a pragmatic framework for the professionalization of college sports that moves well beyond the outdated notion of amateurism is already taking shape. As our values have changed surrounding college sports, so too have our practices, especially those of the NCAA.

A professional model for big-time college athletics is emerging in three parts: the stipend, intellectual property, and prizes.

Starting in 2015, the NCAA allowed Division I schools (the top-level programs) to pay students a stipend called "cost of attendance" to cover expenses not included in scholarship packages.[1] These payments are intended to close the gap between an athletic scholarship and what the government defines as the cost of attending a university, which includes things such as the cost of transportation and school supplies. At the University of Colorado, where I teach, the annual "cost of attendance" is about $4,000 for out-of-state scholarship athletes, and in-state it is $3,300. These additional payments to athletes vary across programs; for instance, the University of California, Los Angeles, a public school, pays as much as $6,000, while the private University of Southern California pays less than $2,000, even though both schools are in Los Angeles.

These payments were created, arguably, as a pre-emptive response by the NCAA to the O'Bannon litigation. To refresh your memory: the O'Bannon litigation involves issues of compensation for the use of an athlete's name, image, and likeness, arising out of video games. The NCAA was also prompted to introduce the cost of attendance payments because it received a lot of bad publicity when Shabazz Napier, a basketball player at the University of Connecticut, complained on national TV after winning the 2014 March Madness tournament of "hungry nights" caused by a lack of food and money under his existing scholarship package.

Looking to the future, if the O'Bannon case or similar litigation leads to a judgment that the NCAA must treat college athletes like employees or increase their compensation in some other way, the NCAA may be forced to augment the cost-of-attendance stipends or even pay salaries to athletes.

One sensible approach would be to treat college athletes like another group of students who work on campus in support of the university mission—graduate students. Universities routinely set stipends for graduate students who work twenty hours a week, often under the watchful eye of federal research agencies. A maximum amount for such stipends in federal grant applications is typically regulated by research agencies such as the National Science Foundation and the National Institutes of Health.

The NCAA could allow scholarship athletes to receive stipends similar to those received by graduate students. Such stipends rarely exceed $30,000 per year. The NCAA could set the maximum undergraduate sports stipend equal to each university's minimum stipend amount for its graduate students, in order to discourage a "stipend war" among universities.

The budgetary consequences would not be outrageous. For instance, at Ohio State University, the minimum graduate student stipend is $13,500,[2] while at Stanford, a private university, it is about $27,000, which just about mirrors the 2 to 1 ratio in current cost-of-attendance numbers that the federal government has calculated between the two schools.[3] If Ohio State carried the maximum number of NCAA-allowed athletic scholarships,[*] then then additional cost of stipends would be about $6 million, or about a 4 percent increase in its nearly $150 million athletics budget. The increase to Stanford's budget would be larger, due to its higher stipends, adding about $12

---

[*] The NCAA regulates the number of scholarships that each school can offer for each varsity sport, and these numbers are influenced by factors such as historical precedent and federal legislation (Title IX) that serve to regulate a balance between men's and women's sports on campus.

million to its reported $100 million athletics budget.[4] Most schools do not carry the maximum set of scholarships, however, and schools could award partial stipends just like graduate programs do, so the financial impact could be managed with different resources and priorities depending on a school's budget.

Some college athletes are more responsible than others for the revenue generated by athletic programs, so a case could be made that athletes in the so-called revenue sports—football and men's and women's basketball—should have an opportunity to receive greater compensation. This could happen in two ways, both of which have existing precedents: prizes and intellectual property.

It is not widely known, and the NCAA doesn't advertise the fact, but the NCAA Division I rule book allows athletes to receive awards for participating in and winning championships.[5] For instance, a university and its conference are each allowed to give an athlete an award for winning a conference ($325) or an NCAA championship ($415). Thus, an athlete who wins both championships in a season could receive cash awards totaling $1,480. In addition, the parents of athletes who make their way to the Final Four basketball tournament get $3,000 (plus another $1,000 if the team reaches the final); parents of athletes who reach the college football playoffs get $3,000.[6] Participants in bowl games and the NCAA basketball tournament have access to "gift suites," where athletes can collect merchandise prizes including "recliners, jewelry, TVs, headphones and speakers."[7] *Sports Business Daily* estimates that some of these athletes have ended up with as much as $4,000 in gifts.

When you add up the potential institutional, conference, and NCAA awards, and add in the parent payments and gift suites, the most successful athletes might take home close to $10,000 in prizes under existing rules. In fact, the NCAA has no limit on awards to participants in NCAA postseason tournaments or championships.

Thus, it seems clear that, under the NCAA, amateurism is already a relic of a bygone era; what has yet to occur is for the NCAA to admit as much. Viewing big-time college athletes as anything other than a form of professionals requires a willingness to turn a blind eye to reality—and a willingness to endure the legal and financial repercussions of upholding this fantasy. In 2015, the NCAA spent

$25 million on external legal bills, and most of that was to defend it-self against challenges to amateurism. To put this in perspective, $25 million is the same amount the NCAA would have to spend if it paid about $10,000 for each scholarship athlete who participated in the college football playoffs and men's and women's NCAA tournaments.

Under current NCAA rules and practices, it could be only a short procedural step to institute meaningful cash prizes for all NCAA championships, with significant money earmarked for participants in March Madness and the College Football Playoff, which both earn billions of dollars annually. Awarding $10,000 to each of the 884 men's scholarship basketball players who make it to the NCAA tour-nament would mean parting with just over 1 percent of the NCAA's current annual March Madness TV contract—a contract that will increase from $770 million per year to $1.1 billion per year starting in 2024.[8] Arguments that the money isn't there or that payments would bankrupt universities just don't hold up.

Another source of variable compensation is related to the focus of the O'Bannon lawsuit: the commercial value of an athlete's name, image, and likeness. As chapter 4 suggests, the NCAA, a body made up of university members, could change its regulations to treat col-lege athletes in much the same way that the NCAA's member uni-versities already treat faculty and students in regard to intellectual property. For example, a team of researchers at UCLA recently sold a drug developed on campus for more than $1 billion, making both the researchers and the university rich.[9] The sharing of revenue from intellectual property in equal parts among the campus, the academic department, and the researcher has helped align incen-tives among researchers and universities, creating a virtuous circle. A similar revenue-sharing setup could benefit the college athlete with commercial potential, while also benefitting the athletics de-partment and the wider campus. Such revenue, when captured by universities, could be used help to defray the cost of stipends.

Typically, university athletics departments have staff focused on licensing and trademarks, and it would not be a big change to include athletes under this umbrella. The economic value of the name, image, and likeness of the vast majority of college athletes is close to zero. It is the same way with professors and their intellectual property. Yet, every once in a while an athlete will have outsized commercial value that is uncaptured. Recall that Texas A&M estimated Jonny Manziel's 2012 Heisman Trophy season to be worth $37 million to the university.[10] Capturing some part of this value would benefit the university and its athletics program— and the athlete.

In 2015, the Pac-12 conference put forward a proposal to the NCAA to allow college athletes to profit from their name, image, and likeness.[11] That proposal was eventually withdrawn due to a lack of support across the conferences, but it signaled openness to the idea. A virtuous cycle that aligns the incentives of athletes, athletics departments, and universities, capturing revenue from intellectual property, could help to stimulate untapped windfalls, just as it has on the research side of campuses under US law since 1980.

For decades, the NCAA has held firm to its outdated and mythological notion of amateurism. Cracks in the foundation of that notion have appeared, but the NCAA has pressed ahead, seemingly undaunted. Olympic athletes transformed from amateurs to professionals during the 1970s; the Olympics are today more popular than ever, and few complain about the fact that participants earn a living through their sport. The Olympic experience shows us that one day the fig leaf of amateurism might be there, but the next day it might be gone, never to be seen again.

If change does occur, it would be wise to have options in place for what might come next, as not all possible paths are equally desirable. Congress or the courts might force change to occur in unexpected ways, such as turning college sports into a de facto minor league for the NFL, NBA, and WNBA.

Although it is not yet clear exactly how college sports will evolve, it seems safe to say that the amateur ideal invoked by the NCAA is already being replaced with a version of professionalism. It is time for the NCAA, as well as college athletes, to jump into this discussion with both feet (rather than paddling around the edge) and to help lead the debate in a way that leads to constructive change reflecting modern values.

When Values Are Contested, Bringing Debates into the Open

In the other battlefields explored in this book, discussions about outdated values have yet to come as far as they have in the field of college sports. In some cases, no one has yet even asked if the values that are invoked to justify rules might be outdated. In other cases, the question has been raised but the discussion is still at an early stage. In yet other cases, a debate has ignited but then has been quickly stamped out by a governing body fearful of where it might lead.

For instance, in chapter 7, I briefly mention Markus Rehm, the German long-jumper who leaps off of a prosthetic leg. His quest to jump in the Rio Olympics in 2016 was turned down by the IAAF several months before the games; the IAAF cited the fact that he had not shown that he does not receive an advantage by jumping off of his blade. The double negative in the previous sentence might seem confusing, but it is accurate. In announcing the decision, the IAAF's president, Sebastian Coe, explained: "[Rehm] has to prove that the prosthetic that he uses does not give him a competitive advantage and at this stage he has not."[12] The IAAF decision is reflective of the values of purity (in this case, the long-standing bias against athletes with prosthetics in the Olympics) and autonomy (as reflected in the fact that the IAAF made its decision with little effort to be transparent or inclusive). Rehm differs from Oscar Pistorius, the blade runner, in that Rehm leaps off of his prosthetic leg—and those jumps are among the farthest of any athlete in the Olympics or Paralympics. The inclusion of Pistorius in the London 2012 games might have been a matter of fairness; letting Rehm compete in the Olympics might mean rewriting the record books. Some leaps may be just too far.

Recall that in the Pistorius case, the burden of proof had been on the IAAF, not the athlete, to demonstrate the presence of an advantage provided by technology. Chapter 7 discusses how Pistorius secured participation in the 2012 London Olympics by winning an appeal against the IAAF before the Court of Arbitration for Sport (CAS). The IAAF had originally prohibited Pistorius from participating in London, but after Pistorius appealed, CAS overturned that ban. In that decision, CAS determined that it was the responsibility of the IAAF to show that, "on the balance of probabilities," Pistorius gained an advantage by running on his blades. The research commissioned by the IAAF did not show such an advantage conclusively. As a result, CAS ruled that Pistorius was able to compete in the London Games, where he reached the semifinals of the 400 meters.

This precedent was overturned in 2015, when the IAAF quietly introduced a new rule that in such cases reverses the burden of proof. The switch placed the burden of proof on the athlete instead of the governing body. The new rule—which we might call the Rehm rule, given its timing—states that an athlete with a prosthetic limb (specifically, a "mechanical aid") cannot participate in IAAF events "unless the athlete can establish on the balance of probabilities that the use of an aid would not provide him with an overall competitive advantage over an athlete not using such aid."[13] This new rule effectively slammed the door to participation by Paralympians with prosthetics from participating in the Olympic Games.

Even if an athlete might have the resources to enlist researchers to carefully study his or her performance, the IAAF requires the athlete to do something that is very difficult, and often altogether impossible—to prove a negative. In the case of Pistorius, CAS concluded that "the IAAF rightly accepted the burden of proof" to show that a prosthetic offered an advantage in order to deny an athlete from participating in the Olympics. The evidence produced by the IAAF was "overall, inconclusive."[14]

A German scientist who studied Rehm's jumping ability in early 2016 concluded that it was "difficult, if not impossible" to show any advantage gained by the use of the prosthetic. Another researcher commented that in the studies of Rehm's jumping, "detecting an advantage or a disadvantage is an impossible task."[15] Yet the very same scientific conclusions that allowed Pistorius to participate in London in 2012 were used to deny Rehm from participating in Rio in 2016. The most important difference between the two cases is not the science but the shifting of the burden of proof to show advantage from the IAAF to Rehm, who must show the absence of advantage. But in this instance, showing the absence of advantage is not possible.*

In the case of Rehm, the IAAF sidestepped a discussion over the inclusion of Paralympians who run on prosthetics in the Olympic Games by introducing a new rule that effectively means that no athletes with prosthetics, ever again, can participate in the Olympics. The new rule is certainly consistent with the value of purity in sport—if one considers prosthetics to be impurities—but what has not been not discussed, at least not out in the open, is whether the decision is consistent with the broader societal values of making sport inclusive, using evidence in decision making, and making important decisions out in the open rather than behind closed doors.

There was no open debate in the Rehm case. Officials in the IAAF decided among themselves who is allowed to participate in the Olympics and who is not. That is autonomy at work. Most people don't know that the Rehm rule was even put into place, not just because IAAF didn't advertise it, but also because it is hard to see people who aren't allowed to participate in the Olympics.

In contrast, in 2016, Caster Semenya began running faster than she had since bursting on the scene in 2009 in Berlin. Her reemergence at the highest levels of track and field reinvigorated a debate over her inclusion in the Olympic Games focused on who is classified as a woman. The more successful women like Semenya are, the more debate and discussion will take place. Unlike Rehm, Semenya was seen, and often seen running away from her competitors. The IAAF was unable to exclude Semenya and other women, as chapter 8 explains. For decades, the sports world tried (and succeeded) in keeping women who might raise eligibility questions away from

---

* More technically, consider the following hypothesis: H1: Rehm's prosthetic offers him no advantage. To evaluate this hypothesis, you would design a study to disprove it, that is, to seek to identify the existence of an advantage. If you can identify an advantage, then the hypothesis is incorrect. The studies that were conducted could not identify an advantage. So, scientifically, one would say that the hypothesis has not been disproven. But saying that something has not been disproven is not, according to the IAAF, the same as saying something is proven (even on a "balance of probabilities"). If an inability to disprove H1 is not sufficient to secure IAAF approval, then proving the absence of advantage appears to be impossible under the IAAF's Rehm rule.

competition. But challenges to existing values led to a debate that has resulted in sport becoming more inclusive.

Issues related to match fixing, discussed in chapter 5, are somewhere in between debates over technological augmentation and sex testing in terms of open and transparent discussion. The conversation is motivated primarily by occasional allegations (often hazy and uncorroborated) of the fix being in for some match or competition, typically in tennis or soccer in Europe, or in cricket in some other parts of the world. Some decision makers have taken the lead in opening a discussion of the threat of match fixing, but as chapter 5 argues, this debate is hamstrung by a definition of sport manipulation that relies on the notion of "uncertainty of outcome." It will be difficult to assess the scale of the problem associated with match fixing unless we know it when we see it, can measure it, and can assess the consequences of possible interventions. A big scandal, such as allegations of fixing in the NFL or the English Premier League, would surely be enough to motivate a wider discussion. Absent such a major scandal, match fixing may remain a niche issue at the edge.

For decades, the issue of doping has ebbed and flowed as a major issue in sport. Today, it is undoubtedly a major issue, perhaps *the* major issue, confronting international sport. The bombshell allegations against Russian track and field, which were fueled by a steady stream of ever-more shocking revelations in 2015 and 2016, forced WADA, the IAAF, and the IOC to respond. Before the 2016 Rio Olympics, the IOC promised to hold an "Extraordinary World Conference on Doping" sometime in 2017.[16] A major international conference would dramatically increase the chances of an open and wide-ranging discussion about antidoping and the institutions that are supposed to oversee sport.

Crisis may cast a cloud over sport, but the resulting debates are its silver lining, offering the promise of new paths forward and a chance for values to change and for changed values to have impact.

Last Words:
Three Principles for Living at the Edge

We have explored what it means to cheat, suggested a vocabulary for discussions at the edge, and looked at five different battlefields where wars are taking place in modern sport. To conclude, let me suggest three principles for governing at the edge between performance and ethics in the twenty-first century. Embracing principles doesn't necessarily mean that we will discover answers, but principles can help us think and act better together.

Principle #1: Values Underlie Rules and Rules Underlie Sport

Chapter 3 offers a definition of cheating as the violation of the constitutive rules of a game. It is important to distinguish cheating from simply breaking rules in a game, competitiveness, or even cynical play, because cheating, as defined here, threatens the very legitimacy of sport.

Chapter 3 suggests a vocabulary that might help us be precise about the issues at stake in debates about sport. This vocabulary includes:

- *Constitutive rules:* Rules about rules
- *Regulatory rules:* Rules that govern game play
- *Norms:* Broadly held societal expectations for behavior
- *Cheating:* The violation of constitutive rules
- *Ordinary play:* A competition in practice
- *Penalty:* A sanction imposed for the violation of regulatory rules
- *Cynical play:* A violation of both regulatory rules and norms
- *Gamesmanship:* A violation of norms but not of regulatory rules
- *Rules hole:* A contingency not covered by existing rules

Chapter 3 also introduces three lessons learned about the application of rules in sport:

- People respond to incentives.

- Rules have unintended consequences.
- Rules are always imperfect.

If we use the same vocabulary and learn the same lessons, we'll be able to discuss problems with more focus and clarity. Let's revisit the issue of doping in sport to illustrate.

The value of purity drives antidoping efforts in athletics, as reflected in the phrase used to describe antidoping's chief goal: "clean athletes." But not all athletes share this value. For instance, three-time Olympic silver medalist (2004, 2008, 2012) Tatyana Firova, who ran for Russia in the 400 meters, commented in 2016 amid the allegations surrounding her nation's role in systematic doping, "A normal person can take banned substances if they want to. So why can't athletes take them as well? How else can we achieve high results?"[17] Not surprisingly, given these comments, in a drug retest conducted in 2016, Firova's 2008 samples came up positive. As chapter 5 describes, Firova is far from alone in the world of sports, with evidence indicating that hundreds, if not thousands, of athletes across many nations and sports break the rules regulating doping. Because doping rules are constitutive rules, these athletes are cheating.

Cheating by these athletes strongly indicates that the norms within sport are not well aligned with the rules that govern sport. Athletes face powerful incentives to secure a performance edge because the rewards are high and the risks are low. One reason for this disparity is that the technologies of doping are ahead of the ability of antidoping regulators to enforce the rules. Athletes will dope. And they will be enabled to do so by coaches and even governments.

In crafting rules, antidoping officials focus almost exclusively on individual athletes, neglecting, almost entirely, the possibility of state-sponsored doping. For track and field, this oversight forced the IAAF, when the systematic nature of Russian doping was revealed, to launch ad hoc investigations and undertake further rule making in the lead up to the Rio Olympics.[18] In stark contrast, the federation that governs international weight lifting, a sport historically plagued by doping, instituted a set of clear rules in 2015 that quantify how many individual doping violations (nine or more) would lead to an entire nation being suspended by the Olympics. When Bulgaria was hit with eleven violations in 2015, it was banned from Rio, and its appeal was rejected by CAS.[19] Arguably, weight lifting was far more prepared for systemic doping than track and field.

What works for weight lifting and Bulgaria might not work in other contexts. Russia is a significant sporting nation, and track and field is widely considered to be the crown jewel of the Olympic Games. Would nations agree to be bound in a highly visible sport like track and field by a predetermined threshold of individual doping violations? The consequences could be severe: the nation with the most athletes sanctioned for doping in 2014 (the most recent year data were available) was Russia; trailing it were India, Italy, France, and China.[20] In addition to doped athletes, another reason for the large number of sanctions is that Russian athletes were tested more often than those in other countries.* The adoption of a weight lifting-style sanction on nations across other sports would have consequences (including unintended ones), and thus, like many issues related to doping, is an option that needs to be discussed in a way that is both transparent and inclusive.

The future of antidoping is unclear except for the fact that the regime that is in place to regulate doping is a work in progress. What is clear is that the issue is plagued by the gap between observed norms and codified rules. As chapter 9 indicates, antidoping rules are not being implemented based on evidence. The challenges revealed in the lead-up to the 2016 Olympic Games in Rio won't be resolved in the years that follow without careful attention to the values that underlie antidoping, how those values influence constitutive rules, and the implications of those rules for the future of sport.

---

* Because drug tests are given "strategically," as we learned in chapter 6, we might assume that the Russians were tested more often than others because of the (now clearly seen) well-founded suspicions of guilt. However, the setting of a threshold for a nation's suspension would likely require some sort of equity in testing across nations.

Principle #2: Athlete Participation in Governance Is Essential

If there is one group of stakeholders whose voice needs to be heard more loudly in debates over sport at the edge, it is athletes. In some case, such as the players associations of the US professional leagues and professional tennis and golf, athletes already have a strong voice and notable presence in the governance of their sport. When US golfer Dustin Johnson was told by the USGA during the 2016 US Open that he might (or might not) be assessed a penalty during the last stages of a closely fought final round, dozens of professional golfers took to Twitter to criticize the process. Top golfers Jordan Spieth, Rory McIlroy, Rickie Fowler, and Tiger Woods came to Johnson's defense. Their statements appear to have influenced the USGA to apologize for the controversy after Johnson had taken the trophy.[21]

The strong voice of athletes in golf is not found across all sports. Contrast this with soccer, in which very few athletes have voiced opinions on the FIFA scandal. Real Madrid's Cristiano Ronaldo, one of the world's top players, was asked about the FIFA scandal in an interview with CNN Español, and he stormed out, yelling, "Speak about FIFA? I don't care about FIFA and Qatar. I don't give a f---."[22] The famously volatile Ronaldo may have uttered an extreme reaction, but judging by the remarkable silence among professional soccer players on the FIFA scandal, his views may be representative. One reason that sports governance failures persist is that athletes closest to those bodies stand by silently when scandals erupt.

Not all athletes have the privileges or platform that elite soccer players and golfers do. In many other contexts, the athlete's voice is hard to hear, such as in US college sports and the Olympic movement. Former US elite runner Lauren Fleishman has offered several reasons why athletes don't speak out more about doping—reasons that help us understand why athletes do not speak out on other issues as well.[23]

First, athletes want to believe that their governing bodies can be trusted to take care of things: "After all, we have to report every hour of every day of our lives to antidoping agencies who can show up at any moment unannounced to take our blood and urine, so surely they must have this under control." Wanting to believe, however, is not the same as believing, and as scandals and poor decision making continue to plague sporting bodies, athletes are thinking twice about extending blind trust. Fleishman explains that the mixed messages often sent by governing bodies (such as exhortations to "play true" even though everyone in the sport knows that many athletes are doping with abandon) can be paralyzing to athletes who may have had their trust weakened, but don't know who is on their side.

Second, athletes are afraid of the consequences of speaking out. Kara Goucher, the US distance runner who came forward in 2015 as a whistle blower with allegations against Nike and her former coach Alberto Salazar, explained: "A big fear of never wanting to come forward is that people will question everything that I did. And that'll keep you silent."[24] Goucher broke her silence and suffered the consequences—not just criticism; her performances suffered due to the stress and distraction. Fleishman argues that there is an edge here too: athletes are worried that when they speak out, they cross an "invisible line that moves a person from pursuit of excellence to pursuit of change." Of course, a lack of empowerment and standing also stands in the way of athletes taking more responsibility for the governance of their sports.

Yet, some athletes *are* speaking out about sport. They may do it through organizations that represent the interests of athletes, such as FIFPro, which represents professional soccer players, or UNI Global Union, which represents workers around the world, including athletes.[25] But athletes are not always a welcome voice in the governance of sport. For instance, in 2016, Beckie Scott, the chair of the WADA Athletes' Committee, called upon WADA to expand its investigation into systematic doping in Russia. After making this request, she was "marginalized" by WADA's president, Craig Reedie, according to one source, and treated "abysmally," according to another. The *Guardian* reported that Reedie has been accused of "dismissing her calls for an independent commission review into other Russian sports, breaking with convention at the last Wada board meeting to deny her a chance to speak, and . . . [saying] 'shut that girl up' when she pressed for more investigations into Russia."[26]

One antidoping official told me that athletes could not be trusted to participate more in the setting of antidoping regulations because if they did, "there would not be any regulations at all."*

The most compelling argument for athletes to have a greater voice in governing sport is that they are the stakeholders who are most directly affected by decisions about sport. The track, the court, the field—these are their workplaces, and they should have a say in the rules that are applied there. The athlete's voice is not the only voice that we need to hear in debates at the edge, but it is definitely one worth hearing more clearly, loudly, and frequently.

Principle #3: Governance at the Edge Is Always a Work in Progress

The various challenges faced by sport are many, yet they should be viewed as opportunities to align sport more closely with shared values. Where we disagree about how rules should be written or implemented, our shared commitment to sporting competition provides an impetus to discuss, to negotiate, and to resolve.

If values underpin rules, and rules make sport possible, then it is governance that links together values, rules, and sport. For much of the history of sport, athletes have not been alone in thinking that the bodies that oversee sport have everything under control. With the exception of a few dedicated investigative journalists, the creation and enforcement of rules took place out of sight, and people paid little attention. Things have changed. The front pages of major newspapers nowadays carry reports of FIFA's incompetence and corruption, stories about the NFL's dispute resolution process for deflated footballs, and a wealth of other newsworthy tales about how badly sport is being run. Sporting bodies today are expected to be more transparent, and stakeholders demand greater accountability.

---

* There is some truth in this assertion, because antidoping regulations that are the result of collective bargaining processes are generally weaker than those imposed with less athlete involvement; see A. H. Selig and R. D. Manfred, "Regulation of Nutritional Supplements in Professional Sports," *Stanford Law and Policy Review* 15 (2004), 35. Nonetheless, less-strong regulations are not the same as toothless ones.

The governance of sport is always going to be a work in progress, and the battle between securing a performance edge while not crossing the ethical line is timeless. Many of the issues that arise at the edge are wicked problems, and they defy solution. But that doesn't mean that we can't make a difference. Instead of throwing up our hands in cynicism and despair, we—fans, athletes, officials—need to work together to make sure the sports we love are played according to rules that reflect values we share. Can we save the soul of sport? You bet we can. We just need to up our game.

Acknowledgments

Writing a book requires a lot of help, and *The Edge* required more than many. The book's origin can be traced to my decision to start full-time blogging and writing about sports governance issues in 2011. Since then, many dozens of people have graciously given of their time and expertise to help me learn more about this fascinating field.

I apologize to all those whom I have missed in the list below, and, as is usual in such things, all responsibility for errors of fact, poor argumentation, and unpopular perspectives lies with me alone. Thanks go out to those few people who have shared advice and information but have asked not to be named. You know who you are, and I'm grateful.

The book has benefited in large and small ways from Catalin Grigoras, Jeff Smith, Ricardo Simmons, Andrew Muscato, Bonita Mersiades, James Corbett, Jamie Fuller, Lance Armstrong, Travis Tygart, Annie Skinner, Jon Nissen-Meyer, Kara Goucher, Maggie Durand, Jesus Dapena, Catherine MacLean, Peter van Eenoo, Henrik Brant, Maria Surballe, Thierry Boghosian, Casey Malone, Walter DiGregorio, Max Boykoff, Jack Graham, Estes Banks, Mario Goijman, Jean-Loup Chappelet, Richard Ings, Doug Beal, Erik Boye, Tad Boyle, David Plati, Neill Woelk, Steve Maxwell, Deborah Unger, Gareth Sweeney, Andreas Selliaas, Robin Ann Shirley, Henrik Brant, Rowland Jack, Spencer Harris, James Kitching, Bill Mallon, Simon Gleave, Andrew Jennings, Richard McLaren, Ammar Moussa, Richard Pound, Alena Grabowski, Mike MacIntyre, Andy Schwarz, Dave Ridpath, Maureen Weston, James Corbett, and Ross Tucker.

In recent years, I have had the pleasure to get to know and speak with a large number of reporters who cover sports (and issues related to sports). I have endless respect for these individuals, their knowledge, and their professionalism, especially as the field of journalism has suffered immense changes over the past decades. I can't name these people all here, but I have learned a lot from them and, it is safe to say, this book would not have been possible to write without their work exploring a side of sports that most people never see. Some of their work is cited in these pages, and much more could have been.

Similarly, there are many scholars who have worked in the esoteric fields of sports studies whose research has proven essential for understanding many of the issues in this book. I've had the pleasure of meeting and corresponding with some of these scholars, and reading and learning from the works of others. As scholarship focused on sports grows, it will build on a solid foundation laid by those who have come before.

Thanks to my blog and to Twitter, I've had access to and received advice from countless experts—some in journalism and academia and many outside these fields—whose counsel is reflected in this book. I can't name you all (and don't even know some of you), but your efforts are appreciated.

A few friends, family, and colleagues took on the thankless task of reading some or all of the manuscript in draft form, including Daryl Adair, Jay Bilas, Paul Dimeo, Bill Mallon, Oliver Luck, Ryan Rodenberg, Carl Bialik, Julie Pielke, Jon Nissen-Meyer, and Roger Pielke Sr. Their comments and suggestions improved the final product immeasurably and saved me from more than a few boneheaded mistakes and poor arguments.

A few people are deserving of extra special thanks. When I had my midlife crisis, instead of buying a red Corvette, I decided to change directions and focus my research, writing, and teaching on sports issues. Several people supported me in this career change when they had no real reason to do so, other than being great people. I'd like to offer special thanks to Nick Harris, Walter Palmer, Simon Kuper, Stefan Szymanski, and Jens Sejer Andersen. Each person is not only incredibly accomplished and talented but also generous with his time and advice. I would not be doing what I am doing today without their support. I am deeply grateful.

The team at the Athletics Department of the University of Colorado, Boulder has provided a welcoming and supportive campus home. There are many people to thank, but none more than Rick George, Lance George, Ceal Barry, and Emily Canova. I hope to be able to return the support that they have shown to me as we work together in the years to come. Thanks, too, to the University of Colorado, Boulder (and its CIRES), especially Phil DiStefano, Russ Moore, John Stevenson, and Waleed Abdalati, who have gone along with my penchant for applied policy research over the years and have offered unwavering support along the way.

At Roaring Forties Press, Deirdre Greene and Nigel Quinney have been all an author could wish for in a publisher and editor. It has been my good fortune to work with them. Many thanks also to Stephen Barbara and Emma Schlee at Inkwell, whose guidance and support have been essential.

Behind the scenes, but present on every page is the work of Ami Nacu-Schmidt, a colleague who has been as reliable and accomplished as anyone I've worked with over more than the fifteen years since I joined the Colorado faculty. Thanks, too, to a support team that has included Victoria Duke, Nancy Filice, Bobbie Klein, and RobinAnn Moser and that has provided expert assistance with the notes and references.

This book has benefitted from papers, essays, blog posts, and other writing of mine over the years, some of which has been adopted and updated for inclusion in this book. These earlier writings benefitted from comments and critiques by students, colleagues, and the extended peer review community.

Last to acknowledge, but first in every other respect, are my family—Megan, Jacob, Calvin, and Julie—who finally get a book that people want to discuss at the dinner table.

Photo Credits

Page 154: By Christopher Johnson (Lionel Messi) [CC BY-SA 2.0 (http://creativecommons.org/licenses/by-sa/2.0)], via Wikimedia Commons.

Page 155: By Will Clayton from Blackburn, UK (Blade Runner (Oscar Pistorius)) [CC BY 2.0 (http://creativecommons.org/licenses/by/2.0)], via Wikimedia Commons.

Page 178: © Chell Hill.

Page 204: Simon Q derivative work: Materialscientist [CC BY 2.0 (http://creativecommons.org/licenses/by/2.0)], via Wikimedia Commons.

Page 230: By Marcello Casal JR/ABr [CC BY 3.0 br (http://creativecommons.org/licenses/by/3.0/br/deed.en)], via Wikimedia Commons.

Page 242: By Olivia Lempe [GFDL (http://www.gnu.org/copyleft/fdl.html) or CC BY-SA 3.0 (http://creativecommons.org/licenses/by-sa/3.0)], via Wikimedia Commons.

Notes

Prologue

1. Victor Conte, Twitter post, August 18, 2015, https://twitter.com/VictorConte/status/633553012884017152.

2. An ESPN film about Coach Bill McCartney and his Colorado football team does a nice job of explaining that era in Boulder: Jim Podhoretz, dir., "The Gospel According to Mac," ESPN 30 for 30 Film (November 2015); http://espn.go.com/30for30/film?page=thegospelaccordingtomac.

3. United Nations Education, Scientific and Cultural Organization, "International Convention against Doping in Sport," http://www.unesco.org/new/en/social-and-human-sciences/themes/anti-doping/international-convention-against-doping-in-sport/.

Chapter 1

1. The phrase is attributed originally to "Red" Sanders, football coach at the University of California, Los Angeles (UCLA) in the early 1950s; J. Sayre, "He Flies on One Wing," *Sports Illustrated*, December 26, 1955.

2. Earnhardt is often given credit for this quote, but it has long been in use; Steve Wulf, "Sporting a New Look," *Sports Illustrated Vault*, April 4, 1994, http://www.si.com/vault/1994/04/04/130772/nl-centralhouston-astros-sporting-a-new-look.

3. Professional Golf Association (PGA), "Heath Slocum PGA Tour Career Summary," 1995–2016, http://www.pgatour.com/players/player.22293.heath-slocum.html/career.

4. R. A. Smith, "Harvard and Columbia and a Reconsideration of the 1905–06 Football Crisis," *Journal of Sport History* 8, no. 3 (1981): 5–19.

5. K. L. Shropshire, "Legislation for the Glory of Sport: Amateurism and Compensation," *Seton Hall Journal of Sports Law* 1, no. 7 (1991).

6. Reuben Fischer-Baum, "Infographic: Is Your State's Highest-Paid Employee a Coach? (Probably)," *Deadspin* (May 9, 2013), http://deadspin.com/infographic-is-your-states-highest-paid-employee-a-co-489635228.

7. Robby Soave, "Three Highest-Paid Pentagon Officials Are All Football Coaches," *The Daily Caller* (June 18, 2013), http://dailycaller.com/2013/06/18/three-highest-paid-pentagon-officials-are-all-football-coaches/.

8. Sam Weber, "Top 100 Highest-Paid Athlete Endorsers of 2015," *Opendorse* (August 6, 2015), http://opendorse.com/blog/highest-paid-athlete-endorsers/.

9. Quoted in Jim Parry, "The Religio Athletae, Olympism, and Peace," in *Sport and Spirituality: An Introduction,* ed. Jim Parry, Simon Robinson, Nick Watson, and Mark West (London: Routledge, 2007), 204.

10. Pro-Football Reference.Com, "Pro-Football Statistics and History," http://www.pro-football-reference.com/.

11. National Football League Combine Results, "Historical NFL Scouting Combine Data," http://nflcombineresults.com/.

12. Dan Wetzel, "Roger Goodell's Manipulation of Tom Brady's Testimony Leaves NFL on Slippery Slope," *Yahoo Sports,* August 5, 2015, http://sports.yahoo.com/news/roger-goodell-s-manipulation-of-tom-brady-s-testimony-leaves-nfl-on-slippery-slope-214409591-nfl.html.

13. Frank Schwab, "Joe Montana: Deflate-gate 'No Big Deal,' His 49ers Used Illegal Silicone," *Yahoo Sports,* June 8, 2015, http://sports.yahoo.com/blogs/nfl-shutdowncorner/joe-montana--deflate-gate--no-big-deal---his-49ers-used-illegal-silicone-155630060.html.

14. Frank Schwab, "Charles Haley Prefers Montana to Brady: 'Joe Didn't Have to Cheat,'" *Yahoo Sports,* February 5, 2015, http://sports.yahoo.com/blogs/nfl-shutdown-corner/charles-haley-prefers-montana-to-brady---joe-didn-t-have-to-cheat-175309538.html.

15. Eric Edholm, "Jerry Rice Calls Out 'Cheating' Patriots But Admitted to Using Stickum," *Yahoo Sports,* February 6, 2015, http://sports.yahoo.com/blogs/nfl-shutdown-corner/jerry-rice-calls-out--cheating--patriots-but-admitted-to-using-stickum-200324269.html.

16. National Collegiate Athletic Association (NCAA), "Amateurism," http://www.ncaa.org/amateurism.

17. Donna M. Desrochers, "Academic Spending Versus Athletic Spending: Who Wins?" *Delta Cost Project at American Institutes for Research,* January 2013, http://www.deltacostproject.org/products/academic-spending-vs-athletic-spending-who-wins.

18. Steve Berkowitz and Andrew Kreighbaum, "College Athletes Cashing in with Millions in New Benefits," *USA Today,* August 19, 2015, http://www.usatoday.com/story/sports/college/2015/08/18/ncaa-cost--attendance-meals-2015/31904839/.

19. Heidi Blake and John Templon, "The Tennis Racket," *Buzzfeed,* January 17, 2016, http://www.buzzfeed.com/heidiblake/the-tennis-racket.

20. Andrea Tan, "Soccer Referee Jailed for 6 Months in Match-Fixing Case," *Bloomberg Business Week,* June 10, 2013, http://www.bloomberg.com/news/articles/2013-06-11/soccer-referee-jailed-for-6-months-in-match-fixing-case.

21. Deutsche Welle (DW), "Disgraced Referee Hoyzer Jailed after Losing Appeal Hearing," December 15, 2006, http://www.dw.com/en/disgraced-referee-hoyzer-jailed-after-losing-appeal-hearing/a-2273305.

22. Dan Colasimone, "10 Reasons Why Juventus Are Not to Blame for the Controversy in Serie A," *Bleacher Report,* October 13, 2014, http://bleacherreport.com/articles/2229593-10-reasons-why-juventus-are-not-to-blame-for-the-controversy-in-serie-a.

23. "List of Cricketers Banned for Corruption," Wikipedia, https://en.wikipedia.org/wiki/List_of_cricketers_banned_for_match_fixing.

24. Firdose Moonda, "South Africa Sports Minister Offers CSA State Assistance in Fixing Probe," *ESPN CRICINFO,* February 23, 2016, http://www.espncricinfo.com/southafrica/content/story/975621.html.

25. Weekly Media Recap, "Match-Fixing Update: Illegal Betting Raids Across Asia, But FIFA Reports No Evidence As Yet of Match-Fixing At World Cup Brazil," *Law in Sport,* June 16–22, 2014, http://www.lawinsport.com/blog/interpol-integrity-in-sport/item/match-fixing-update-illegal-betting-raids-across-asia-but-fifa-reports-no-evidence-as-yet-of-match-fixing-at-world-cup-brazil.

Chapter 2

1. Oxford English Dictionary (OED), "Definition of the word *disport*," Oxford University Press, http://www.oed.com/view/Entry/55101#eid6436274.

2. O. W. Right, trans., *The Thoughts, Letters, and Opuscules of Blaise Pascal* (Hurd and Houghton, 1869), 198, https://play.google.com/store/books/details?id=HbwNAQAAIAAJ&rdid=book -HbwNAQAAIAAJ&rdot=1.

3. OED, "Definition of the word *sport*," http://www.oed.com/view/Entry/187476?rskey= Zhxt6e&result=1&isAdvanced=false#eid.

4. P. Downward, A. Dawson, and T. Dejonghe, *Sports Economics: Theory, Evidence, and Policy* (London: Routledge, 2009), 62.

5. Daniel Kaplan, "NFL Projecting Revenue Increase of $1B over 2014," *Street & Smith's Sports Business Daily Global Journal*, March 9, 2015, 1, http://www.sportsbusinessdaily.com/ Journal/Issues/2015/03/09/Leagues-and-Governing-Bodies/NFL-revenue.aspx.

6. Daniel Kaplan, "Goodell Sets Revenue Goal of $25B by 2027 for NFL," *Street & Smith's Sports Business Daily Global Journal*, April 5, 2010, http://www.sportsbusinessdaily.com/Journal/ Issues/2010/04/20100405/This-Weeks-News/Goodell-Sets-Revenue-Goal-Of-$25B-By- 2027-For-NFL.aspx.

7. International Air Transport Association (IATA), "Scheduled Passengers Carried," *World Air Transport Statistics (WATS)*, 59th ed. (2014), https://www.iata.org/publications/pages/wats- passenger-carried.aspx; *Sustainable Business Review*, "$12 Billion Revenue Expected in 2015: Turkish Airlines," http://www.tsbreview.com/12-billion-revenue-expected-in-2015-turkish -airlines/.

8. Helaine Olen, "Can You Still Trust the Starbucks Index?" *Slate*, November 5, 2015, http:// www.slate.com/articles/business/the_bills/2015/11/starbucks_sales_are_up_peet_s_is_ buying_up_competitors_can_coffee_tell_us.html.

9. "Apple Reports Record Fourth Quarter Results," *Apple Press Library*, October 27, 2015, http://www.apple.com/pr/library/2015/10/27Apple-Reports-Record-Fourth-Quarter- Results.html.

10. Eric Chemi, "If the NFL Were a Real Business," *Bloomberg*, September 12, 2014, http://www. bloomberg.com/bw/articles/2014-09-12/if-the-nfl-were-a-real-business.

11. Eric Chemi, "Does Roger Goodell Truly Deserve $74 Million?" *Bloomberg*, September 12, 2014, http://www.bloomberg.com/bw/articles/2014-09-12/does-roger-goodell-really- deserve-74-million.

12. US GDP data can be found here: The White House Budget Historicals, Office of Management and Budget, "United States Gross Domestic Product (US GDP)," https://www.whitehouse. gov/omb/budget/Historicals.

13. Plunkett Research, "Industry Statistics Sports and Recreation Business Statistics Analysis," http://www.plunkettresearch.com/statistics/sports-industry/.

14. Ibid.

15. For a comprehensive treatment, see S. Szymanski, *Money and Soccer: A Soccernomics Guide: Why Swansea City and Brescia Will Never Win the Champions' League, Why Manchester City, Roma, and Paris St. Germain Are on the Rise, and Why Real Madrid, Bayern Munich, and Arsenal Dominate* (New York: Nation Books, 2015).

16. C. S. Stepp, "Why Do People Read Newspapers?" *American Journalism Review* (Dec/Jan 2004), http://ajrarchive.org/article_printable.asp?id=3505.

17. Dave Nagle, "In 2015, ESPN Repeats as Cables Best in Prime Time," *ESPN Media Zone* press release, December 31, 2015, http://espnmediazone.com/us/press-releases/2015/12/in- 2015-espn-repeats-as-cables-best-in-prime-time/.

18. "List of Most Watched Television Broadcasts," Wikipedia, https://en.wikipedia.org/wiki/List_of_most_watched_television_broadcasts#China.

19. J. Dapena, *The Evolution of High Jumping Technique: Biomechanical Analysis* (Extremadura, Spain: ISBS, 2002). This section benefits from an interview with Dapena in addition to his published work.

20. Steve Kilgallon, "The Flop That Won Gold," Stuff.co.nz, http://www.stuff.co.nz/sport/other-sports/4368844/The-flop-that-won-gold.

21. J. Dapena, personal correspondence with author.

22. H. W. Rittel and M. M. Webber, "Dilemmas in a General Theory of Planning," *Policy Sciences 4*, no. 2 (1973): 155–169.

23. International Association of Athletics Federations (IAAF), Records and Lists, "Senior Outdoor 2015 100 Metres Men," http://www.iaaf.org/records/toplists/Sprints/100-metres/outdoor/men/Senior/2015.

24. Owen Gibson, "Usain Bolt Beats Justin Gatlin to 100m Gold in 'Clash of Good against Evil,'" *Guardian*, August 24, 2015, http://www.theguardian.com/sport/2015/aug/23/usain-bolt-wins-100m-in-clash-of-good-against-evil.

25. Ross Tucker, "The Gatlin Dilemma," *Science of Sport*, May 18, 2015, http://sportsscientists.com/2015/05/the-gatlin-dilemma/.

26. AFP, "Doping Ban 'A Gift and a Curse' Admits in Form Gatlin," *Bangkok Post, Archive*, July 16, 2015, http://www.bangkokpost.com/news/sports/625168/doping-ban-a-gift-and-a-curse-admits-in-form-gatlin.

27. IAAF, "Doha Press Conference Highlights—IAAF Diamond League," May 5, 2016, http://www.iaaf.org/home.

    For my original analysis, see "Gatlin's Geriatric Sprinting Exceptionalism," *The Least Thing* (blog) May 19, 2015, http://leastthing.blogspot.com/2015/05/gatlins-geriatric-sprinting.html.

28. "Gatlin and Farah Head Up Glittering Monaco Meet," *Daily Nation*, July 16, 2016, http://www.nation.co.ke/sports/athletics/Justin-Gatlin-Mo-Farah-head-up-glittering-Monaco-Diamond-meet/-/1100/2791854/-/m2f412z/-/index.html.

29. Rob Harris, "CAS Overturns Britain's Lifetime Olympic Bans," *USA Today*, April 30, 2012, http://usatoday30.usatoday.com/sports/olympics/story/2012-04-30/Britain-doping-ban/54641894/1.

30. DW, "German Parliament Passes Anti-Doping Law," November 13, 2015, http://www.dw.com/en/german-parliament-passes-anti-doping-law/a-18848283.

31. "Olympism in Action," Olympic.Org, http://www.olympic.org/olympism-in-action.

32. Olympic Games Museum, "The Olympic Oath 1920–1980," http://olympic-museum.de/oath/theoath.htm.

33. Timothy Burke, "Here's the 'Integrity of the Game' Honor Code the NFL Says Brady Broke," *Deadspin*, August 4, 2015, http://deadspin.com/heres-the-integrity-of-the-game-honor-code-the-nfl-sa-1722162689.

34. See, for example, S. Loland and H. Hoppeler, "Justifying Anti-Doping: The Fair Opportunity Principle and the Biology of Performance Enhancement," *European Journal of Sport Science 12*, no. 4 (2012): 347–353; and J. Savulescu, B. Foddy, and M. Clayton, "Why We Should Allow Performance Enhancing Drugs in Sport," *British Journal of Sports Medicine 38*, no. 6 (2004): 666–670.

35. 1 Timothy, chapter 2, verse 5, King James Bible Online.Org.

36. J. D. Drummond, "The Characteristics of Amateur and Professional," *International Journal of Music Education*, no. 1 (1990): 3–8.

37. B. L. Goff, W. F. Shughart, W. F., and R. D. Tollison, "Disqualification by Decree: Amateur Rules as Barriers to Entry," *Journal of Institutional and Theoretical Economics (JITE)/Zeitschrift für die gesamte Staatswissenschaft* 144, no. 3 (1998): 515–523.

38. L. Allison, *The Changing Politics of Sport* (Manchester: Manchester University Press, 1993), 7.

39. J. A. Arieti, "Nudity in Greek Athletics," *The Classical World* (Oxford: Oxford University Press, 1993), 431–436.

40. Kavitha A. Davidson, "Peyton Manning's Absurd Doping Scandal," *Bloomberg View*, December 28, 2015, http://www.bloombergview.com/articles/2015-12-28/who-cares-if-peyton-manning-takes-hgh-.

41. J. L. Chappelet, *Autonomy of Sport in Europe* (Strasbourg: Council of Europe, 2010).

42. Ibid.

43. Ryan Rodenberg, "When It's Legal to Rig a Sports Game (and Why It Shouldn't Be)," *Atlantic*, February 14, 2013, http://www.theatlantic.com/entertainment/archive/2013/02/when-its-legal-to-rig-a-sports-game-and-why-it-shouldnt-be/273152/.

44. I first learned of this episode in M. Oriard, *Bowled Over: Big-Time College Football from the Sixties to the BCS Era* (Chaper Hill: University of North Carolina Press, 2009). See also Phil White, "The Black 14: Race, Politics, Religion and Wyoming Football," http://www.wyohistory.org/essays/black-14-race-politics-religion-and-wyoming-football.

45. David Matthews, "In the 1960's, a College Football Protest Ended with 14 Black Players Kicked Off the Team," *Fusion*, November 3, 1969, http://fusion.net/story/229542/missouri-protest-black-14-wyoming/.

46. Oriard, *Bowled Over*.

47. http://universe.byu.edu/2005/11/22/racial-issues-heat-up-byu-accused-of-racism-blacks-get-priesthood-in-70s/.

48. White, "The Black 14."

49. Jason Horowitz, "The Genesis of a Church's Stand on Race," *Washington Post*, February 28, 2012, https://www.washingtonpost.com/politics/the-genesis-of-a-churchs-stand-on-race/2012/02/22/gIQAQZXyfR_story.html.

50. "BYU Cougars Football," Wikipedia, http://en.wikipedia.org/wiki/BYU_Cougars_football.

51. Oriard, *Bowled Over*.

Chapter 3

1. "Capriati 'Angry and Disappointed' After Sharapova Fails Drug Test," Tennis.com, March 8, 2016, http://www.tennis.com/pro-game/2016/03/capriati-angry-and-disappointed-after-sharapova-drug-test/57825/.

2. Russell Fuller, "John McEnroe Says 'No-Brainer' for Players to Use Legal Drugs," British Broadcasting Corporation (BBC), March 13, 2016, http://www.bbc.co.uk/sport/tennis/35797018.

3. Courtney Nguyen, "Victoria Azarenka's Medical Timeout Causes Controversy at Aussie Open," *Sports Illustrated*, January 24, 2013, http://www.si.com/tennis/beyond-baseline/2013/01/24/victoria-azarenka-medical-timeout-australian-open.

4. "Was Azarenka 'Cheating' Within the Rules?" *USA Today*, January 24, 2013, http://www.usatoday.com/story/sports/tennis/2013/01/24/australian-open-victoria-azarenka-sloane-stephens-medical-timeout/1860827/.

5. Chris Fowler, Twitter post, January 23, 2013, https://twitter.com/cbfowler/status/294333051008323585.

6. S. G. French, "Kant's Constitutive-Regulative Distinction," *The Monist* (1967): 623–639.

7. J. R. Searle, *Speech Acts: An Essay in the Philosophy of Language* (Cambridge: Cambridge University Press, 1969), 626, emphasis in original.

8. "Memorandum, Articles of Association, and Bye-laws of ITF Limited Trading as the International Tennis Federation," http://www.itftennis.com/media/221225/221225.pdf.

9. International Tennis Federation (ITF), "2016 Rules of Tennis," Tennis.com, http://www.itftennis.com/officiating/rulebooks/rules-of-tennis.aspx.

10. "An Olympics Qualifying 'Rules Hole,'" *The Least Thing*, June 26, 2012, http://leastthing.blogspot.com/2012/06/olympics-qualifying-rules-hole.html.

11. Much has been written on norms in society; see, for example, C. Bicchieri, *The Grammar of Society: The Nature and Dynamics of Social Norms* (Cambridge: Cambridge University Press, 2005).

12. Francisco Larios, "Introducing the NBA's 'Flopping' Rules to Football," *Law in Sport*, http://www.lawinsport.com/articles/regulation-a-governance/item/introducing-the-nba-s-flopping-rules-to-football.

13. For a more technical discussion in the context of sport, see A. Fink and D. J. Smith, "Norms in Sports Contests: The Tour de France," *Journal of Sport Management* 26, no. 1 (2012): 43–52. More broadly, much has been written on rules, norms, and their intercomplexities in regard to policy and decision making.

14. Jack Bell, "Luiz Adriano Falls Afoul of Fair Play," *New York Times*, November 27, 2012, http://goal.blogs.nytimes.com/2012/11/27/luiz-adriano-falls-afoul-of-fair-play/.

15. Ibid.

16. "Luiz Adriano Suspended for One Match," Union of European Football Associations (UEFA), November 27, 2012, http://www.uefa.org/disciplinary/news/newsid=1899812.html.

17. "Ozzie Guillen Suspended Five Games," ESPN, April 10, 2012, http://espn.go.com/mlb/story/_/id/7795152/ozzie-guillen-miami-marlins-suspended-five-games.

18. "Jeitinho," Wikipedia, https://en.wikipedia.org/wiki/Jeitinho.

19. Miguel Delaney, "In Spanish There's a Phrase for What Suarez Gets up To . . . ," *Independent*, January 12, 2013, http://www.independent.co.uk/sport/football/premier-league/in-spanish-theres-a-phrase-for-what-suarez-gets-up-to-8449344.html.

20. Ben Lindbergh, "The Art of Pitch Framing," *Grantland*, May 16, 2013, http://grantland.com/features/studying-art-pitch-framing-catchers-such-francisco-cervelli-chris-stewart-jose-molina-others/.

21. Emily Benammar, "Dean Richards Ban: How 'Bloodgate' Saga Unfolded," *Telegraph*, August 18, 2009, http://www.telegraph.co.uk/sport/rugbyunion/club/6047832/Dean-Richards-ban-how-Bloodgate-saga-unfolded.html.

22. L. Anderson, "Bloodgate: Were the Punishments Fair?" *British Journal of Sports Medicine* 45, no. 12 (2011): 948–949.

23. Jonathan Wilson, "The Question: Why Is the Modern Offside Law a Work of Genius?" *Guardian*, April 13, 2010, http://www.theguardian.com/sport/blog/2010/apr/13/the-question-why-is-offside-law-genius.

24. "New Offside Rule Good for Football, Says Referees' Chief Mike Riley," *Sky Sports*, August 8, 2015, http://www.skysports.com/football/news/11095/9935364/former-referee-dermot-gallagher-backs-offside-rule-change.

25. This anecdote is told in I. Preston and S. Szymanski, "Cheating in Contests," *Oxford Review of Economic Policy* 19, no. 4 (2003): 612–624.

26. Chris J. McKain, "Shell Caribbean Cup 1994," *RSSF*, http://www.rsssf.com/tabless/shell-car94.html.

27. Preston and Szymanski, Cheating in Contests.

28. Chris J. McKain, "Shell Caribbean Cup 1994," *RSSF,* http://www.rsssf.com/tabless/shell-car94.html.

29. As quoted in S. Gardiner, S. Boyes, U. Naidoo, J. O'Leary, and R. Welch, *Sports Law* (New York: Routledge, 2012).

30. Andreas Selliaas, "A Tactical Blunder," Play the Game, March 8, 2012, http://www.playthe-game.org/news/detailed/a-tactical-blunder-5430.html.

31. An exploration of this "law" can be found in R. K. Merton, "The Unanticipated Consequences of Purposive Social Action," *American Sociological Review* 1, no. 6 (1936): 894–904.

32. "Larysa Latynina," Sports Reference, http://www.sports-reference.com/olympics/athletes/la/larysa-latynina-1.html.

33. "Larisa Latynina," Wayback Machine Internet Archive, http://web.archive.org/web/20061027054302/http://www.intlgymnast.com/legends/latynina.html.

34. V. Anderson, "Female Gymnasts: Older and Healthier," *The Physician and Sports Medicine* 25, no. 3 (1997).

35. Quoted in Anderson, "Female Gymnasts." See also C. M. Dresler, K. Forbes, P. J. O'Connor, R. D. Lewis, M . A. Glueck, and I. R. Tofler, "Physical and Emotional Problems of Elite Female Gymnasts," *New England Journal of Medicine* 336 (1997): 140–142.

36. "Achilles Heel," *Economist,* March 19, 2013, http://www.economist.com/blogs/gametheory/2013/03/gymnastics.

37. Ibid.

38. T. Ackland, B. Elliott, and J. Richards, "Gymnastics: Growth in Body Size Affects Rotational Performance in Women's Gymnastics," *Sports Biomechanics* 2, no. 2 (2003): 163–176.

39. O. Donti, A. Donti, and K. Theodorakou, "A Review of the Changes of the Evaluation System Affecting Artistic Gymnasts' Basic Preparation: The Aspect of Choreography Preparation," *Science of Gymnastics* (2014).

40. "Achilles Heel."

41. Joanne C. Gerstner, "Flashback Friday: Age Controversy Follows Chinese Gymnasts," *New York Times,* June 8, 2012, http://london2012.blogs.nytimes.com/2012/06/08/flashback-friday-age-controversy-follows-chinese-gymnasts/.

42. Juliet Macur, "Medal of Underage Chinese Gymnast Revoked," *New York Times,* February 26, 2010, http://www.nytimes.com/2010/02/27/sports/olympics/27gymnasts.html.

43. Sam Borden, "A Photo Finish Too Close to Call, Even by Camera," *New York Times,* June 24, 2012, http://www.nytimes.com/2012/06/25/sports/olympics/2012-olympics-allyson-felix-and-jeneba-tarmoh-100-meter.html.

44. "Dead-Heat Procedures Announced," USA Track & Field, June 24, 2012, http://www.usatf.org/News/Dead-heat-procedures-announced.aspx.

45. "Allyson Felix Biography," USA Track & Field, http://www.usatf.org/Athlete-Bios/Allyson-Felix.aspx.

46. Jere Longman, "A Coin Flip? A Runoff? Talk about Amateur," *New York Times,* June 25, 2012, http://www.nytimes.com/2012/06/26/sports/olympics/london-olympics-a-coin-flip-a-runoff-talk-about-amateur.html.

47. Mark Maske, "Tuck Rule Hard to Grasp," *Washington Post,* October 15, 2005, http://www.washingtonpost.com/wp-dyn/content/article/2005/10/14/AR2005101401828.html.

48. "The Tuck Rule—10 Year Anniversary," https://www.youtube.com/watch?v=5lNI-Uq_fww.

49. "'Tuck Rule' Eliminated by Wide Margin at NFL Annual Meeting," NFL, March 20, 2013, http://www.nfl.com/news/story/0ap1000000152253/article/tuck-rule-eliminated-by-wide-margin-at-nfl-annual-meeting.

Chapter 4

1. Tom Farrey, "Kain Colter Starts Union Movement," ESPN, January 28, 2014, http://espn. go.com/espn/otl/story/_/id/10363430/outside-lines-northwestern-wildcats-football-players-trying-join-labor-union.

2. Donald Remy, "NCAA Responds to Union Proposal," NCAA Media Center press release, http://www.ncaa.org/about/resources/media-center/press-releases/ncaa-responds-union-proposal.

3. Peter Sung Ohr, "United States Government before the National Labor Relations Board Region 13, Decision and Direction of Election," ESPN, March 26, 2014, http://www.espn. go.com/pdf/2014/0326/espn_uniondecision.PDF.

4. John Kline, "Kline Statement: Hearing on 'Big Labor on College Campuses: Examining the Consequences of Unionizing Student Athletes,' " Education and the Workforce Committee, May 9, 2014, http://edworkforce.house.gov/news/documentsingle. aspx?DocumentID=379217.

5. Gabrielle Levy, "Klein: Unionizing Student-Athletes Is 'Not the Answer,'" United Press International (UPI), May 8, 2014, http://www.upi.com/Top_News/US/2014/05/08/Klein-Unionizing-student-athletes-is-not-the-answer/2571399565578/.

6. Jon Solomon, "Q & A: What the O'Bannon Ruling Means for NCAA, Schools and Athletes," CBSSports.com, August 9, 2014, http://www.cbssports.com/collegefootball/writer/jon-solomon/24654805/qa-what-the-obannon-ruling-means-for-the-ncaa-schools-and-athletes.

7. Steve Eder and Ben Strauss, "Understanding Ed O'Bannon's Suit against the NCAA," *New York Times*, June 9, 2014, http://www.nytimes.com/2014/06/10/sports/ncaabasketball/understanding-ed-obannons-suit-against-the-ncaa.html.

8. Ben Strauss, "NLRB Rejects Northwestern Football Players' Union Bid," *New York Times*, August 17, 2015, http://www.nytimes.com/2015/08/18/sports/ncaafootball/nlrb-says-northwestern-football-players-cannot-unionize.html.

9. "Northwestern University," National Labor Relations Board, Cases & Decisions, August, 17, 2015, https://www.nlrb.gov/case/13-RC-121359.

10. Michael McCann, "What the Appeals Court Ruling Means for O'Bannon's Ongoing NCAA Lawsuit," *Sports Illustrated*, September 30, 2015, http://www.si.com/college-basketball /2015/09/30/ed-obannon-ncaa-lawsuit-appeals-court-ruling.

11. Case documents can be found at United States Courts for the Ninth Circuit, Court of Appeals, "Edward O'Bannon, Jr. v. NCAA 14-16601," https://www.ca9.uscourts.gov/content/view.php?pk_id=0000000757.

12. Steve Berkowitz and Andrew Kreighbaum, "College Athletes Cashing in with Millions in New Benefits," *USA Today*, August 19, 2015, http://www.usatoday.com/story /sports/college/2015/08/18/ncaa-cost--attendance-meals-2015/31904839/.

13. "Cost of Attendance Q & A for College Athletes," NCAA, September 3, 2015, http://www. ncaa.com/news/ncaa/article/2015-09-03/cost-attendance-qa.

14. The prehistory of US college sports goes back further; see Frederick Rudolph, *The American College and University: A History* (Athens: University of Georgia Press, 1962).

15. R. A. Smith, *Sports & Freedom* (Oxford: Oxford University Press, 1988).

16. R. K. Smith, "Brief History of the National Collegiate Athletic Association's Role in Regulating Intercollegiate Athletics," *Marquette Sports Law Review* 11, no. 9 (2000).

17. H. A. Scott, *Competitive Sports in Schools and Colleges* (New York: Harper, 1951).

18. Smith, "Brief History."

19. R. N. Davis, "Academics and Athletics on a Collision Course," *North Dakota Law Review* 66, no. 239 (1990).

20. *San Francisco Call*, November 27, 1905, http://chroniclingamerica.loc.gov/lccn/ sn85066387/1905-11-27/ed-1/seq-1/. Other accounts claim eighteen deaths in 1905. For comparison, Gregg Easterbrook cites data showing that, from 2001 to 2011, football caused 163 deaths, of which 130 were at the high school level. See G. Easterbrook, *The King of Sports: Why Football Must Be Reformed* (New York: Thomas Dunne Books, 2013).

21. R. A. Smith, "Harvard and Columbia and a Reconsideration of the 1905–06 Football Crisis," *Journal of Sport History* 8, no. 3 (1981): 5–19.

22. John J. Miller, "How Teddy Roosevelt Saved Football," *Wall Street Journal*, April 21, 2011, http://online.wsj.com/news/articles/SB10001424052748703712504576242431663682162.

23. Theodore Roosevelt, "Boys to Men," *Lapham's Quarterly* (1900), http://www.laphamsquarterly .org/youth/boys-men.

24. G. M. Lewis, "Theodore Roosevelt's Role in the 1905 Football Controversy," *Research Quarterly: American Association for Health, Physical Education and Recreation* 40, no. 4 (1969): 717–724.

25. Smith, "Harvard and Columbia."

26. Lewis, "Theodore Roosevelt's Role."

27. Franklin Foer and Chris Hughes, "Barack Obama Is Not Pleased: The President on His Enemies, the Media, and the Future of Football," *New Republic*, January 26, 2013, http://www. newrepublic.com/article/112190/obama-interview-2013-sit-down-president.

28. "NCAA Reaches Proposed Settlement in Concussion Lawsuit," NCAA, July 30, 2014, http://www.ncaa.com/news/ncaa/article/2014-07-30/ncaa-reaches-proposed-settlement-concussion-lawsuit.

29. Steve Berkowitz and Dan Wolken, "White House to Meet with College Athletics Officials," *USA Today*, January 12, 2015, http://www.usatoday.com/story/sports/college/2015/01/11/ ncaa-white-house-president-obama/21595607/.

30. K. E. Broyles, "NCAA Regulation of Intercollegiate Athletics: Time for a New Game Plan," *Alabama Law Review* 46 (1994): 487.

31. Marc Edelman, "The NCAA's 'Death Penalty' Sanction—Reasonable Self-Governance or an Illegal Group Boycott in Disguise?" *Lewis & Clark Law Review* (Spring 2014).

32. Lewis, "Theodore Roosevelt's Role."

33. R. K. Smith, "National Collegiate Athletic Association's Death Penalty: How Educators Punish Themselves and Others," *Indiana Law Journal* 62 (1986): 985.

34. "Championships," NCAA, http://www.ncaa.org/about/what-we-do/championships.

35. Broyles, "NCAA Regulation of Intercollegiate Athletics."

36. "Flashback: SMU Gets NCAA 'Death Penalty'; Worse than Penn State?" *Dallas News*, February 26, 1987, http://www.dallasnews.com/sports/college-sports/smu-mustangs/20120723-flashback-smu-gets-ncaa-death-penalty-worse-than-penn-state.ece.

37. "Timeline of the UNC Investigation," *News & Observer*, http://www.newsobserver.com/ unc-scandal/.

38. Doug Lederman, "Bad Apples or More? NCAA Punished Nearly Half of Universities with Big-Time Football Programs for Major Violations in Last Decade—with Uptick in Academic Wrongdoing," *Inside Higher Ed*, February 7, 2011, https://www.insidehighered. com/news/2011/02/07/ncaa_punishes_almost_half_of_members_of_football_bowl_ subdivision_for_major_rules_violations.

39. "Major Infraction Case Search," NCAA Legislative Services Database, https://web1.ncaa. org/LSDBi/exec/miSearch.

40. Stu Durando, "Life after the NCAA's Death Penalty at MacMurray," *St. Louis Post-Dispatch*, September 16, 2011, http://www.stltoday.com/sports/college/article_1ce13601-eb4c-5a7f-a407-3d5a6e472237.html.

41. Data in the graph are from Brent Schrotenboer, "Simply Complex: With Hundreds of Pages of NCAA Rules, and New Legislation Being Added Each Year, It's No Wonder that College Athletic Programs Are Constantly Tripping over Compliance Issues," *San Diego Union Tribune*, February 10, 2008, http://legacy.sandiegouniontribune.com/sports/20080210-9999-1s10ncaa.html. For 2016, the data come from the NCAA Policy Manuals for Divisions I, II, and III, "NCAA Manuals and Rule Books," http://www.ncaapublications.com/.

42. Pete Iacobelli, "South Carolina Reports 22 Minor NCAA Violations," *South Carolina Now*, August 2, 2014, http://www.scnow.com/news/state/article_ad0f4bf8-1a68-11e4-a161-0017a43b2370.html.

43. "NCAA Takes First Step to Simplify, Deregulate Complex Rulebook," NCAA, January 20, 2013, http://www.ncaa.com/news/ncaa/article/2013-01-20/ncaa-takes-first-step-simplify-deregulate-complex-rulebook.

44. "Amateurism."

45. L. Allison, *Amateurism in Sport: An Analysis and a Defence* (Hove, UK: Psychology Press, 2001).

46. Ben Koh, "Amateurism and Anti-Doping: A Cautionary Tale," *Law in Sport*, July 2, 2013, ahttp://www.lawinsport.com/features/item/amateurism-and-anti-doping-a-cautionary-tale.

47. D. C. Young, *The Olympic Myth of Greek Amateur Athletics* (Chicago: Ares, 1984). Young who argues that the ancient Greeks did not even have a word for "amateur." As cited in K. L. Shropshire, "Legislation for the Glory of Sport: Amateurism and Compensation," *Seton Hall Journal of Sport Law* 1, no. 7 (1991).

48. Shropshire, "Legislation for the Glory of Sport."

49. The official website of Ivy League Athletics is at http://ivyleague.prestosports.com/information/psa/index.

50. Greg Echlin, "Walter Byers Legacy Virtually Ignored at NCAA Office," KCUR, August 28, 2012, http://kcur.org/post/walter-byers-legacy-virtually-ignored-ncaa-office, quoting from Walter Byers, *Unsportsmanlike Conduct: Exploiting College Athletes* (Ann Arbor: University of Michigan Press, 1995).

51. For a hard-hitting critique along these lines, see Patrick Hruby, "Four Years a Student-Athlete: The Racial Injustice of Big-Time College Sports," *Vice Sports*, April 4, 2016, https://sports.vice.com/en_us/article/four-years-a-student-athlete-the-racial-injustice-of-big-time-college-sports.

52. Quoted in Lewis, "Theodore Roosevelt's Role."

53. Cited in Smith, "National Collegiate Athletic Association's Death Penalty."

54. Shropshire, "Legislation for the Glory of Sport."

55. The full code of 1906 is reproduced in ibid., note 45.

56. V. A. Fitt, "NCAA's Lost Cause and the Legal Ease of Redefining Amateurism," *Duke Law Journal* 59 (2009): 555.

57. Smith, "Harvard and Columbia."

58. Michael Oriard, *Bowled Over: Big-Time College Football from the Sixties to the BCS Era* (Chapel Hill: University of North Carolina Press, 2009).

59. A. A. Stagg, "Should Any Student in Good Standing Be Permitted to Play in Inter-Collegiate Athletics Contests?" *American Physical Education Review* 14 (1909): 100–108.

60. Blair Kerkhoff, "Ex-Mizzou System President Tim Wolfe: Football Team Threw 'Gasoline on a Small Fire,'" *Kansas City Star*, January 27, 2016, http://www.kansascity.com/sports/college/sec/university-of-missouri/article56836933.html.

61. Knight Commission on Intercollegiate Athletics, "Football Bowl Subdivision (FBS): Athletics Spending and Institutional Funding to Athletics Growing Faster Than Academic Spending," October 19, 2011, http://chronicle.com/items/biz/pdf/Fig_FBS_10.19.11.pdf.

62. "National Collegiate Athletic Association (NCAA) Finances," *USA Today,* http://sports.usatoday.com/ncaa/finances/. These data do not include private universities and others not required to make their financial data public. The data are based on the accounting rules in place at individual universities.

63. As quoted in Taylor Branch, *The Cartel* (San Francisco: Byliner, 2011), 54.

64. Ibid.

65. Smith, "National Collegiate Athletic Association's Death Penalty."

66. "CBS Sports, Turner Broadcasting, NCAA Reach 14-Year Agreement," NCAA, January 12, 2011, http://www.ncaa.com/news/basketball-men/2010-04-21/cbs-sports-turner-broadcasting-ncaa-reach-14-year-agreement.

67. "Turner, CBS and the NCAA Reach Long-Term Multimedia Rights Extension for NCAA Division I Men's Basketball Championship: New Agreement Extends Television, Digital and Marketing Rights Through 2032," NCAA, April 12, 2016, http://www.ncaa.com/news/basketball-men/article/2016-04-12/turner-cbs-and-ncaa-reach-long-term-multimedia-rights

68. The data come from the NCAA via Bloomberg: David Ingold and Adam Pearce, "March Madness Makers and Takers: The Way the NCAA Distributes the Staggering Revenue from the Basketball Tournament Has Created a Polarized System Where Some Schools Make Money and Others Just Take It," Bloomberg.com, March 18, 2015, http://www.bloomberg.com/graphics/2015-march-madness-basketball-fund/.

69. Ira Boudway, "ESPN's College Football Playoff Money Machine Is Just Getting Started," Bloomberg.com, January 13, 2015, http://www.bloomberg.com/news/articles/2015-01-13/espns-college-football-playoff-money-machine-is-just-getting-started.

70. Igor Guryashkin, "Tipping the Scales," ESPN, November 2, 2013, http://espn.go.com/mens-college-basketball/story/_/id/9912120/louisville-cardinals-move-acc-2014-only-make-more-money-espn-magazine.

71. "Study: End of Football Season Produced $37 Million in Media Exposure for Texas A&M," Texas A&M University Athletics, January 18, 2013, http://www.12thman.com/ViewArticle.dbml?ATCLID=206020080.

72. Steve Berkowitz, "NCAA Increases Value of Scholarships in Historic Vote," *USA Today,* January 17, 2015, http://www.usatoday.com/story/sports/college/2015/01/17/ncaa-convention-cost-of-attendance-student-athletes-scholarships/21921073/.

73. "Innovation's Golden Goose," *Economist,* December 12, 2002, http://www.economist.com/node/1476653.

74. Birch Bayh, Joseph P. Allen, and Howard W. Bremer, "Universities, Inventors, and the Bayh-Dole Act," *Life Sciences Law & Industry Report* 3, no. 24 (December 18, 2009), http://allen-assoc.com/documents/LifeSciences_InventorsUniversitiesandBayh-Dole.pdf.

75. Mark Schlabach, "Varsity Athletes Get Class Credit, Some Colleges Give Grades for Playing," *Washington Post,* August 26, 2004, http://www.washingtonpost.com/wp-dyn/articles/A33987-2004Aug25.html.

76. Ben Strauss, "Football Major, Basketball Minor?" *New York Times,* February 1, 2015, http://www.nytimes.com/2015/02/08/education/edlife/football-major-basketball-minor.html.

77. "Getting a Degree in Football?" National Public Radio (NPR), December 6, 2012, http://www.npr.org/2012/12/06/166655698/getting-a-degree-in-football.

78. B. J. Cardinal, S. D. Sorensen, and M. K. Cardinal, "Historical Perspective and Current Status of the Physical Education Graduation Requirement at American 4-Year Colleges and Universities," *Research Quarterly for Exercise and Sport* 83, no. 4 (2012): 503–512.

79. Ibid, 509.
80. For comparison, see John Infante, "A Student-Focused NCAA Needs Athletics Majors," Athletic Scholarships.net, October 16, 2012, http://www.athleticscholarships.net/2012/10/16/student-focused-ncaa-needs-athletics-majors.htm.
81. Strauss, "Football Major, Basketball Minor?"
82. John V. Lombardi, "Time for a Sports Degree," InsideHigherEd.com, April 3, 2014, https://www.insidehighered.com/views/2014/04/03/universities-should-create-sports-performance-degree-athletes-essay.

Chapter 5

1. See "Chelyabinsk Meteor" Wikipedia, https://en.wikipedia.org/wiki/Chelyabinsk_meteor.
2. Jonathan Abrams, "All the Kings' Men," Grantland, May 7, 2014, http://grantland.com/features/2002-western-conference-oral-history-los-angeles-lakers-sacramento-kings/.
3. Ibid.
4. Roland Beech, "Reviewing the Calls: Lakers-Kings Game 6," 82games.com, http://www.82games.com/lakerskingsgame6.htm.
5. Sam Amick, "Spurs-Thunder Game 5 Ending Mired in Officiating Controversy, Yet Again," USA Today, May 11, 2016, http://www.usatoday.com/story/sports/nba/playoffs/2016/05/11/spurs-thunder-game-5-ending-officiating-controversy-no-call/84217938/
6. Alan Schwarz and William K. Rashbaum, "National Basketball Association (NBA) Referee Is the Focus of a Federal Inquiry," New York Times, July 21, 2007, http://www.nytimes.com/2007/07/21/sports/basketball/21referee.html.
7. Pat Jordan, "Does This ExCon Know the National Basketball Association (NBA) Better Than LeBron?" New York Magazine, June 14, 2015, http://nymag.com/daily/intelligencer/2015/06/tim-donaghy-gamblings-golden-boy.html.
8. Chris Sheridan, "2002 Lakers-Kings Game 6 at Heart of Donaghy Allegations," ESPN, June 11, 2008, http://sports.espn.go.com/nba/news/story?id=3436401.
9. Wayne Drehs, "Expert Explains the Many Ways a Crooked Referee Could Fix Bets," ESPN, July 23, 2007, http://sports.espn.go.com/nba/news/story?page=expertexplainsNBAbets.
10. French Press Agency (AFP), "Global Sports Gambling Worth 'Up to $3 Trillion,'" Daily Mail, April 15, 2015, http://www.dailymail.co.uk/wires/afp/article-3040540/Global-sports-gambling-worth-3-trillion.html.
11. EGBA, "Sports Betting." See also http://www.nbcnews.com/news/other/think-sports-gambling-isnt-big-money-wanna-bet-f6C10634316; and Andrew Vacca, "Sports Betting: Why the United States Should Go All In," Willamette Sport Law Journal 11 (2014): 1–7.
12. Sean Ingle, "Revealed: Tennis Umpires Secretly Banned over Gambling Scam," Guardian, February 9, 2016, https://www.theguardian.com/sport/2016/feb/09/revealed-tennis-umpires-secretly-banned-gambling-scam.
13. "Pro Circuit Tournament Calendar," International Tennis Federation, May 2016, http://www.itftennis.com/procircuit/tournaments/men's-calendar.aspx.
14. Carl Bialik, "Inside the Shadowy World of High-Speed Tennis Betting," FiveThirtyEight.com, May 29, 2014, http://fivethirtyeight.com/features/inside-the-shadowy-world-of-high-speed-tennis-betting/.
15. For a running list of incidents related to match fixing, see "List of Match Fixing Incidents," Wikipedia, https://en.wikipedia.org/wiki/List_of_match_fixing_incidents.
16. Chris Eaton, "Match-Fixing a Bigger Problem in Sport Than Doping, Says Chris Eaton, FIFA's Former Head of Security," Telegraph UK, May 16, 2016, http://www.telegraph.co.uk/sport/

football/10507193/Match-fixing-a-bigger-problem-in-sport-than-doping-says-Chris-Eaton-Fifas-former-head-of-security.html.

17. "Jacques Rogge: Sport's Integrity Is Being Eroded by Cheats. We Have to Act Now," *Independent*, February 28, 2011, http://www.independent.co.uk/sport/olympics/jacques-rogge-sports-integrity-is-being-eroded-by-cheats-we-have-to-act-now-2228557.html.

18. Kevin Carpenter, "Match-Fixing: The Biggest Threat to Sport in the 21st Century?" Interpol.int, *Media Files* 2 (2012), http://www.interpol.int/Media/Files/INTERPOL-Expertise/IGLC/Match-fixing-biggest-threat.

19. KEA European Affairs, "Match-Fixing in Sport: A Mapping of Criminal Law Provisions in EU 27," (March 2012), http://www.keanet.eu/docs/study-sports-fraud-final-version_en.pdf.

20. "Chart of Signatures and Ratifications of Treaty 215, Council of Europe Convention on the Manipulation of Sports Competitions," Council of Europe (COE), http://www.coe.int/en/web/conventions/full-list/-/conventions/treaty/215/signatures.

21. "The Anti-Coping Convention: An Instrument of International Co-Operation," COE, http://www.coe.int/t/dg4/sport/doping/convention_en.asp.

22. "Explanatory Report to the Council of Europe Convention on the Manipulation of Sports Competitions," COE, https://rm.coe.int/CoERMPublicCommonSearchServices/DisplayDCTMContent?documentId=09000016800d383f.

23 "Le Tissier in Failed Betting Scam," BBC, September, 3, 2009, http://news.bbc.co.uk/sport2/hi/football/teams/s/southampton/8236108.stm.

24. Roger A. Pielke Jr., *The Honest Broker: Making Sense of Science in Policy and Politics* (New York: Cambridge University Press, 2007).

25. "James Blake: If True, This Scandal Will Be Extremely Damaging to Tennis," *The Doug Gottlieb Show*, January 21, 2016, http://gottlieb.radio.cbssports.com/2016/01/21/james-blake-if-true-this-scandal-will-be-extremely-damaging-to-tennis/.

26. "Australian Open—Novak Djokovic, Press Conference" (FastScripts Transcript by ASAP Sports), ASAPtext.com, https://asaptext.com/orgs/ausopen/browse_file.php?browse_file_name=./transcripts/4380.html.

27. "2007 ATP Tour," Wikipedia, https://en.wikipedia.org/wiki/2007_ATP_Tour#ATP_prize_money_leaders.

28. "Novak Djokovic Overview," Association of Tennis Professionals, http://www.atpworldtour.com/en/players/novak-djokovic/d643/overview.

29. Judson Woods and Henry Johnson, "Measuring Salary Inequality Across Major Sports Leagues," Harvard Sports Analysis Collective, January 20, 2014, http://harvardsportsanalysis.org/?p=4573.

30. For details and background, see, for example, Lorenzo Giovanni Bellu, "Inequality Analysis: The Gini Index," EasyPol On-line Resource Materials for Policy Making, Module 040, http://www.fao.org/docs/up/easypol/329/gini_index_040en.pdf.

31. "Income Distribution and Poverty," Organization for Economic Co-Operation and Development, http://stats.oecd.org/Index.aspx?DataSetCode=IDD.

32. Douglas Robson, "Women's Tennis Association (WTA), Payout Distribution Leans Toward Winner-Take-All," *USA Today*, September 17, 2013, http://www.usatoday.com/story/sports/tennis/2013/09/17/wta-prize-money-distribution/2825259/.

33. Ibid.

34. "The Cost of Fixing a Tennis Match," Heavy Topspin (blog), January 25, 2016, http://www.tennisabstract.com/blog/2016/01/25/the-cost-of-fixing-a-tennis-match/.

35. Association of Tennis Professionals, http://www.atpworldtour.com/News/Tennis/2013/04/17/Wimbledon-2013-Prize-Money-Increase.aspx.

36. The data for table 5.1 are from spotrac.com, http://www.spotrac.com, and Jake Cohen, "Sports Charity Partners 2016, RightToPlay, MLS'S CBA Negotiations: Federal Mediation, Salary Cap and Steps Toward Free Agency," *Law in Sport*, March 27, 2015, http://www.lawinsport.com/sports/item/major-league-soccer-s-collective-bargaining-negotiations-federal-mediation-salary-cap-and-steps-toward-free-agency?category_id=152.

37. See "Three Ex-Toledo Players Get Probation in Point-Shaving Case," Foxsports.com, April 1, 2015, http://www.foxsports.com/college-football/story/toledo-rockets-point-shaving-scandal-three-former-football-players-sentenced-to-probation-033115; and "An Inside Look at Alleged Point Shaving scheme at U of San Diego," *Sports Illustrated*, January 25, 2002, http://www.si.com/more-sports/2012/01/25/operation-hookshot.

38. David Butler, "Why Match Fixing Won't Happen in the Premier League," *Economics of Sport*, November 11, 2013, http://www.sportseconomics.org/sports-economics/why-match-fixing-wont-happen-in-the-premier-league.

39. Holly Watt and Claire Newell, "Delroy Facey Charged with Conspiracy to Bribe Football Players," *Telegraph*, September 1, 2014, http://www.telegraph.co.uk/sport/football/11068142/Delroy-Facey-charged-with-conspiracy-to-bribe-football-players.html.

40. D. Bernhardt and S. Heston, "Point Shaving in College Basketball: A Cautionary Tale for Forensic Economics," *Economic Inquiry 48*, no. 1 (2010): 14–25.

41. See Justin Wolfers, "Point Shaving: Corruption in NCAA Basketball," *American Economic Review* (2006): 279–283; and J. Gibbs, "Point Shaving in the NBA: An Economic Analysis of the National Basketball Association's Point Spread Betting Market," unpublished working paper, Stanford University, 2007. For critiques of these papers, see G. Diemer and M. A. Leeds, "Failing to Cover: Point Shaving or Statistical Abnormality?" *International Journal of Sport Finance 8*, no. 3 (2013): 175; Bernhardt and Heston, "Point Shaving in College Basketball"; and R. Borghesi, R. Paul, and A. P. Weinbach, "Totals Markets as Evidence against Widespread Point Shaving," *Journal of Prediction Markets 4*, no. 2 (2010): 15–22.

42. Bernhardt and Heston, "Point Shaving in College Basketball."

43. Richard Ings, interview with the author, January 25, 2016.

44. Mike O'Kane, "ESSA Q4 2015 Integrity Report," 2015, http://www.eu-ssa.org/wp-content/uploads/QR4-BROCHURE-WEB.pdf. The ESSA review focused on European betting houses. A focus on Asian and illegal betting would certainly turn up suspicious competitions.

45. For recent instances, see, for example, Ben Gladwell, "Match Fixing 'Cancer' Hasn't Been Eliminated—Italian Prosecutor," ESPN, May 5, 2016, http://www.espnfc.com/italian-serie-a/story/2865186/match-fixing-cancer-hasnt-been-eliminated-italian-prosecutor, and http://www.foxnews.com/world/2016/04/19/turkey-38-arrested-for-framing-fenerbahce-with-scandal.html.

46. "Investigators Identify 380 Fixed Football Matches," *Guardian*, February 4, 2013, https://www.theguardian.com/football/2013/feb/04/europol-investigation-football-matchfixing. More generally, see D. Hill, *The Fix* (Toronto: McClelland & Stewart, 2010).

47. https://www.theguardian.com/football/2013/feb/06/debrecen-keeper-liverpool-denies-fix.

48. "List of Cricketers Banned for Corruption," Wikipedia, https://en.wikipedia.org/wiki/List_of_cricketers_banned_for_corruption.

49. Shantanu Guha Ray, "Cricket and Match-Fixing: It's as Routine as Groundsman Laying a Pitch: But Does Anyone Really Care?" FirstPost.com, March 8, 2016, http://www.firstpost.com/sports/cricket-and-fixing-its-as-routine-as-groundsman-laying-a-pitch-but-does-anyone-really-care-2662652.html.

50. "Global Attendances, Best Attended Domestic Sports Leagues in the World (By Average Attendance Per Game), *Sporting Intelligence*, May 18, 2015, http://www.sportingintelligence.com/finance-biz/business-intelligence/global-attendances/.

51. S. Szymanski, "The Economic Design of Sporting Contests," *Journal of Economic Literature* 41, (2003): 1137–1187.

52. A more formal, recent review can be found in Murray Dalziel, Paul Downward, Richard Parrish, Geoff Pearson, and Anna Semens, "Study on the Assessment of Union of European Football Associations (UEFA) 'Home Grown Player Rule' Negotiated Procedure EAC/07/2012," University of Liverpool and Edge Hill University, April 30, 2013, http://ec.europa.eu/sport/library/studies/final-rpt-april2013-homegrownplayer.pdf.

53. "Full National Football League (NFL) Statement into 'Bounty' Program Run by New Orleans Saints," *Times-Picayune*, March 2, 2012, http://www.nola.com/saints/index.ssf/2012/03/full_nfl_statement_into_bounty.html.

54. Howard Fendrich, "NFL Bounties Amount to Incentive System Run Amok," *USA Today*, March 6, 2012, http://usatoday30.usatoday.com/sports/football/nfl/2012-03-05-4169161926_x.htm.

55. Greg Bishop, "Bounties Called 'Inmates Governing Themselves,'" *New York Times*, March 3, 2012, http://www.nytimes.com/2012/03/04/sports/football/former-jets-player-calls-bounties-inmates-governing-themselves.html.

56. Matthew Futterman, "Little Booty in Saints' Bounties," *Wall Street Journal*, March 6, 2012, http://online.wsj.com/article/SB10001424052970203370604577263580381162426.html.

57. "National Football League (NFL) Announces Management Discipline in New Orleans Saints 'Bounty' Matter," NFL Labor Files, March 21, 2012, http://nfllabor.files.wordpress.com/2012/03/saints-2012.pdf.

58. "Constitution and Bylaws of the National Football League," Effective February 1, 1970 (2006 Rev.), NFL, http://static.nfl.com/static/content/public/static/html/careers/pdf/co_.pdf, at. 36–37.

Chapter 6

1. Tom Cary, "Lance Armstrong: I've Admitted to It All and I Have Suffered Enough—It's Now Time to Draw Line in the Sand," *Telegraph*, June 10, 2015, http://www.telegraph.co.uk/sport/othersports/cycling/lancearmstrong/11666570/Lance-Armstrong-Ive-admitted-to-it-all-and-I-have-suffered-enough-its-now-time-to-draw-line-in-the-sand.html.

2. Lance Armstrong, interview with the author, January 19, 2016.

3. "Paul Kimmage at 2009 Amgen Tour of California," February 13, 2009, https://www.youtube.com/watch?v=y6Ai6t6R1_w.

4. "Tysse Tested Positive for Doping," RusaAthletics.com, July 22, 2010, http://eng.rusathletics.com/nov/news.7215.htm.

5. "Award Delivered by the Court of Arbitration for Sport in the Arbitration Between Erik Tysse and Norwegian Athletics Federation," Centrostudisport.it, http://www.centrostudisport.it/PDF/TAS_CAS_ULTIMO/85.pdf .

6. "Erik Tysse, Athlete Profile," IAAF, http://www.iaaf.org/athletes/norway/erik-tysse-134850.

7. Jon Nissen-Meyer, Erik Boye, Bjarne Østerud, and Tore Skotland, "World Anti-Doping Agency (WADA) Accredited Doping Analyses Cannot Always Be Trusted: Weak Evidence," *Lab Times*, January 18, 2013, http://www.labtimes.org/labtimes/issues/lt2013/lt01/lt_2013_01_18_23.pdf.

8. Vik Ostein, "35 Professors Supporting Tysse," *Bergens Tidende*, February 25, 2011, http://www.bt.no/lokallokal/arnaogosteroy/sport/35-professorer-stotter-Tysse-1756746.html.

9. Jon Nissen-Meyer, personal communication, February 11, 2016.

10. Werner Franke and Hans Heid, letter to CAS, June 29, 2011.

11. Natalie St. Cyr Clarke, "Do World Anti-Doping Agency (WADA) Anti-Doping Regulations Restrict Athletes' Access to Impartial Experts?" *Law in Sport,* May 19, 2016, http://www.lawinsport.com/articles/item/do-wada-s-anti-doping-regulations-restrict-athletes-access-to-impartial-experts

12. H. T. Waaler, H. Siem, and O. O. Aalen, "Can We Trust Doping Tests?" *Journal of the Norwegian Medical Association,* September 20, 2011, http://tidsskriftet.no/article/2144625/en_GB.

13. Claudio Gatti, "Officials Covered Up Italian Olympian's Doping, Investigators Say," *New York Times,* June 18, 2013, http://www.nytimes.com/2013/06/19/sports/olympics/officials-accused-of-covering-up-italian-olympians-doping.html.

14. "World Anti-Doping Agency (WADA) Doping Test Lab: Weird Analysis," *Lab Times,* September 18, 2015, http://www.labtimes.org/epaper/LT_15_05.pdf.

15. "Revisiting a Doping Cover-Up: A Guest Post by Jon Nissen-Meyer, University of Oslo," *The Least Thing,* May 17, 2016, http://leastthing.blogspot.com/2016/05/revisiting-doping-cover-up-guest-post.html. In 2016, Schwazer again tested positive in 2016 in advance of the Rio games.

16. Sandro Donati, "Anti-Doping; The Fraud Behind the Stage," Play the Game, November 15, 2000, http://www.playthegame.org/news/news-articles/2000/anti-doping-the-fraud-behind-the-stage/.

17. Letter in the author's possession.

18. Ibid.

19. See "Only a Few . . . " *Lab Times,* November 25, 2015, http://www.labtimes.org/epaper/LT_15_06.pdf. Subsequently, three more were suspended: South Africa, Portugal, and China. See "Accredited Laboratories," WADA, https://www.wada-ama.org/en/what-we-do/science-medical/laboratories/accredited-laboratories. This number is sure to be out of date when you read this, as WADA laboratories are being declared noncompliant on a frequent basis.

20. Charles E. Yesalis and Michael S. Bahrke. "History of Doping in Sport," *International Sports Studies* 24, no. 1 (2002): 42–76.

21. In their wonderful biography of Edward Payson Weston, Nick and Helen Harris, along with Paul Marshall, document the rise of a sport that few are aware of today. Nick Harris, Helen Harris, and Paul Marshall, *A Man in a Hurry: The Extraordinary Life and Times of Edward Payson Weston, the World's Greatest Walker* (London: DeCoubertin, 2012). Special thanks to Nick for introducing me to Weston and for sharing some of the original documentation that he relied on.

22. Helen Harris, "Walking Tall: The World's Greatest Pedestrian," *Express,* August 2, 2012, www.express.co.uk/comment/expresscomment/336949/Walking-tall-The-world-s-greatest-pedestrian.

23. Yesalis and Bahrke, "History of Doping in Sport."

24. See ibid.; J. Hoberman, *Mortal Engines* (New York: Free Press, 1992); T. Donohoe and N. Johnson, *Foul Play? Drug Use in Sport* (Oxford: Blackwell, 1986); and L. Prokop, "The Struggle against Doping and Its History," *Journal of Sports Medicine and Physical Fitness 10* (1970): 45–48.

25. Yesalis and Bahrke, in "History of Doping in Sport," indicate that there is some uncertainty to this claim.

26. https://web.archive.org/web/20151113153601/https://www.wada-ama.org/en/who-we-are/a-brief-history-of-anti-doping.

27. A comprehensively referenced resource on the history of doping in the Olympic movement since 1960 is T. M. Hunt, "Drug Games: The International Politics of Doping," PhD dis-

sertation, University of Texas, 2007, http://www.lib.utexas.edu/etd/d/2007/huntt51425/huntt51425.pdf.

28. Quoted in Hoberman, *Mortal Engines*, 131–132.

29. E. Halchin, *Anti-Doping Policies: The Olympics and Selected Professional Sports* (Washington, DC: Congressional Research Service, 2007).

30. B. Gilbert, "Problems in a Turned on World," *Sports Illustrated*, June 23, 1969.

31. Rick Weinberg, "Jordan Battles Flu, Makes Jazz Sick," ESPN, June 23, 2004, http://sports.espn.go.com/espn/espn25/story?page=moments/79.

32. "Chicago Bulls at Utah Jazz Box Score, June 11, 1997," *Basketball Reference*, http://www.basketball-reference.com/boxscores/199706110UTA.html.

33. Weinberg, "Jordan Battles Flu, Makes Jazz Sick."

34. Paul Dimeo, "The Truth About Knud: Revisiting an Anti-Doping Myth," *Sports Integrity Initiative*, March 1, 2016, http://www.sportsintegrityinitiative.com/the-truth-about-knud-revisiting-an-anti-doping-myth/.

35. Jere Longman, "US Seeks Redress for 1976 Doping in Olympics," *New York Times*, October 25, 1998, http://www.nytimes.com/1998/10/25/sports/olympics-us-seeks-redress-for-1976-doping-in-olympics.html

36. "Medal Winners," databsedolympics.com, http://www.databaseolympics.com/sport/sportevent.htm?sp=SWI&enum=530.

37. Werner W. Franke and Brigitte Berendonk, "Hormonal Doping and Androgenization of Athletes: A Secret Program of the German Democratic Republic Government," *Clinical Chemistry* 43, no. 7 (July 1997): 1262–1279.

38. Both quotes are from Neil Amdur, "E. German Women's Success Stirs U.S. Anger," *New York Times*, August 1, 1976.

39. Barrie Houlihan, "The World Anti-Doping Agency: Prospects for Success," in *Drugs and Doping in Sport: Socio-Legal Perspectives* (The Hague: Cavendish, 2001), 125–145.

40. Houlihan, "The World Anti-Doping Agency," 127.

41. Rebecca R. Ruiz and Michael Schwirtz, "Russian Insider Says State-Run Doping Fueled Olympic Gold," *New York Times*, May 12, 2016, http://www.nytimes.com/2016/05/13/sports/russia-doping-sochi-olympics-2014.html?_r=0.

42. James Connor, Jules Woolf, and Jason Mazanov, "Would They Dope? Revisiting the Goldman Dilemma," *British Journal of Sports Medicine*, January 23, 2013, http://www.oliverfinlay.com/assets/pdf/connor%20(2013)%20would%20they%20dope.%20%20revisiting%20the%20goldman%20dilemma.pdf.

43. Tim Rohan, "Antidoping Agency Delays Publication of Research," *New York Times*, August 22, 2013, http://www.nytimes.com/2013/08/23/sports/research-finds-wide-doping-study-withheld.html.

44. "Gather Data to Reveal True Extent of Doping in Sport," *Nature*, January 28, 2015, http://www.nature.com/news/gather-data-to-reveal-true-extent-of-doping-in-sport-1.16798.

45. The official was the manager of scientific affairs for the national antidoping organization of the Netherlands. See Olivier de Hon, Harm Kuipers, and Maarten van Bottenburg, "Prevalence of Doping Use in Elite Sports: A Review of Numbers and Methods," Link.springer.com, August 29, 2014, http://link.springer.com/article/10.1007%2Fs40279-014-0247-x.

46. Gilbert, "Problems in a Turned on World."

47. "Resources, Implementation of Code 2015," WADA, http://www.wada-ama.org/Documents/World_Anti-Doping_Program/WADP-The-Code/WADA_Anti-Doping_CODE_2009_EN.pdf.

48. Houlihan, "The World Anti-Doping Agency."

49. "Whereabours," WADA, https://www.wada-ama.org/en/questions-answers/whereabouts #node-540.

50. "Murray Attacks 'Draconian' Anti-Doping Rules," *Guardian*, February 5, 2009, http://www.theguardian.com/sport/2009/feb/06/tennis-andy-murray-anti-doping.

51. Dennis Galema, "Top Dutch Judo Athlete, Henk Grol: Degrading Doping Control," *Antidoping Reform*, June 26, 2014, http://antidopingreform.com/2014/06/26/top-dutch-judo-athlete-henk-grol-degrading-doping-control/.

52. Paul Dimeo and Verner Moller, "Anti-Doping: Is the Curse Worse Than the Disease?" *The Outer Line*, September 8, 2014, http://www.theouterline.com/anti-doping-is-the-cure-worse-than-the-disease/.

53. "Notes from Sparks Ruling on Armstrong vs. US Anti-Doping Agency (USADA), *The Least Thing*, August 21, 2012, http://leastthing.blogspot.com/2012/08/notes-from-sparks-ruling-on-armstrong.html.

54. "Integrity Trumps Tragedy: Why US Anti-Doping Agency (USADA) Should Seek a Deal with Lance Armstrong," *The Least Thing*, January 21, 2013, http://leastthing.blogspot.com/2013/01/integrirty-trumps-tragedy-why-usada.html.

55. Dimeo and Moller, "Anti-Doping."

56. Ibid.

57. Teddy Cutler, "Cycling in the EPO Era: 65 Per Cent 'Juiced' . . . and Probably More," *Sporting Intelligence*, December 13, 2014, http://www.sportingintelligence.com/2014/12/31/cycling-in-the-epo-era-65-per-cent-dirty-and-probably-more-311201/. Despite the allegations, the article concludes, "One of the most loyal of all Lance Armstrong's lieutenants, Ekimov has never given evidence against Armstrong nor been definitively nailed down himself as a doper."

58. "Jan Ullrich Finally Admits to Using 'Treatment,' Says It Was to Level Playing Field," *Velo News*, June 22, 2013, updated October 30, 2014, http://velonews.competitor.com/2013/06/news/jan-ullrich-finally-admits-to-using-treatment-says-it-was-to-level-playing-field_291690.

59. "Event Results," Olympic.org, http://www.olympic.org/content/results-and-medalists/eventresultpagegeneral/?athletename=&country=&sport2=31494&games2=&event2=31497&mengender=true&womengender=true&mixedgender=true&goldmedal=true&silvermedal=true&bronzemedal=true&teamclassification=true&individualclassification=true&winter=true&summer=true.

60. Philip Hersh, "Scoundrels and Their Scandals—OpEd," *Around the Rings*, December 29, 2015, http://aroundtherings.com/site/A__54289/Title__Scoundrels-and-Their-Scandals----OpEd/292/Articles.

61. https://www.wada-ama.org/en/questions-answers/2015-world-anti-doping-code.

62. Mara Yamauchi, Twitter post, May 17, 2016, https://twitter.com/mara_yamauchi/status /732683821657817088.

63. Mary Pilon, " '04 Drug Test May Give US Olympic Gold," *New York Times*, December 5, 2012, http://www.nytimes.com/2012/12/06/sports/four-2004-olympians-stripped-of-medals-in-doping-re-test.html?_r=0.

64. Tom Kalil, "Funding What Works: The Importance of Low-Cost Randomized Controlled Trials," The White House, July 9, 2014, http://www.whitehouse.gov/blog/2014/07/09/maximizing-impact-social-spending-using-evidence-based-policy-and-low-cost-randomize.

65. "Lack of Effectiveness of Testing Programs," WADA, December 5, 2013, https://www.wada-ama.org/en/resources/world-anti-doping-program/lack-of-effectiveness-of-testing-programs#.VChiVPmwI8w.

66. Pete Madden, "The Professional Golf Association (PGA) Tour's Drug: Testing Policy Needs a Big Fix," Golf.com, January 27, 2016, http://www.golf.com/golf-plus/pga-tours-drug-testing -policy-needs-big-fix.

67. Lance Armstrong, interview with the author, January 19, 2016.

Chapter 7

1. Josh McHugh, "Blade Runner," *Wired*, March 2007, http://archive.wired.com/wired/ archive/15.03/blade.html.

2. Guillem Balague, "Lionel Messi's Improbably Progression from Struggling Youngster to World Super Star," *Telegraph*, December 2, 2013, http://www.telegraph.co.uk/sport/football /players/lionel-messi/10487181/Lionel-Messis-improbable-progression-from-struggling-youngster-to-world-super-star.html.

3. National Library of Medicine, "Growth Hormone Deficiency: Children," updated July 10, 2015, http://www.nlm.nih.gov/medlineplus/ency/article/001176.htm.

4. Court of Arbitration for Sport (CAS), "Arbitration CAS 2008/A/1480 Pistorius v/IAAF, Award of 16 May 2008," http://amlawdaily.typepad.com/amlawdaily/files/oscar_pistorius_ decision.pdf.

5. J. M. Tanner, "Human Growth Hormone," *Nature* 237 (1972): 433–439.

6. Carol Pogash, "A Personal Call to a Prosthetic Invention," *New York Times*, July 2, 2008, http://www.nytimes.com/2008/07/02/sports/olympics/02cheetah.html.

7. Chris Taylor, "A Big Hand," *Guardian*, November 5, 2005, http://www.theguardian.com/ football/2005/nov/06/sport.argentina.

8. IAAF, "IAAF and Oscar Pistorius to Cooperate on Future Research," July 26, 2007, http:// www.iaaf.org/news/news/iaaf-and-oscar-pistorius-to-co-operate-on-fut.

9. CAS, "Arbitration CAS 2008/A/1480 Pistorius v/IAAF."

10. M. A. Peters, *See to Play* (Minneapolis: Bascom Hill Publishing Group, 2012).

11. William Saletan, "The Beam in Your Eye: If Steroids are Cheating, Why Isn't LASIK?" *Slate*, April 18, 2005, http://www.slate.com/articles/health_and_science/human_nature /2005/04/the_beam_in_your_eye.2.html.

12. Owen Gibson, "Oscar Pistorius Blades Row Reignited by South African Officials," *Guardian*, September 5, 2012, http://www.theguardian.com/sport/2012/sep/05/oscar-pistorius-blades-row.

13. Sarah Gearhart, "Tennessee Teen Amputee Excels in Three Sports While Wearing a Prosthetic Leg," *USA Today*, November 19, 2014, http://usatodayhss.com/2014/tennessee-teen-amputee-athlete-football-basketball-baseball.

14. Sean Ingle, "Amputee Long Jumper Markus Rehm's Olympic Hopes Boosted by Glasgow Win," *Guardian*, February 21, 2016, https://www.theguardian.com/sport/2016/feb/21/ olympic-long-jump-paralympic-glasgow-markus-rehm.

15. "'EliteXC: Renegade' Results—KJ Noons Upsets Nick Diaz for 160-Pound Title," mmajunkie.com, November 11, 2007, http://mmajunkie.com/2007/11/elitexc -renegade-results-kj-noons-upsets-nick-diaz-for-160-pound-title.

16. Jake Rossen, "The Cutting Edge: How Mixed Martial Arts (MMA) Fighters Face Pugilistic Plastic Surgery," *Wired*, March 9, 2011, http://www.wired.com/2011/03/mma-plastic-surgery/.

17. For example, Tim Kawakami, "New Man: Boxer Has Plastic Surgery to Reduce Effect of Cuts," *Los Angeles Times*, April 14, 1994, http://articles.latimes.com/1994-04-14/sports/ sp-45954_1_cosmetic-surgery.

18. R. M. Schneiderman, "Cut-Prone Fighters Turn to Surgery to Limit Bleeding," *New York Times*, July 10, 2009, http://www.nytimes.com/2009/07/11/sports/11surgery.html.

19. "Nick Diaz," Wikipedia, https://en.wikipedia.org/wiki/Nick_Diaz.

20. "Plastic Surgery in Mixed Martial Arts (MMA)," mmafutures.com, http://mmafutures.com/plastic-surgery-in-mma/.

21. C. S. Ahmad, W. J. Grantham, and R. M. Greiwe, "Public Perceptions of Tommy John Surgery," *The Physician and Sports Medicine* 40, no. 2 (2012): 64–72.

22. Stephania Bell, "What We've Missed about Tommy John Surgery," ESPN, April 9, 2015, http://espn.go.com/mlb/story/_/id/12648769/what-missed-tommy-john-surgery.

23. B. J. Erickson, et al., "Rate of Return to Pitching and Performance after Tommy John Surgery in Major League Baseball Pitchers,"*American Journal of Sports Medicine* 42, no. 3 (2014): 536–543.

24. Ahmad, Grantham, and Greiwe, "Public Perceptions of Tommy John Surgery."

25. Compare: Bell, "What We've Missed about Tommy John Surgery."

26. Tom Kelly, "Win or Bust: Tennis Star Who Had Breast Reduction Surgery to Help Her Game Is Now Number Three Seed for Wimbledon," *Daily Mail*, June 23, 2014, http://www.dailymail.co.uk/news/article-2665341/Win-bust-Tennis-star-breast-reduction-surgery-help-game-number-three-seed-Wimbledon.html.

27. "How Breast Reduction Saved a Tennis Star's Career," *New York Post*, May 31, 2014, http://nypost.com/2014/05/31/how-breast-reduction-saved-a-tennis-stars-career/.

28. "Jana Rawlinson Sacrifices Breast Implants for Olympics," BBC, January 5, 2010, http://news.bbc.co.uk/sport1/hi/athletics/8441196.stm.

29. R. M. Rodenberg and H. L. Hampton, "Surgical Doping: A Policy Loophole?" *International Journal of Sport Policy and Politics* 5, no. 1 (2013): 145–149.

30. B. R. Allenby and D. Sarewitz, *The Techno-Human Condition* (Cambridge: MIT Press, 2008), and L. Zonneveld, H. Dijstelbloem, and D. Ringoir, eds., *Reshaping the Human Condition: Exploring Human Enhancement* (The Hague: Rathenau Institute, in collaboration with the British Embassy, Science and Innovation Network and the Parliamentary Office of Science and Technology, 2008).

31. M. Hamilton, "Elective Performance Enhancement Surgery for Athletes: Should It Be Resisted?" *Acta Universitatis Palackianae Olomucensis Gymnica* 36, no. 2 (2006): 39–46.

32. "Layman's Guide to Paralympic Classification," Paralympic.org, http://www.paralympic.org/sites/default/files/document/120716152047682_classificationguide_2.pdf.

33. Chicago Sports and Entertainment Partners, "Victoria Arlen, at a glance . . ." http://www.chicagosep.com/Victoria%20Arlen-%20Bio%20-%20Final%20as%20of%2010082013.pdf.

34. Joyce Wang, "Paralympian Gold Medalist Victoria Arlen Joins Entertainment & Sports Programming Network (ESPN) as Features Reporter," ESPNMediaZone.com, December 14, 2015, http://espnmediazone.com/us/press-releases/2015/12/paralympian-gold-medalist-victoria-arlen-joins-espn-as-features-reporter/. She was later diagnosed with a second debilitating condition, acute disseminated encephalomyelitis.

35. "Swimming Classification," Paralympic.org, http://www.paralympic.org/swimming/classification. For an in-depth and highly accessible explanation, see Jeff Commings, "Confused about the Paralympic Classification System? Join the Club," *Swimming World*, August 30, 2012, http://www.swimmingworldmagazine.com/news/confused-about-the-paralympic-classification-system-join-the-club/.

36. James Montague, "The Thin Line: Paralympic Classification Causes Controversy," CNN, August 31, 2012, http://www.cnn.com/2012/08/31/sport/london-2012-paralympics-classification-arlen/index.html.

37. Sarah Lyall, "Swimmer Is Not Disabled Enough," *New York Times*, September 26, 2013, http://www.nytimes.com/2013/09/27/sports/swimmer-is-fighting-a-ruling-she-is-not-disabled-enough.html.

38. Ibid.

39. Ibid.

40. Wang, "Paralympian Gold Medalist."

41. Rebecca E. Morss, Julie L. Demuth, and Jeffrey K. Lazo, "Communicating Uncertainty in Weather Forecasts: A Survey of the US Public," *Weather and Forecasting* 23 (2008): 974–991.

42. Harry Collins and Robert Evans, "Welcome to the Hawk-Eye Page, Hawk Eye Debate," Cardiff School of Social Sciences, July 2008, http://www.cf.ac.uk/socsi/contactsandpeople/harrycollins/expertise-project/hawk-eye-debate.html.

43. Christopher Hitchens, "World Cup 1966: Geoff Hurst's Controversial Goal in Color," YouTube.com, http://youtu.be/0Uhe_l1h3w8.

44. Ian Reid and Andrew Zisserman, "Goad-Directed Video Metrology," Robots.ox.ac.uk, 1996, http://www.robots.ox.ac.uk/~vgg/publications/papers/reid96.pdf.

45. Anna Edwards, "Furious French Open Player Takes a Photo of Mark Left by Ball After Umpire Says His Shot Was Out," *Daily Mail*, May 28, 2013, http://www.dailymail.co.uk/news/article-2332122/French-Open-2013-Sergiy-Stakhovsky-takes-photo-mark-left-ball-umpire-says-shot-out.html.

46. J. Hamrick and J. Rasp, "The Connection Between Race and Called Strikes and Balls," *Journal of Sports Economics* 16, no. 7 (2015): 714–734.

47. "The Boise State Robbery," *The Least Thing*, February 11, 2016, http://leastthing.blogspot.com/2016/02/the-boise-state-robbery.html

48. Matt Verderame, "Reviewable and Non-Reviewable Plays: How It Works in the National Football League (NFL)," *Sports Blog Nation*, February 2, 2014, http://www.sbnation.com/nfl/2014/2/2/5360810/super-bowl-2014-reviewable-plays-nonreviewable-broncos-seahawks.

49. Noah Davis and Michael Lopez, "Umpires Are Less Blind Than They Used to Be," FiveThirtyEight.com, August 19, 2015, http://fivethirtyeight.com/features/umpires-are-less-blind-than-they-used-to-be/.

50. Alex Shultz, "Rise of the Machines? Baseball Weighs Use of Automated Strike Zone," *Los Angeles Times*, August 10, 2015, http://www.latimes.com/sports/la-sp-automated-strike-zone-20150810-story.html.

51. Dan Szymborski, "Automated Strike Zone an Improvement Baseball Needs," ESPN.go.com, January 19, 2016, http://espn.go.com/mlb/story/_/id/14599589/re-imagining-baseball-robot-umpires-home-plate.

52. Shultz, "Rise of the Machines?"

53. "Schilling Attacks Ques Tec, Literally," *St. Petersburg Times*, May 26, 2003, http://www.sptimes.com/2003/05/26/Sports/Schilling_attacks_Que.shtml.

54. Jere Longman, "An Amputee Sprinter: Is He Disabled or Too Abled?" *New York Times*, May 15, 2007, http://www.nytimes.com/2007/05/15/sports/othersports/15runner.html.

55. Paul Hochman, "Bionic Legs, i-Limbs, and Other Super Human Prostheses You'll Envy," FastCompany.com, February 1, 2010, http://www.fastcompany.com/1514543/bionic-legs-i-limbs-and-other-super-human-prostheses-youll-envy.

56. S. Camporesi, "Oscar Pistorius, Enhancement and Post-Humans," *Journal of Medical Ethics* 34, no. 9 (2008): 639.

57. C. Cooper, *Run, Swim, Throw, Cheat: The Science Behind Drugs in Sport* (Oxford: Oxford University Press, 2012).

Chapter 8

1. Debabrata Mohanty, Jonathan Selvaraj, and Nihal Koshie, "I Am Who I Am: Dutee Chand," *Indian Express*, September 29, 2014, http://indianexpress.com/article/sports/sport-others/big-picture-i-am-who-i-am/.

2. Taipei Sixteenth Asian Athletics Junior Championships 2014, Women Results, http://163.17.55.13/taipei2014/score_query.php?action=sub_all&htm=18&ItNo=&grp_num=100&grp_name=%A4k%A4l&cate=tf&ID=.

3. Mohanty, Selvaraj, and Koshie, "I Am Who I Am."

4. The AFI is India's track and field federation under the IAAF. See Mohanty, Selvaraj, and Koshie, "I Am Who I Am."

5. IAAF, "Regulations Governing Eligibility of Females with Hyperandrogenism to Compete in Women's Competition," in force from May 1, 2011, http://www.iaaf.org/about-iaaf/documents/medical.

6. CAS, "Interim Arbitral Award between Ms. Dutee Chand versus Athletics Federation of India (AFI) and the International Association of Athletics Federations (IAAF)," 2014, http://www.tas-cas.org/fileadmin/user_upload/award_internet.pdf.

7. Patricia Campbell Warner, *When the Girls Came Out to Play: The Birth of Modern American Sportswear* (Amherst: University of Massachusetts Press, 2006), 85.

8. International Olympic Committee (IOC), "Olympic Charter," in force from September 9, 2013, http://www.olympic.org/Documents/olympic_charter_en.pdf.

9. IOC, "Factsheet: Women in the Olympic Movement," Olympic.org, updated January 2016, http://www.olympic.org/Documents/Reference_documents_Factsheets/Women_in_Olympic_Movement.pdf.

10. Ibid., 5.

11 "Factsheet: Women in Leadership Positions within SportAccord Members," Sport-Accord.com, http://www.sportaccord.com/multimedia/docs/2013/02/SportAccord_Women_in_Leadership_Positions_Factsheet_February_2013_2.pdf.

12. World Health Organization (WHO), "Gender and Genetics, Genetic Components of Sex and Gender," 2015, http://www.who.int/genomics/gender/en/index1.html, and Deutscher Ethikrat, "Intersexuality," German Ethics Council, February 23, 2012, http://www.ethikrat.org/files/opinion-intersexuality.pdf.

13. For a comprehensive treatment of this history, see Lindsay Parks Pieper, *Sex Testing: Gender Policing in Women's Sports* (Champaign: University of Illinois Press, 2016).

14. See IAAF, "Regulations Governing Eligibility of Females with Hyperandrogenism."

15. Christopher Clarey and Gina Kolata, "Gold Awarded Amid Dispute over Runner's Sex in Berlin, Germany," *New York Times*, August 20, 2009, http://www.nytimes.com/2009/08/21/sports/21runner.html.

16. Ariel Levy, "Either/Or: Sports, Sex, and the Case of Caster Semenya," *New Yorker*, November 30, 2009, http://www.newyorker.com/magazine/2009/11/30/eitheror.

17. Clarey and Kolata, "Gold Awarded."

18. Mike Hurst, "Caster Semenya Has Male Sex Organs and No Womb or Ovaries," *Daily Telegraph*, September 11, 2009, http://www.dailytelegraph.com.au/sport/-has-no-womb-or-ovaries/story-e6frexni-1225771672245.

19. IAAF, "Caster Semenya May Compete," July 6, 2010, http://www.iaaf.org/news/iaaf-news/caster-semenya-may-compete.

20. Stephanie Findlay, "Olympics Struggle with 'Policing Femininity,'" *Star*, December 26, 2012, http://www.thestar.com/sports/olympics/2012/06/08/olympics_struggle_with_policing_femininity.html.

21. IAAF, "Hyperandrogenism Regulations: Explanatory Notes," http://www.iaaf.org/about-iaaf/documents/medical.

22. See IAAF, "Regulations Governing Eligibility of Females with Hyperandrogenism."

23. Ibid.

24. Findlay, "Olympics Struggle."

25. Ibid.

26. Ian Chadband, "Caster Semenya Finds a Silver Lining after Misjudged Start in the 800m Final," *Telegraph*, August 12, 2012, http://www.telegraph.co.uk/sport/olympics/athletics/9470212/London-2012-Olympics-Caster-Semenya-finds-a-silver-lining-after-misjudged-start-in-the-800m-final.html.

27. IAAF, "Senior Outdoor 2016 800 Metres Women Record & Lists," http://www.iaaf.org/records/toplists/middle-long/800-metres/outdoor/women/senior/2016.

28. See Mohanty, Selvaraj, and Koshie, "I Am Who I Am."

29. Vanessa Heggie, "Testing Sex and Gender in Sports: Reinventing, Reimagining, and Reconstructing Histories," *Endeavour* 34, no. 4 (2010): 157–163.

30. Ole Bjorn Rekdal, "Academic Urban Legends," *Social Studies of Science* 44, no. 4 (2014): 638–654.

31. This quote appears in Lindsay Parks Pieper, "Sex Testing and the Maintenance of Western Femininity in International Sport," *International Journal of the History of Sport* 31, no. 13 (June 2014): 1557–1576.

32. See Heggie, "Testing Sex and Gender in Sports."

33. Myron Genel and Arne Ljungqvist, "Gender Verification of Female Athletes," *Lancet* (December 2005), http://www.thelancet.com/pdfs/journals/lancet/PIIS0140673605678439.pdf.

34. WHO, "Gender and Genetics."

35. See Genel and Ljungqvist, "Gender Verification of Female Athletes."

36. Ibid.

37. Claire F. Sullivan, "Gender Verification and Gender Policies in Elite Sport, Eligibility and 'Fair Play,'" *Journal of Sport & Social Issues* (November 15, 2011), http://jss.sagepub.com/content/35/4/400.short.

38. Eduardo Hay, "Femininity Tests at the Olympic Games," *Olympic Review* (1974), http://library.la84.org/OlympicInformationCenter/OlympicReview/1974/ore76/ore76m.pdf.

39. "IOC Addresses Eligibility of Female Athletes with Hyperandrogenism," *Olympic News*, April 6, 2011, http://en.olympic.cn/news/olympic_news/2011-04-06/2134979.html.

40. George Vecsey, "Remembering Flo Hyman," *New York Times*, February 5, 1988, http://www.nytimes.com/1988/02/05/sports/sports-of-the-times-remembering-flo-hyman.html.

41. David Epstein, *The Sports Gene* (New York: Current, 2013).

42. Shawn Crincoli, "The IAAF Hyperandrogenism Regulations and Discrimination," *World Sports Law Report* 9, no. 6 (2011), http://digitalcommons.tourolaw.edu/cgi/viewcontent.cgi?article=1461&context=scholarlyworks

43. Ibid.

44. Roger Pielke, Jr., *The Honest Broker: Making Sense of Science in Policy and Politics* (New York: Cambridge University Press, 2007).

45. See WHO, "Gender and Genetics."

46. Ethikrat, "Intersexuality"; Katrina Karkazis, "Out of Bounds? A Critique of the New Policies on Hyperandrogenism in Elite Female Athletes," *American Journal of Bioethics* 12, no. 7 (2012), http://www.tandfonline.com/doi/abs/10.1080/15265161.2012.680533; and Alice

Dreger, "Sex Typing for Sport," BioMedSearch.com, March 1, 2010, http://www.biomed-search.com/article/Sex-typing-sport/239530614.html.

47. Stéphane Bermon, Martin Ritzén, Angelica Lindén Hirschberg, and Thomas H. Murray, "Are the New Policies on Hyperandrogenism in Elite Female Athletes Really Out of Bounds? Response to 'Out of Bounds? A Critique of the New Policies on Hyperandrogenism in Elite Female Athletes,'" *American Journal of Bioethics* 13, no. 5 (2013), http://www.tandfonline.com/doi/pdf/10.1080/15265161.2013.776129.

48. "IOC Addresses Eligibility of Female Athletes with Hyperandrogenism," IOC press release, April 5, 2011, https://www.olympic.org/news/ioc-addresses-eligibility-of-female-athletes-with-hyperandrogenism.

49. See IAAF, "Regulations Governing Eligibility of Females with Hyperandrogenism."

50. See also Ben Koh, Daryl Adair, and Peter Sonksen, "Testosterone, Sex and Gender Differentiation in Sport: Where Science and Sports Law Meet," *Law in Sport*, October 14, 2014, http://www.lawinsport.com/articles/item/testosterone-sex-and-gender-differentiation-in-sport-where-science-and-sports-law-meet.

51. See IAAF, "Regulations Governing Eligibility of Females with Hyperandrogenism."

52. Crincoli, "IAAF Hyperandrogenism Regulations and Discrimination."

53. Alvaro Morales, "The Long and Tortuous History of the Discovery of Testosterone and Its Clinical Application," *Journal of Sexual Medicine* 10, no. 4 (2013), https://www.researchgate.net/publication/235381891_The_Long_and_Tortuous_History_of_the_Discovery_of_Testosterone_and_Its_Clinical_Application.

54. Paul Davis and Lisa Edwards, "The New IOC and IAAF Policies on Female Eligibility: Old Emperor, New Clothes?" *Sport, Ethics and Philosophy*, 8, no.1 (2014), http://www.tandfonline.com/doi/abs/10.1080/17511321.2014.899613.

55. Warner, *When the Girls Came Out to Play.*

56. IOC, "Factsheet: Women in the Olympic Movement."

57. IOC, "Women and Sport Commission," 2014, http://www.olympic.org/women-sport-commission.

58. Hay, "Femininity Tests at the Olympic Games."

59. Ibid.

60. Compare Jamie Schulz, "New Standards, Same Refrain: The IAAF's Regulations on Hyperandrogenism," *American Journal of Bioethics*, 12, no. 7 (2012): 32–33; and Davis and Edwards, "The New IOC and IAAF Policies on Female Eligibility."

61. IAAF, "Hyperandrogenism Regulations: Appendices," 2011, http://www.iaaf.org/about-iaaf/documents/medical.

62. Bermon, Ritzén, Hirschberg, and Murray, "New Policies on Hyperandrogenism."

63. Crincoli, "IAAF Hyperandrogenism Regulations and Discrimination."

64. See IAAF, "Regulations Governing Eligibility of Females with Hyperandrogenism."

65. "IOC Addresses Eligibility of Female Athletes."

66. Ibid.

67. See Heggie, "Testing Sex and Gender in Sports."

68. K. Karkazis, R. Jordan-Young, G. Davis, & S. Camporesi, "Out of Bounds? A Critique of the New Policies on Hyperandrogenism in Elite Female Athletes," in *American Journal of Bioethics* 12, no. 7 (2012): 3-16.

69. Alice Dreger, "Sex Typing for Sport," Hastings Center Report, March/April 2010, http://alicedreger.com/sex-testing_files/Dreger%20HCR%20Sport%20of%20Sex.pdf.

70. Alice Dreger, "The Social Construction of Sex and Me," March 1, 2007, http://alicedreger.com/social_construction.html.

71. Compare Rebecca Jordan-Young and Katrina Karkazis, "You Say You're a Woman? That Should be Enough," *New York Times*, June 17, 2012, http://www.nytimes.com/2012/06/18/sports/olympics/olympic-sex-verification-you-say-youre-a-woman-that-should-be-enough.html?_r=1&.

72. IOC, "Olympic Charter"; IAAF, Rule 5: Eligibility to represent a member," http://www.iaaf.org/download/download?filename=68431829-23e2-4829-a7cad4e395f085f0.pdf&urlslug=Rule%205%20amendment?utm_source=GCSResults&utm_medium=googlecse&utm_campaign=Search%20term:%20%27nationality%27,%20Page1&utm_content=Slot4).

73. Roger Pielke, Jr., "US Immigration Policy Negatively Impacts US Soccer," *Law in Sport*, January 12, 2014, http://www.lawinsport.com/articles/regulation-a-governance/item/us-immigration-policy-negatively-impacts-us-soccer.

74. Peter Spiro, "Eliminate Nationality Rules," *New York Times*, December 6, 2012, http://www.nytimes.com/roomfordebate/2012/07/26/which-country-did-you-say-you-were-playing-for-in-the-olympics/eliminate-nationality-rules.

75. See Pielke, "US Immigration Policy."

Chapter 9

1. Nick Mulvenney, "Science Will Prevail in Doping Firestorm: WADA Chief," Reuters, August 21, 2015, http://www.reuters.com/article/us-athletics-world-doping-reedie-idUSKC-N0QQ1H120150821.

2. "Richard W Pound, Play the Game Conference, Cologne, Germany, Responses to Corruption in Sport," Play the Game, October 3, 2011, http://www.playthegame.org/fileadmin/image/PTG2011/Presentation/Richard_Pound_2011.pdf.

3. Marcus Hoy, "Pound Points to Lack of Incentives to Catch Drug Cheats," Play the Game, October 28, 2013, http://www.playthegame.org/news/news-articles/2013/pound-points-to-lack-of-incentives-to-catch-drug-cheats/.

4. Working Group Established Following Foundation Board Meeting of May 18, 2012, "Report to WADA Executive Committee on Lack of Effectiveness of Testing Programs," May 12, 2013, https://wada-main-prod.s3.amazonaws.com/resources/files/2013-05-12-Lack-of-effectiveness-of-testing-WG-Report-Final.pdf.

5. Rebecca R. Ruiz and Michael Schwirtz, "Russian Insider Says State-Run Doping Fueled Olympic Gold," *New York Times*, May 12, 2016, http://www.nytimes.com/2016/05/13/sports/russia-*doping*-sochi-olympics-2014.html.

6. Olivier de Hon, Harm Kuipers, and Maarten van Bottenburg, "Prevalence of Doping Use in Elite Sports: A Review of Numbers and Methods," Link.Springer.com, August 29, 2014, http://link.springer.com/article/10.1007%2Fs40279-014-0247-x.

7. Tim Rohan, "Antidoping Agency Delays Publication of Research," *New York Times*, August 22, 2013, http://www.nytimes.com/2013/08/23/sports/research-finds-wide-doping-study-withheld.html.

8. "Uncomfortable Science and the Embargoed WADA Doping Study," *The Least Thing*, March 16, 2016, http://leastthing.blogspot.com/2016/03/uncomfortable-science-and-embargoed.html.

9. "Report on Lack of Effectiveness of Testing Programs."

10. UNESCO, "International Convention against Doping in Sport," October 19, 2005, http://www.unesco.org/eri/la/convention.asp?KO=31037&language=E, and "International Convention against Doping in Sport," UNESCO, http://www.unesco.org/new/en/social-and-human-sciences/themes/anti-doping/international-convention-against-doping-in-sport/.

11. Treasury and General Government Appropriations Act, 2002, Public Law 107-67, http://www.gpo.gov/fdsys/pkg/GPO-CDOC-107sdoc8/pdf/GPO-CDOC-107sdoc8-1-7-23.pdf.

12. S. 529: A Bill to Designate a United States Anti-Doping Agency, As Ordered Reported by the Senate Committee on Commerce, Science, and Transportation on September 27, 2006, http://www.cbo.gov/sites/default/files/cbofiles/ftpdocs/76xx/doc7633/s529.pdf.

13. Stephane Mandard, "Antoine Vayer: Armstrong? Almost a Small Player to King Miguel," *Le Monde*, June 6, 2013, http://www.lemonde.fr/sport/article/2013/06/06/antoine-vayer-armstrong-presque-un-petit-joueur-a-cote-du-roi-miguel_3425660_3242.html.

14. "Women Faster Than Men in the Pool, and SA's First Medal Is Gold," *Science of Sport*, July 29, 2012, http://www.sportsscientists.com/2012/07/london-day-2-quick-thoughts/.

15. Simon Ernst and Perikles Simon, "Drug Testing and Analysis: A Quantitative Approach for Assessing Significant Improvements in Elite Sprint Performance: Has IGF-1 Entered the Arena?" Wiley Online Library, August 29, 2012, http://onlinelibrary.wiley.com/doi/10.1002/dta.1406/abstract.

16. Perikles Simon, "Loopholes in the Testing System," Play the Game, October 28, 2013, http://www.playthegame.org/fileadmin/image/PtG2013/Presentations/28_October_Monday/28_okt_15.30_Marselissalen_Perikles_Simon.pptx.pdf.

17. Ernst and Simon, "Drug Testing and Analysis."

18. Travis T. Tygart, "Come Clean, Russia, or No Rio," *New York Times*, May 25, 2016, http://www.nytimes.com/2016/05/25/opinion/come-clean-russia-or-no-rio.html?_r=0.

19. "Anti-Doping Official Says US Covered Up," *New York Times*, April 17, 2003, http://www.nytimes.com/2003/04/17/sports/olympics-anti-doping-official-says-us-covered-up.html.

20. Duncan Mackay, "Lewis: 'Who Cares I Failed Drug Test?'" *Guardian*, April 23, 2003, http://www.theguardian.com/sport/2003/apr/24/athletics.duncanmackay.

21. Tim Rohan, "Antidoping Agency Delays Publication of Research," *New York Times*, August 22, 2013, http://www.nytimes.com/2013/08/23/sports/research-finds-wide-doping-study-withheld.html.

22. NPD Group, "For Every Cup of Tea We Drink Out of Home We Now Consume Two-and-Half Cups of Coffee," https://www.npdgroup.co.uk/wps/portal/npd/uk/news/press-releases/for-every-cup-of-tea-we-drink-out-of-home-we-now-consume-two-and-half-cups-of-coffee/.

23. The myth and the quote are both from Bertil B. Fredholm, "Notes on the History of Caffeine Use," *Methylxanthines* (2011): 1–9.

24. Louise M. Burke, "Caffeine and Sports Performance, Applied Physiology, Nutrition, and Metabolism," National Research Council (NRC) Research Press, October 14, 2008, http://www.nrcresearchpress.com/doi/abs/10.1139/h08-130#.V1mnMk32aUk.

25. Jonathan D. Wiles, Michael Tegerdine, and Ian L. Swaine, "The Effects of Caffeine Ingestion on Performance Time, Speed and Power During a Laboratory-Based 1 km Cycling Time-Trial," *Journal of Sports Sciences* (2006), www.kfd.pl/index.php?app=core&module=attach&section...id.

26. "Cycling at the 2012 Summer Olympics—Men's Omnium," Wikipedia, https://en.wikipedia.org/wiki/Cycling_at_the_2012_Summer_Olympics_%E2%80%93_Men%27s_Omnium.

27. "Alex Watson's Positive Drug Test," http://www.aph.gov.au/binaries/senate/committee/ecita_ctte/completed_inquiries/pre1996/pos_drug_aw/01commrep.pdf. Morgan was apparently only the second athlete who received a doping violation for caffeine. The first was Bakhaavaa Buidaa of Mongolia, who was stripped of a silver medal in judo at the 1972 games after failing a urine test.

28. "What Is Doping?" *The Least Thing*, August 8, 2012, http://leastthing.blogspot.com/2012/08/what-is-doping.html.

29. "The limit can sometime be reached by consuming around five regular cups of coffee (100 mg per 8 oz.) a few hours before a drug test." See USADA, http://www.usada.org/substances/wada-ncaa-differences/, and Caffeine Informer, "The Complete Guide to Starbucks Caffeine: A Single Starbucks 12 oz. Coffee Has 260 mg of Caffeine," http://www.caffeineinformer.com/the-complete-guide-to-starbucks-caffeine.

30. WADA, "2016 List of Prohibited Substances and Methods," http://list.wada-ama.org/.

31. WADA "The World Anti-Doping Code: The 2004 Prohibited List, International Standard," March 17, 2004, https://wada-main-prod.s3.amazonaws.com/resources/files/WADA_Prohibited_List_2004_EN.pdf.

32. Sean Cottrell, "An Explanation of How the World Anti-Doping Agency Decides Which Substances Are Included on the Prohibited List," *Law in Sport*, January 27, 2016, http://www.lawinsport.com/features/item/an-explanation-of-how-the-world-anti-doping-agency-decides-which-substances-are-included-on-the-prohibited-list.

33. This quote comes from a transcript of the meeting shared by Walter Palmer.

34. "List of Arbitrators (General List)," Tribunal Arbitral for Sport/Court of Arbitration for Sport (TAS/CAS), http://www.tas-cas.org/en/arbitration/list-of-arbitrators-general-list.html.

35. Roger Pielke, Jr., "How Can FIFA Be Held Accountable?" *Sport Management Review*, December 19, 2012, http://docplayer.net/2748507-Sport-management-review.html.

36. "Independence Scorecard for FIFA's 'Independent' Governance Committee," *The Least Thing*, December 18, 2011, http://leastthing.blogspot.com/2011/12/independence-scorecard-for-fifas.html.

37. "How Much Were FIFA's IGC Members Paid 2012–2013? More than $80,000 Each," *The Least Thing*, June 17, 2015, http://leastthing.blogspot.com/2015/06/how-much-were-fifas-igc-members-paid.html.

38. IAAF, "Code of Ethics," http://www.iaaf.org/download/download?filename=416d2e1e-94f0-4017-a7f0-cde989773f3c.pdf&urlslug=IAAF%20Code%20of%20Ethics%20in%20force%20as%20from%201%20May%202015.

39. Andy Brown, "IAAF Asked Coe to Sign a Conflict of Interests Declaration," Sports Integrity Initiative, December 1, 2015, http://www.sportsintegrityinitiative.com/iaaf-asked-coe-to-sign-a-conflict-of-interests-declaration/?utm_content=buffer2add4&utm_medium=social&utm_source=twitter.com&utm_campaign=buffer.

40. Tripp Mickle and Terry Lefton, "Nike Scores in Brazil with '16 Olympic Deal," *Sports Business Daily*, April 2, 2012, http://m.sportsbusinessdaily.com/Journal/Issues/2012/04/02/Marketing-and-Sponsorship/Nike-Rio.aspx.

41. "FIFA Still Doesn't Get 'Independence,' " *The Least Thing*, December 3, 2015, http://leastthing.blogspot.com/2015/12/fifa-still-doesnt-get-independence.html.

42. Bonita Mersiades, "FIFA Reforms: Easy Pickings, Compromises and Missed Opportunity," *Sporting Intelligence*, February 22, 2016, http://www.sportingintelligence.com/2016/02/22/fifa-reform-easy-pickings-compromises-and-missed-opportunity-220201/.

43. For some good examples, see "What Is a Conflict of Interest?" *The Least Thing*, September 2, 2015, http://leastthing.blogspot.com/2015/09/what-is-conflict-of-interest.html.

44. Steve Fainaru and Mark Fainaru-Wada, "NFL Donations to Brain Research Benefit League-Linked Doctors, Raise Worries About Influence on Science," ESPN, February 4, 2016, http://espn.go.com/espn/otl/story/_/id/14711203/nfl-donations-brain-research-benefit-league-linked-doctors-raise-worries-influence-science-lines.

45. US House of Representatives, Committee on Energy and Commerce, "Democratic Staff Report: The National Football League's Attempt to Influence Funding Decisions at the National Institutes of Health," May 2016, https://democrats energycommerce.house.gov/sites/

democrats.energycommerce.house.gov/files/Democratic%20Staff%20Report%20on%20 NFL%20NIH%20Investigation%205.23.2016.pdf.

46. I describe these roles in my book *The Honest Broker* (New York: Cambridge University Press, 2007).

47. Paul Dimeo, "Opinion: Issues Faced by Critical Academics in Anti-Doping," Sports Integrity Initiative, June 6, 2016, http://www.sportsintegrityinitiative.com/opinion-issues-faced-by-critical-academics-in-anti-doping/.

48. "USAC Announces Changes to Anti-Doping Committee," USA Cycling, June 2, 2016, http://www.usacycling.org/usac-announces-changes-to-anti-doping-committee.htm.

49. Paul Dimeo, "Issues Faced by Critical Academics in Anti-Doping," Sports Integrity Initiative, June 6, 2016, http://www.sportsintegrityinitiative.com/opinion-issues-faced-by-critical-academics-in-anti-doping/.

50. Michael Ask, "INDR Commentary: How Should NADO's and Academics Work Together?" Aarhus University, December 2015, http://ph.au.dk/en/about-the-department-of-public-health/sections/section-for-sport-science/research/research-unit-for-sports-and-physical-culture/international-network-of-doping-research/newsletters/december-2015/indr-commentary-michael-ask/,

Chapter 10

1. Chris Chase, "Americans Don't Care About the FIFA Scandal," *USA Today*, May 29, 2015, http://ftw.usatoday.com/2015/05/fifa-scandal-americans-usa-wont-care-sepp-blatter-election.

2. Kenan Malik, "The Corrupt Rhetoric of the FIFA Scandal," *New York Times*, June 16, 2015, http://www.nytimes.com/2015/06/17/opinion/-2015-06-17-opinion-malik-the-corrupt-rhetoric-of-the-fifa-scandalhtml.html.

3. Rob Hughes, "Future for FIFA: Clearing the Muddy Waters," *New York Times*, June 1, 2011, http://www.nytimes.com/2011/06/02/sports/soccer/02iht-FIFA02.html.

4. Paul Kelso, "Revealed: FIFA's Top Secret Bribery Files on Mohamed Bin Hammam and Jack Warner," *Telegraph*, May 28, 2011, http://www.telegraph.co.uk/sport/football/international/8544176/Revealed-Fifa-s-top-secret-bribery-files-on-Mohamed-Bin-Hammam-and-Jack-Warner.html.

5. Joshua Robinson and Matthew Futterman, "Top FIFA Officials Allegedly Paid Each Other $80 Million," *Wall Street Journal*, June 3, 2016, http://www.wsj.com/articles/three-top-fifa-officials-shared-80-million-in-five-years-investigators-say-1464959109.

6. "Robert Keohane Quote," Coursehero.com, 2006, https://www.coursehero.com/file/p1hvkkk/Robert-Keohane-Definition-Governance-can-be-defined-as-the-making-and/.

7. Grit Hartmann, "IWF President under Suspicion of Financial Mismanagement," Play the Game, May 14, 2013, http://www.playthegame.org/news/news-articles/2013/iwf-president-under-suspicion-of-financial-mismanagement/.

8. Stine Alvad and Jens Sejer Andersen, "FIVB Accused of Violating Statutes to Oust Former Presidential Candidate," Play the Game, October 29, 2014, www.playthegame.org/news/news-articles/2014/fivb-accused-of-violating-statutes-to-oust-former-presidential-candidate; and Nick Butler, "Rio 2016 Volleyball Test Event in Doubt after Corruption Allegations Involving FIVB President," Inside the Games, December 15, 2014, http://www.insidethegames.biz/sports/summer/volleyball/1024363-rio-2016-volleyball-test-event-in-doubt-after-corruption-allegations-involving-fivb-president. For background, see Alvad and Andersen, "FIVB Accused of Violating Statutes," and Kirsten Sparre, "FIVB Stops Practice That Has Enriched Former President Acosta," Play the Game, April 21, 2009, http://www.

playthegame.org/news/news-articles/2009/fivb-stops-practice-that-has-enriched-former-president-acosta/.

9. Reed Albergotti and Vanessa O'Connell, "Wheelmen: Lance Armstrong, the Tour de France, and the Greatest Sports Conspiracy Ever," *Economist*, November 16, 2013, http://www.economist.com/news/books-and-arts/21589851-victor-has-been-spoiled-what-shame.

10. Owen Gibson, "Crisis at IAAF that Threatens to Bring Athletics to Its Knees," *Guardian*, December 13, 2014, http://www.theguardian.com/sport/blog/2014/dec/13/iaaf-crisis-drugs-allegations-athletics.

11. This section benefits from discussions with Jens Sejer Andersen of Play the Game and Mario Goijman. Several others who would prefer to remain anonymous also helped me; thanks to all.

12. Nikki Dryden, "How FINA Spends and Earns—Revisited," *Swim News*, April 8, 2015, https://www.swimnews.com/News/view/10402.

13. Austin Knoblauch, "Jack Warner Allegedly Diverted FIFA Haiti Relief Funds, Report Says," *Los Angeles Times*, June 9, 2015, http://www.latimes.com/sports/sportsnow/la-sp-sn-jack-warner-fifa-haiti-funds-20150609-story.html.

14. Jean-Loup Chappelet, "Autonomy of Sport in Europe," COE, April 2010, http://www.coe.int/t/dg4/epas/resources/6720-0-ID8704-Autonomy%20of%20sport%20assemble.pdf.

15. UNESCO, "International Convention against Doping in Sport," October 19, 2005, http://www.unesco.org/new/en/social-and-human-sciences/themes/anti-doping/international-convention-against-doping-in-sport/.

16. WADA, "Governance," https://www.wada-ama.org/en/who-we-are/governance.

17. WADA, "Implementation of Code 2015," http://www.wada-ama.org/Documents/World_Anti-Doping_Program/WADP-The-Code/WADA_Anti-Doping_CODE_2009_EN.pdf.

18. The US Treasury and General Government Appropriations Act, 2002, Public Law 107-67, Section 644, states: "The Congress of the United States recognizes the United States Anti-Doping Agency (USADA) as the official anti-doping agency for Olympic, Pan American, and Paralympic sport in the United States."

19. Thanks to Annie Skinner at USADA; also see CBO, "Congressional Budget Office Cost Estimate, S.529 A Bill to Designate a United States Anti-Doping Agency," September 27, 2006, http://www.cbo.gov/sites/default/files/cbofiles/ftpdocs/76xx/doc7633/s529.pdf. The US government contributed about $2 million to WADA's $26 million budget in 2013. See http://www.wada-ama.org/PageFiles/18892/WADA_Contributions_2013_update_EN.pdf.

20. USA Cycling, "Policy II: Medical Control," http://www.usacycling.org/policy-ii-medical-control.htm.

21. Government House Documents, "Travis T. Tygart, Chief Executive Officer Biography." http://docs.house.gov/meetings/IF/IF17/20131121/101517/HHRG-113-IF17-Bio-TygartT-20131121.pdf.

22. http://blogs.bicycling.com/blogs/dailylance/travis-tygart-man-who-brought-down-armstrong

23. Albergotti and O'Connell, "Wheelmen."

24. Ibid.

25. Edward E. Hollis III, "United States Olympic Committee and the Suspension of Athletes: Reforming Grievance Procedures under the Amateur Sports Act of 1978," *Indiana Law Journal* (Winter 1995), https://litigation-essentials.lexisnexis.com/webcd/app?action=DocumentDisplay&crawlid=1&doctype=cite&docid=71+Ind.+L.J.+183&srctype=smi&srcid=3B15&key=45d8ebfcd450fe5f152b76d231f439b7.

26. American Arbitration Association, "Sports Arbitration including Olympic Athlete Disputes," https://www.adr.org/aaa/ShowPDF?doc=ADRSTG_004199.

27. The judgment can be found here: "Before the American Arbitration Association, the North American Court of Arbitration for Sport/AAA Panel, United States Anti-Doping Agency and Floyd Landis," http://www.usada.org/wp-content/uploads/Landis-Final-20-09-07-3.pdf. The one arbitrator who found in Landis's favor filed a dissenting view; "United States Anti-Doping Agency v. Floyd Landis, American Arbitration Association No. 30 190 00847 06, North American Court of Arbitration for Sport Panel Award Dates September 20, 2007," http://www.usada.org/wp-content/uploads/LandisFinalDissent.pdf. He was the arbitrator chosen by Landis to sit on the panel; see Bonnie DeSimone, "Who Will Take Part in Landis Hearing," *ESPN.go.com*, May 11, 2007, http://sports.espn.go.com/oly/cycling/columns/story?id=2865881.

28. For some insight on how CAS operates, read "Interview with Matthieu Reeb, Secretary General of the Court of Arbitration for Sport," *Law in Sport*, September 4, 2014, http://www.lawinsport.com/articles/item/interview-with-matthieu-reeb-secretary-general-of-the-court-of-arbitration-for-sport.

29. Louise Reilly, "Introduction to the Court of Arbitration for Sport (CAS) and the Role of National Courts in International Sports Disputes, A Symposium," *Journal of Dispute Resolution* 2012, no. 1 (2012), http://jurisprudence.tas-cas.org/sites/CaseLaw/Shared%20Documents/1394.pdf.

30. Albergotti and O'Connell, "Wheelmen."

31. "Statement from USADA CEO Travis T. Tygart Regarding the US Postal Service Pro Cycling Team Doping Conspiracy," USADA, October 10, 2012, http://cyclinginvestigation.usada.org/.

32. "Notes from Sparks Ruling on Armstrong vs. USADA," *The Least Thing*, August 21, 2012, http://leastthing.blogspot.com/2012/08/notes-from-sparks-ruling-on-armstrong.html.

33. L. Casini, "The Making of a Lex Sportiva by the Court of Arbitration for Sport, in *Lex Sportiva: What Is Sports Law?*, 149–171 (The Hague: TMC Asser, 2012).

34. Matt Slater, "Claudia Pechstein Puts Sport's Supreme Court on Trial," BBC, February 19, 2015, http://www.bbc.com/sport/31447368.

35. Paul Osborne, "German Court Sets Precedent by Allowing Case Involving Speed Skater Accused of Doping," Inside the Games, January 15, 2015, http://www.insidethegames.biz/articles/1024896/german-court-sets-precedent-by-allowing-case-involving-speed-skater-accused-of-doping.

36. CAS, "Code: Statutes of ICAS and CAS," http://www.tas-cas.org/en/icas/code-statutes-of-icas-and-cas.html.

37. Slater, "Claudia Pechstein Puts Sport's Supreme Court on Trial."

38. Rebecca R. Ruiz, "Sports Arbitration Court Ruling against German Speedskater Claudia Pechstein Is Upheld," *New York Times*, June 7, 2016, http://www.nytimes.com/2016/06/08/sports/sports-arbitration-court-ruling-against-german-speedskater-claudia-pechstein-is-upheld.html?_r=0.

39. Jens Sejer Andersen, "The Year That Killed the Autonomy of Sport," Play the Game, December 23, 2015. http://www.playthegame.org/news/comments/2015/021_the-year-that-killed-the-autonomy-of-sport/.

40. Christopher Clarey, "Tennis Umpire Suspended for Corruption Worked at US Open," *New York Times*, February 12, 2016, http://www.nytimes.com/2016/02/13/sports/tennis/tennis-umpire-suspended-for-corruption-worked-at-us-open.html?_r=0.

41. Sportcal/Olympic Marketing Fact File, "Olympic Games Set to Break $8bn Revenues Barrier Four-Year Cycle Ending with London 2012," July 2012, http://www.sportcal.com/pdf/gsi/Sportcal_Issue26_6-9.pdf.

42. Maury Brown, "Major League Baseball Sees Record Revenues Exceed $8 Billion for 2013," Forbes.com, December 17, 2013, http://www.forbes.com/sites/maurybrown/2013/12/17/major-league-baseball-sees-record-revenues-exceed-8-billion-for-2013/#21a95f62179f.

43. "Deloitte Football Money League 2016, Top of the Table," Deloitte.com, January 2016, http://www2.deloitte.com/uk/en/pages/sports-business-group/articles/deloitte-football-money-league.html.

44. "Finances: Financial Reports," FIFA, http://www.fifa.com/aboutfifa/finances/income.html.

45. "Five Year Record," Tesco, June 20, 2016, http://www.tescoplc.com/index.asp?pageid=30.

46. "News Releases and Regulatory Filings, First Quarter 2016 Results," Shell, May 4, 2016, http://www.shell.com/global/aboutshell/investor/news-and-library/2014/fourth-quarter-2013-results-announcement.html.

47. Stefan Szymanski, *Handbook on the Economics of Sport* (Cheltenham, UK: Edward Elgar, 2006).

48. "Changing the Game: Outlook for the Global Sports Market to 2015," Pricewaterhouse-Coopers, http://www.pwc.com/gx/en/hospitality-leisure/changing-the-game-outlook-for-the-global-sports-market-to-2015.jhtml.

49. Mark Pieth, "Governing FIFA, Concept Paper and Report," September 19, 2011, http://www.fifa.com/mm/document/affederation/footballgovernance/01/54/99/69/fifagutachten-en.pdf.

50. For an overview, see Jean-Loup Chappelet and Brenda Kubler-Mabbott, *The International Olympic Committee and the Olympic System: The Governance of World Sport* (New York: Routledge, 2008).

51. "The Organisation," Olympic.org, http://www.olympic.org/content/the-ioc/governance/introductionold/.

52. "Promote Olympism in Society," Olympic.org, http://www.olympic.org/olympism-in-action.

53. "Sports: Summer Sports/Winter Sports," Olympic.org, http://www.olympic.org/sports.

54. Katharina Bart, "Swiss to Increase Oversight of FIFA, Other Sports Bodies," Reuters, December 5, 2014, http://www.reuters.com/article/2014/12/05/us-soccer-fifa-switzerland-idUSKCN0JJ1II20141205.

55. "News," Olympic.org, http://www.olympic.org/news/ioc-and-un-secretariat-agree-historic-deal/230542.

56. Chappelet and Kubler-Mabbott, *International Olympic Committee*, ch. 6.

57. Federal Department of Foreign Affairs, "International Organizationsin Switzerland," https://www.eda.admin.ch/eda/en/fdfa/foreign-policy/international-organizations/international-organizations-switzerland.html. For historical background, see M. M. Gunter (1976), "Switzerland and the United Nations," *International Organization* 30, no. 1 (1976): 129–152.

58. Nick Butler, "IAAF Should Have Acted Quicker to Deal with '19th Century' Governance Structure, Claims Pound," Inside the Games, January 8, 2016, http://www.insidethegames.biz/articles/1033066/iaaf-should-have-acted-quicker-to-deal-with-19th-century-governance-structure-claims-pound.

59. "Salaries, Allowances, Benefits and Job Classification," UN, http://www.un.org/Depts/OHRM/salaries_allowances/salary.htm.

60. "Nestle Cuts Chief Executive Paul Bulcke's Pay amid Swiss Scrutiny," ForTrade.com, http://www.ft.com/intl/cms/s/0/6ae9ca98-a93c-11e3-b87c-00144feab7de.html.

61. "Further Thoughts on Sepp Blatter's FIFA Salary," *The Least Thing*, June 17, 2013, http://leastthing.blogspot.com/2013/06/further-thoughts-on-sepp-blatters-fifa.html.

62. "Blatter Named in $80m FIFA Secret Bonus Investigation," *Financial Times*, June 3, 2016, http://www.ft.com/fastft/2016/06/03/blatter-named-in-80m-fifa-secret-bonus-investigation/.

63. Pieth, "Governing FIFA."

64. Andrew Warshaw, "FIFA on Alert as Swiss Tighten Laws to Keep a Closer Eye on Sports Bodies," *Inside World Football*, December 15, 2014, http://www.insideworldfootball.com/fifa/16033-fifa-on-alert-as-swiss-tighten-laws-to-keep-a-closer-eye-on-sports-bodies.

65. "FIFA and Olympic Leaders Face New Financial Checks," BBC, December 12, 2014, http://www.bbc.com/news/business-30451609.

66. For example, see Transparency International, "Global Corruption Report: Sport," 2016, http://www.reuters.com/article/2011/05/31/us-soccer-fifa-idUSTRE74S16320110531.

67. Roger Pielke Jr., "How Can FIFA Be Held Accountable?" *Sport Management Review* 16, no. 3 (2013): 255–267.

68. Robert O. Keohane, "Global Governance and Democratic Accountability," in *Contemporary Political Philosophy: An Anthology*, 2nd ed., ed. Robert E Goodwin and Phillip Pettit (Oxford: Blackwell, 2006).

69. Details of the IOC scandal are drawn from the excellent history by Bill Mallon, "The Olympic Bribery Scandal," *Journal of Olympic History* (2000), http://library.la84.org/SportsLibrary/JOH/JOHv8n2/johv8n2f.pdf

70. Ibid.

71. Transparency International, "Global Corruption Report: Sport."

Chapter 11

1. Jon Solomon, "Cost of Attendance Results: The Chase to Pay College Players," CBSSports .com, August 20, 2015, http://www.cbssports.com/collegefootball/writer/jon-solomon/25275500/cost-of-attendance-results-the-chase-to-legally-pay-college-players.

2. "Minimum Stipend for Graduate Associates," Ohio State University Graduate School, http://www.gradsch.ohio-state.edu/minimum-stipend-for-graduate-associates.html.

3. "Salary Rates for Graduate Research & Teaching Assistantships," Stanford University, Graduate Academic Policies and Procedures, http://gap.stanford.edu/RATAsalary.html.

4. "The Price of Athletics at Stanford," *Stanford Daily*, February 22, 2015, http://www.stanforddaily.com/2015/02/22/the-price-of-athletics-at-stanford/.

5. NCAA, *National Collegiate Athletic Association (NCAA) Division Manual*, January 2015–16, http://www.ncaapublications.com/productdownloads/D116JAN.pdfhttp://www.ncaapublications.com/productdownloads/D116JAN.pdf.

6. "NCAA to Pay for Family Travel Under Pilot Program," NCAA, January 6, 2015, http://www.ncaa.org/about/resources/media-center/news/ncaa-pay-family-travel-under-pilot-program.

7. David Broughton, "Gift Suite Adds to Men's Final Four," *Sports Business Daily*, March 7, 2016, http://www.sportsbusinessdaily.com/Journal/Issues/2016/03/07/Colleges/Final-Four-gift-suite.aspx.

8. Associated Press, "NCAA Tournament Deal with CBS, Turner Extended through 2032," ESPN.go.com, April 12, 2016, http://espn.go.com/mens-college-basketball/story/_/id/15190549/ncaa-tournament-deal-cbs-turner-extended-2032.

9. Phil Hampton, "UCLA Sells Royalty Rights Connected with Cancer Drug to Royalty Pharma," UCLA.newsroom.edu, March 4, 2016, http://newsroom.ucla.edu/releases/ucla-sells-royalty-rights-connected-with-cancer-drug-to-royalty-pharma.

10. "End of Football Season Produced $37 Million in Media Exposure for Texas A&M," Texas A&M, January 18, 2013, http://today.tamu.edu/2013/01/18/study-end-of-football-season -produced-37-million-in-media-exposure-for-texas-am/.

11. Jon Solomon, "Pac-12 Tables Proposal for Players to be Able to Profit off Name," CBSSports. com, January 12, 2016, http://www.cbssports.com/collegefootball/writer/jon-solomon /25446855/ncaa-convention-preview-concern-over-players-profiting-off-their-names.

12. "Markus Rehm Dealt Blow in Bid to Make Rio Olympics," *Athletics Weekly*, June 17, 2016, http://www.athleticsweekly.com/featured/markus-rehm-dealt-blow-in-bid-to-make-rio-olympics-45035/.

13. IAAF, *Competition Rules, 2016–17* (Monaco: IAAF, n.d.), http://www.iaaf.org/download/ download?filename=89ed4cba-6b5e-49fe-a43e-9f5487b77a84.pdf&urlslug=IAAF%20 Competition%20Rules%202016-2017%2C%20in%20force%20from%201%20November %202015.

14. "Markus Rehm and the Limits of Science," *The Least Thing*, June 2, 2016, http://leastthing. blogspot.com/2016/06/markus-rehm-and-limits-of-science.html.

15. Ibid.

16. "Declaration of the Olympic Summit, Five-Point Plan to Ensure a Level Playing Field for Athletes at the Olympic Games Rio 2016," Olympic.org, June 21, 2016, https://www.olympic .org/news/declaration-of-the-olympic-summit.

17. John Sparks, "Russian Athlete: Why Can't We Take Drugs?" Sky.News.com, June 8, 2016, http://news.sky.com/story/1707958/russian-athlete-why-cant-we-take-drugs.

18. IAAF, "Key Moments: Rusaf Suspension and Reinstatement Process," IAAF.org. June 16, 2016, http://www.iaaf.org/news/press-release/rusaf-suspension-and-reinstatement-timeline.

19. "The Bulgarian Precedent," *The Least Thing*, June 20, 2016, http://leastthing.blogspot. com/2016/06/the-bulgarian-precedent.html.

20. "2014 Anti-Doping Rule Violations (ADRVs) Report," WADA, February 21, 2016, https:// wada-main-prod.s3.amazonaws.com/resources/files/wada-2014-adrv-report-en.pdf.

21. Sean Zak, "Spieth, McIlroy, Pros React to Dustin Johnson Putting Controversy," Golf.com, June 19, 2016, http://www.golf.com/tour-and-news/dustin-johnson-putting-controversy-spieth-mcilroy-pros-react.

22. "Cristiano Ronaldo Doesn't Care about the FIFA Scandal," ESPNfc.us, August 2, 2015, http://www.espnfc.us/blog/the-toe-poke/65/post/2545900/cristiano-ronaldo-doesnt-care-about-the-fifa-scandal.

23. Lauren Fleshman, "Why Athletes Don't Speak Out about Doping," Asklauren fleshman.com, December 1, 2015, http://asklaurenfleshman.com/2015/12/why-athletes-dont-speak-out-about-doping/.

24. Bonnie D. Ford, "Athletes, Others Who Raise Doping Concerns in Sports Often Left Whistling into the Wind," ESPN.go.com, June 15, 2016, http://espn.go.com/espn/otl/story/_/ id/16209580/doping-whistleblowers-such-stepanovs-kara-goucher-often-left-dangling-taking-sports-bodies-governing-bodies.

25. Brendan Schwab, "Organised Athletes: A Critical Voice in Sports Governance," Transparency.org, http://www.transparency.org/files/content/feature/6.9_OrganisedAthletes_ Schwab_GCRSport.pdf.

26. Sean Ingle, "Athletes 'Have Lost Faith' in IOC and Wada over Russia Failures," *Guardian*, June 14, 2016, https://www.theguardian.com/sport/2016/jun/14/athletes-letter-doping-wada-ioc-russia-decision.

For Further Reading

Many references throughout this book document the sources of specific facts and arguments. This brief section highlights a few readings that I recommend as next stops for those who want to dig deeper into and learn more about the themes and issues covered in this book.

On the efforts by athletes to achieve a performance edge, David Epstein's *The Sports Gene* (Penguin, 2013) is both fascinating and readable.

On the history of college sports (the subject of much writing), I have read nothing better than Ronald Smith's *Sports and Freedom* (Oxford University Press, 1988). Because the amateur issue in college sports is in flux, more recent treatments are quickly out of date, but a plethora of books offers polemicism on all sides of the debate. The academic literature, particularly in the field of law, offers a steady stream of technical analyses of debates surrounding employment, compensation, and the rights of college athletes.

There are many books about doping in sport, and there might be a dozen about Lance Armstrong alone. One general overview that I found to be particularly good is Chris Cooper's *Run, Swim, Throw, Cheat* (Oxford University Press, 2012).

Match fixing is not yet the subject of any one authoritative volume, but the European Commission is keeping a close eye on the issue at http://ec.europa.eu/sport/policy/organisation_of_sport/match_fixing_en.htm.

Similarly, there are no comprehensive treatments of the role of technology in sport. More generally, on the fusion of humans and technology, Braden Allenby and Daniel Sarewitz provide a provocative perspective in *The Techno-Human Condition* (MIT Press, 2011).

Lindsay Parks Piper recently published an excellent overview of the history and the issues associated with sex testing in sport in the aptly named *Sex Testing* (University of Illinois Press, 2016).

The role of science in decision making is the subject of a voluminous literature, but little has been directly applied to sports. I wrote a well-received book on science, policy, and politics titled *The Honest Broker* (Cambridge University Press, 2007) that goes deeper into some of the themes that I highlight in this volume. Be on the watch for the second edition of that book, which will have considerable new material and into which I hope to smuggle some sports examples.

Sports governance is a rapidly growing subject. An excellent overview is the *Global Corruption Report: Sport* by Transparency International (Routledge, 2016). Play the Game, based in Denmark, holds the world's top sports governance conference every odd year, and Play the Game's website—www.playthegame.org—is an excellent resource for anyone who wants to stay abreast of this rapidly changing area.

I blog and tweet regularly on the issues covered in this book, and in both settings I try to point out analyses worth reading and people worth following. In turn, I invite you to do the same for me: You can find me online at http://leastthing.blogspot.com and on Twitter at @rogerpielkejr.

Index

Williams, Tom, 62
Wilshere, Jack, 194
Winfrey, Oprah, 241
Wolfers, Justin, 113
"woman-ness," biological criteria for, 192
women
  intersex, 255
  role of in the Olympics, 189
women's 100m run, 69–70
women's 400m individual medley, *140*, 208
women's sports, 73
Women's Tennis Association (WTA), 111
Woods, Tiger, 4, 7, 247, 268
World Anti-Doping Agency (WADA), 16, 40, 53, 126–133, 138, 141–143, 148, 156, 162, 201–205, 207–209, 211, 215–216, 228, 231, 237–238, 241, 250, 264
  Athletes' Committee, 269
  code, 215, 225, 238
  prohibited list, 20, 213–214, 223–224

World Championships, 2015 (Beijing), 37
World Cup (soccer). *See under* FIFA
World Gymnastics Championships (1957), 67
World Health Organization (WHO), 176
World Tennis Association (WTA), 161
World Track and Field Championships (2009; Berlin), 177
Wrage, Alexandra, 216
Wyoming Fourteen, 45–47

Yahoo Sports, 13
Yale University, 78–80, 86
Yamauchi. Mara, 146
Ye Shiwen, 208
Yeager, Steve, 61
Young, David, 85

ZDF (Germany), 131

About the Author

Roger Pielke, Jr., directs the Sports Governance Center, housed in the Athletics Department at the University of Colorado. He is the author, coauthor, or coeditor of seven books, including *The Honest Broker: Making Sense of Science in Policy and Politics* and *The Climate Fix: What Scientists and Politicians Won't Tell You About Global Warming*. Roger is an active blogger, and he regularly contributes *to* the *New York Times*, the *Wall Street Journal*, *USA Today*, *Sporting Intelligence*, the *Financial Times*, and the *Guardian*. He lives in Boulder.

Praise for
The Edge

The War against Cheating and Corruption
in the Cutthroat World of Elite Sports

"Pielke's accessible and conversational writing style will have Joe Fan eagerly flipping pages."—*Foreword* magazine

"A fascinating exploration of how technology and the constant desire for competitive advantage are undermining our notions of what constitutes fair play. But this isn't just a book about sports—it's a book that challenges readers to think about the codes by which they live their own lives."—Richard Bradley, *The Greatest Game: The Yankees, the Red Sox, and the Playoff of '78*

"This book, with its case studies and data, should be required reading for all involved in college sports."—Jay Bilas, ESPN

"This is a book that should reach informed experts on sports governance as well as ordinary curious fans. Pielke writes with an academic's erudition and a journalist's style and eye for detail. Sport is lucky to have him."—Simon Kuper, author of *Soccernomics*

"Packed with fascinating detail and case studies still unfolding, there's no better primer on cheating and corruption in 21st-century sport. . . . It is a bold argument, and one as entertaining as [it is] compelling. And necessary."—Nick Harris, *UK Mail*

"The clear thinking and analysis . . . in *The Edge* should be compulsory reading. . . . *The Edge* shows us that the time is ripe for a new conversation."—Tracy Holmes, ABC Australia